SPEAKING TO EACH OTHER

VOLUME ONE

Speaking To Each Other

Essays by

RICHARD HOGGART

VOLUME I

About Society

1970

Chatto & Windus

LONDON

PUBLISHED BY
CHATTO & WINDUS LTD.
40 WILLIAM IV STREET
LONDON W.C.2

*

CLARKE, IRWIN & CO. LTD.
TORONTO

SBN 7011 1463 0

© Richard Hoggart 1970

PRINTED IN GREAT BRITAIN BY
NORTHUMBERLAND PRESS LIMITED
GATESHEAD

CONTENTS

For
Simon, Nicola and Paul

ACKNOWLEDGEMENTS

The essays in this volume have, with one or two exceptions, all been published previously in a somewhat different form. Acknowledgement is made to the following sources of original publication:

GROWING UP: *Breakthrough*, ed. R. Goldman, Routledge & Kegan Paul, 1966.

A SENSE OF OCCASION: Reprinted by permission of MacGibbon & Kee from *Conviction*, ed. N. Mackenzie, 1958.

CHANGES IN WORKING CLASS LIFE: Analyse et Prévision, *Prognosis* 19, under the title MY NEIGHBOURS IN 1970. Copyright 1961 by Futuribles—S.E.D.E.I.S., Paris. Reprinted by permission.

THE CONDITION OF ENGLAND QUESTION: *Times Educational Supplement*, February 19th, 1965, under the title WHAT WE THINK OF IT AS WE LIVE IT. Reprinted by permission.

IMAGES OF THE PROVINCES: *The Guardian*, October 17th, 1967, under the title PROPER FERDINANDS.

EDUCATION IN THE NEXT FEW DECADES: *Esso Magazine*, Winter 1966/67.

HIGHER EDUCATION AND CULTURAL CHANGE: Delivered as the 44th Earl Grey Memorial Lecture, 1965. Reprinted by permission of the University of Newcastle.

TWO WAYS OF LOOKING: Given as a speech at the First Bath Conference 1965 under the title VALUES AND VIRTUES. Subsequently published in *Technology and Society*, ed. G. Walters and K. Hudson, 1966, Bath University Press. By permission.

MARSHALL MCLUHAN AND MAKING CHOICES: *The Listener*, December 3rd, 1964.

PROFESSOR BANTOCK AND AUTHORITY: *New Society*, October 5th, 1967.

PROFESSOR MARCUS AND CULTURAL READING: *The Guardian*, January 20th, 1967.

SPEAKING TO EACH OTHER

MR. GORER AND ATTITUDES TO DEATH: *New Society*, April 29th, 1965.

MRS. LEAVIS AND THE DANGERS OF NARROWNESS: *The Guardian*, November 5th, 1965.

CULTURE—DEAD AND ALIVE: *The Observer*, May 14th, 1961.

MASS COMMUNICATIONS IN BRITAIN: *Pelican Guide to English Literature*, Vol. 7, ed. B. Ford, 1961.

THE USES OF TELEVISION: From a talk originally given as the William F. Harvey Memorial Lecture at Fircroft College, Birmingham in June 1959. Published in substantially revised form in *Encounter*, Vol. XIV-1, January 1960.

TELEVISION AS THE ARCHETYPE OF MASS COMMUNICATIONS: *International Encyclopaedia of the Social Sciences*, 1968.

THE BBC AND SOCIETY: *The Listener*, August 5th, 1965.

DIFFICULTIES OF DEMOCRATIC DEBATE: From a talk given as a Jubilee address at Columbia Teachers College, New York. Published in *Teachers College Record*, Vol. 64/8, May 1963.

THE DAILY MIRROR AND ITS READERS: *New Society*, October 27th, 1966.

THE GUARDIANS AND THE NEW POPULISM: *Censorship*, Vol. I-1, Autumn 1964.

THE CASE AGAINST ADVERTISING: *Advertisers' Weekly*, 229-2720, October 1st, 1965.

THE ARGUMENT ABOUT EFFECTS: Delivered as a public lecture for the Cambridge University Faculty of Divinity, November 1966.

THE ARTS AND STATE SUPPORT: *Essays on Reform*, ed. B. Crick, Oxford University Press, 1967. Reprinted by permission.

PREFACE

ALL but three or four of these essays were written during the last ten years; they represent just over a third of my published writing in that period. Looking at their dates, I notice that two in three of the essays about culture were written between 1965 and 1967, and half of those about literature between 1963 and 1966. So 1965 and 1966 seem to have been fuller years than usual. During 1968 almost all the essays were greatly amended, for publication, chiefly by pruning; and some have been given new titles.

Most were prompted by particular occasions: a request for a long essay or special lecture, or for a book review. I virtually never accept such an invitation unless it gives the chance to work somewhere near my main interests. I am a slow writer and can hardly ever afford to 'knock something out' in a spirit of only casual interest.

I can see, now that these essays have been put side by side, that I tend to work at the same group of themes again and again, though from different angles. At least, this is what I have done in the past decade. So there is a good deal of interweaving and movement of cross-currents in and between these two volumes.

The main social themes seem to circle around how one understands, interprets and evaluates cultural change—as seen in attitudes to class and education, the debate about 'brows', mass communications, 'public voices' (who speaks to whom, about what, and in what tones of voice?), and in questions about intellectual freedom and responsibility in a commercial democracy.

Where the literary essays are about particular authors, their special interest for someone with my kind of outlook is self-evident. The others seem as often as not to settle on such subjects as the peculiar nature of the 'subjective' literary imagination and its contribution to understanding society;

9

or—and this I really do want to take much further if I can—
they are about questions of tone and how very much a reading
of tone can reveal.

I have noticed some changes—some quite marked changes
—in my own attitudes over the decade, and some changes of
style. I've noted also some recurrent patterns in my ways of
thinking, of approaching problems; and so some recurrent
habits of style. But I'm not yet sure what these contrasting
characteristics mean.

I owe a great deal to a great many people, but most of all
to the following nine, whom I want to thank as strongly as
ever I can: Catharine Carver, Stuart Hall, Eleanor Insch,
G. E. T. Mayfield, Felicity Reeve, Roy Shaw, Mary Weate,
my daughter Nicola and my wife Mary.

October 1969   Richard Hoggart

GROWING UP

I was born just north of the centre of Leeds, in a district called Chapeltown, which seems to have become a lower-middle-class suburb but at that time contained the remnants of a village. It was a village that had been enveloped in, I suppose, the late-nineteenth century. As you came off the main road you dropped down a widish lane, and on the right were a few stone-built houses and cottages and courts. Ours was No. 48, Potternewton Lane, in a little court to itself. Cramped in the corner was this old-fashioned house, which may have been a farm labourer's house at one time.

The area was half-surrounded by working-class terrace houses of the slightly better late-nineteenth century kind. Immediately in front of us there was a field and I remember as a boy (I must have been about five) seeing a cow calve in this field. That was only about a mile and a half to two miles from the centre of Leeds. I went back a few years ago and, of course, the field doesn't exist; it's been obliterated by a lot of semis.

The house itself had a living-room and, at the back of it, a scullery with a single cold tap. The stairs rose out of the living-room and that had a big old-fashioned range. There was a room over the living-room and, if I remember correctly, a small room over the scullery. That's where my mother and the three of us lived. There was an outside lavatory which I think was an earth closet. It was funny, near the middle of a city full of huddled working-class brick dwellings, to have this tiny court almost to ourselves. The story of the cow rather overstresses the rural quality. It was very much a pocket and we were very much part of Leeds. We were near one of the big tram depots, and I remember seeing the men picketing there during the 1926 strike. But still the flags in the yard and the stone of the house gave a kind of West Riding rural quality to it.

11

I don't really remember how the sleeping arrangements went, but I suspect that my sister slept with my mother and my brother with me. I was born in September 1918, my sister a couple of years later and my brother almost a couple of years before. My father had been a soldier; he must have died about 1921. From then on my mother was looking after us on her own. I can't really say I remember my father. Sometimes I think I do and then I wonder whether I'm remembering photographs of him. But my mother I remember fairly well. Most of the time she was tired and ill. We were living wholly on public assistance. I remember one relative who seemed well-to-do to us. She may have worked in Montague Burton's factory or one of the other big tailoring firms for about £2 a week. That seemed affluence. And I remember someone producing a small packet of mixed biscuits—before that, I had only seen them in shop windows. If my mother wanted to cheer us up or get us over an awkward hump or keep us quiet for a while she would give us a half-slice of bread, with a bit of margarine and some tinned, condensed milk on it. It was cheap foreign condensed milk and had a special character of its own: the sugar they laced it with somehow hadn't melted and it had a gritty quality.

We children usually just wandered around the roads in Chapeltown or Potternewton. If we wanted to make something of an expedition we would go about a mile, across the main road, to a park. I imagine we were a fairly closed-in family. A widow and her three children—just managing on public assistance—were bound to be slightly separated from others.

My father was the next to eldest child of a family of ten, and his mother was one of the older ones of a family of nine or ten. She was born and brought up in Boston Spa, which is a few miles outside Leeds. It was rather a feudal place, a village with landowners and the remnants of a ruling gentry. My grandmother, my father's mother, was the daughter of a farm-hand—although I think probably a sort of foreman—and she married her cousin, who was also of that village. He was from a big family, too. Then they became part of a representative movement we all know about. I imagine their marriage was in the early 1870's (she was born in the '50's). This young woman with her husband came to Leeds or Sheffield first, drawn like so many to the big industrial centres. He was a fairly talented man, I gather, in that he had an inventive streak; and he moved around more than a normal labourer would. Finally they settled in Leeds.

We've got a family legend of a common kind—that he invented something. (I think it was a way of picking up huge steel sheets so that as they rose there was no danger of the clamp giving way, dropping the sheets and killing men. His device caused the clamp to tighten as the sheets rose higher and higher and this, my older relatives used to say, is still used.) The story ends that he didn't get his dues for it, that he was paid a small lump sum by the works and no royalties. Other stories suggest that he was an independent-minded man. I've heard recently, from an aunt who is now in her nineties, an account of how he got the sack at Loughborough. He was working as a craftsman in a big factory, making machines for boots and shoes. The foreman handed back something he had made. He thought it was good and that the foreman was insecure and only trying to establish his authority. My grandfather is said to have stood up and answered: "Well, you can do it yourself," then thrown it at the foreman's feet, demanded his cards and walked out. So they were on the move again. My grandmother had her ten children in several different parts of the country. Once in Leeds, they settled in the big, industrial-barrack region of Hunslet, and that is where—very much later—I come in. When we were living in Potternewton, my mother would very occasionally take us on the double tram-ride—from Potternewton into town, then on to the Hunslet tram to see my grandmother. I don't remember my grandfather at all, though you could say that his spirit lived on in the house for years. Families like that had a strong sense of the father's importance. "My father always used to say . . ." was a common opening remark.

13

My own father too seemed to have various jobs. I think he served in the Boer War, but in what capacity I don't know. On my own birth certificate he's shown as a house painter. But I imagine this is something he happened to be doing at the time I was born. For patches he was certainly in the Regular Army. But that, of course, was one of the things working men who couldn't settle, or simply couldn't find work, often did for a spell. Then he went to the First World War. I think he had a period in the Pay Corps. At one time he was a Sergeant, it may have been in the infantry. His army record must be all right, because I got a grant for clothing from the British Legion when I was a student at Leeds and they presumably looked up the records. The story is that he got Maltese fever in Malta, though again this may be one of those pieces of family folk-lore. You expected to send one of your family abroad to tramp around the Empire with the troops; you half expected him to pick up strange diseases. Again, some of my family say that if everybody had had their rights, we'd have had a pension for my father's Maltese fever. I think they tried, and the Government said it wasn't certain that his death was due to the fever. I gather there was a long-standing chest trouble. I have to 'watch my chest' and this may be a legacy. My father was probably in his middle-forties when he died. I don't think he married young. I'm told he met my mother in York when he was doing a spell of military service. His surviving sisters talk about him as though he was a man of great self-determination but with a certain kind of wildness.

As to my grandparents on my mother's side, I am even more vague. The story is that my mother was of a 'better class' family. I think that may be true so long as you realize the fine shadings you can have in that phrase 'better class'. She was certainly from Liverpool: my brother and I once went over for a week just after my mother died to stay with some of her relatives. They seemed to range from lower-middle to quite comfortable middle class; and they didn't seem to feel upstarts. We stayed in an area which looked to us well-to-do. I think it was probably a respectable, lower-middle-class, terrace region with bay-windowed houses, small gardens, and narrow halls. But to have a hall, with a bit of stained glass, was rather grand. This was one of my mother's sisters, and she was very kind. She took us to see her daughter, who had married the captain of a banana boat, and lived in a 'semi' in a comfortable modern part of Liverpool.

So my mother's family were not poor working-class. My relatives on the Hoggart side, when they mention my mother, say things like, "Ah! She was a lady, was your mother." They talk about her voice, and they say that once I began to lose my Leeds accent the intonations I kept were those of my mother. What she was doing in York I don't really know. I've heard it said that she went away from home because it was frustrating and that she decided to make her own way. The story is that when my father met her she was serving in the canteen of a soldiers' barracks or something like that. From his photographs, he seems to have been a well-set-up man with a thick moustache and, in those tight 1914 jackets, a strong-looking Tommy Sergeant sort of person. He was a good-sized man as well. I don't know whether she was swept off her feet. She was a slim woman. I remember the long dark dresses that she used to wear, that swished, and those lace-up boots. I've got a sense of her way of talking, a way which wasn't Leeds working class; but that may be something I've invented from hearing people describe it. I do remember one or two little incidents when her relatives asked my brother and me —they called us 'Addie's kids'—over for the week's holiday. All in all they were kind and anxious to give us a good time. But just once or twice I got the sense that we were the children of Addie who had stepped down in the world. I don't think they were conscious of making us feel that way; only, I remember little conversations I overheard. Children have ears the size of footballs, especially if they're looked after by strange adults.

But to come back to our house when my mother was alive. Hardly anything happened, as you can imagine, and a visitor was unusual. My mother used to draw her small amount of money and, under the system in those days, I think part of it was given in coupons which she had to spend at certain speci-fied grocers' shops, such as the Maypole. This was money from the Board of Guardians, as they then were. She used to go down about once a week, I suppose to an office, to collect it, though people did occasionally appear from the Local Author-ity. Our food was about as basic as it could be: tinned cocoa and condensed milk at about threepence a tin. There were no luxuries. I think she had to be very shrewd to keep the boat steady and that she must have had great pride. She was always anxious not to be looked down upon. I've not ever heard that she earned any extra money; she was hardly well enough. She always had chest trouble and died of bronchitis.

For breakfast, we had a piece of bread and, if there was dripping, dripping and a cup of cocoa. The cocoa was cheap, and gritty like the condensed milk; but it was a sensible thing to give us. I remember that, when we had meat, it was usually very cheap stew; but this, after all, is peasant fare all over Europe and is, in fact, very nourishing. Tea was usually bread and butter and there might possibly be a jar of cheap jam. We had a cup of cocoa at night. This seems the sort of diet that would have commended itself to those Quakers who are interested in the diet of the working class, in that within its limits it provided a lot of nourishment. We never saw fish and chips or shop-prepared food of that kind. I have a photo-graph of myself round about that time and did look healthy; in fact, I was chubby. I remember that I used to go to a shop next door—an old woman kept it—and she always called me 'Sonny Jim'. Of course, we were cheaply dressed; but we were 'neat and tidy and well cared for'. My mother used to get clothing cheques as well as food cheques, from the Board of Guardians. I remember once she dressed us two boys in those sailor suits which used to be so popular. That must have been at Whitsuntide, the annual occasion for children's new clothes. She was terribly proud of us and she was always ready to fight for her brood. She took us, in the sailor suits, to see my grandmother; and one of my aunts still remembers how on such occasions she used to sit with her back straight and want us to be admired. The day my sister had to have glasses, I remember my mother sitting and crying. All her pride and her sense of self-identity must have been bound up with her three kids.

We had no radio in the home, and if there were any books I never noticed them. There was a lot of children's chatter but not much conversation because hardly anybody ever came in. I suppose we chattered about school, but it was a closed world. My mother was certainly not an intellectual. It is very hard to see down this long tunnel; I imagine she would have seemed withdrawn to strangers, because she was rather grey and under-par much of the time, but fighting to keep a good face on things. I remember coming in one day and finding her lying on the clip-rug in front of the hearth. Her chest was really playing her up and she'd been coughing. I'm not sure if it was consumption, but it was at least bad bronchitis. We were frightened because we didn't know what it was. I suspect she was well on her way to her last illness. Then everything goes hazy, because children are like dumb animals when things like that happen. I suppose I saw my mother in her coffin; it was normal, but I can't remember. I do remember relatives converging from Hunslet and then, of course, from Liverpool, when she died. I suspect she was buried from my grandmother's home in Hunslet. This makes me think that she probably died in hospital but that arrangements were made for the coffin to be brought by the undertaker to my grandmother's, and that they just gave up our old house. It would revert to the landlord, I expect, and be let again for the usual few shillings a week. I don't remember the funeral itself but I remember the funeral day clearly. I remember the great crowd in my grandmother's because it brought together my father's sisters and brothers, the Hoggart group, and some from Liverpool.

Then I moved to my grandmother's in Hunslet. That area was mid- to late-nineteenth century, Industrial Revolution, cheap speculative housing for workers. There are areas like this all over the big industrial cities, especially from the Midlands upwards. It's just been knocked down, in these last two years. There was the centre of Leeds and you crossed the river, going south, and got into the heavy industrial area where the gasworks were, the railway sidings, the canals and the main arterials to London. We were off the right hand side, about one mile from the city centre. You came off the road and started walking up a slight incline and you were in row after row of symmetrical, brick, back-to-back houses with cobbled streets, corner shops and a little Board School. As it happened—there's always an oddity—at one point there was a Roman Catholic school in the middle of it all, and just at the back of this, between it and the cobbled street, they'd put a small row of brick houses which they didn't make back-to-back because, I suppose, they couldn't have back access to them. They were through-houses with tiny open yards and then a wall to the Catholic school playground. We were in one of those, the end one. It was an advantage, having the end one, because it meant that we had a side-yard which you could have even put a handcart in, or if you had been a window cleaner you could have kept your ladders there. The yard was 'L' shaped. Everybody else had a bit of yard with old palings they'd made out of orange boxes, and one kept pigeons.

There were two lavatories in our yard; the left hand one was shared by us and the people next door. They were, when I arrived, earth closets but were later made into cheap water closets. The yard was in some sense common because the 'rubbish hole' was there, between the two lavatories. We had, in the house itself, a living-room into which you walked straight off the street, and behind that a scullery. I think we had a cellar too. There were narrow stairs coming out of the living-room. Upstairs, there was a front bedroom over the living-room and a back bedroom over the scullery. But the thing that made the house cost a shilling or one and sixpence a week more than the other houses in that street, or that area, was that there was an attic which went over both living-room and scullery. This, of course, was spacious by comparison with any other room. When she'd moved in there, my grandmother must have been better off than she had ever been; that is, her children were grown up and her husband still working. They'd moved to this house because they felt able to pay the odd shilling and sixpence a week more. At some date somebody had put a bath in the attic. This was unusual. We had a screen made out of a large clothes-horse which had been covered in left-over bits of wallpaper. It was put round the bath so that someone could have a bath when somebody else was in bed. That was where I slept. If the neighbours had something special on—say, a daughter getting married—they would ask whether she could have a bath.

We were broken up as a family that day at my mother's funeral, in my grandmother's living-room. I remember the conversation about what should be done with us. I can remember someone saying that orphanages were very good nowadays, and that we'd probably be better looked after there than in any individual family. Of course, a child felt immediately threatened and isolated. But the majority wouldn't hear of this; all their traditions were against it. What they were feeling, I think, was that nothing could make up for 'belonging to somebody' rather than being part of a public institution. I was the only one who went to my grandmother. My sister went to a half-aunt in the next street. My brother went to Sheffield, to my grandmother's oldest daughter, the second of her children. She had eleven children of her own; and her husband was a railway waggon driver. Sheffield was a long, long way from Leeds, about forty miles. I saw my sister fairly often of course, in the next street. I went over to Sheffield to see my brother at odd intervals, perhaps once a year for a few days during the school holidays. He came over once or twice. I lived with my grandmother until she died, having gone to her when I was seven or eight. She died in January 1937, just after I had gone up to Leeds University.

There were six at my grandmother's: myself, a grand-daughter from Sheffield looking for work (this was during the slump), and three unmarried children of my grandmother, ranging in age from about thirty to fifty.

I can't remember much about the schooling in Chapel-town, except that I enjoyed it. It was the nearest local school and had a stone plaque saying that this was a Board School built after the 1870 Act or something to that effect. I can't remember feeling that I was more intelligent than any of the others. At seven or eight, when I changed homes, I went to what they called Jack Lane Elementary School in Hunslet. I remember the shock of this South Leeds slum school, which again suggests that the Chapeltown area might not have been solidly, toughly, working-class. I remember being beaten by the inevitable bully, for 'talking posh' in Hunslet. Interest-ing, because I must have had a broad Leeds voice; but there would be just that edge to it which the Hunslet ear picked up and thought was upstaging them. I was on the whole unhappy at Jack Lane. There was one particular bully, who took it out of me viciously and gave me my first taste of anti-Semitism, which is quite a strong strain in some areas of working-class life. I'm not a Jew, but he decided for some reason to say I was. I think the basic reason was that he looked like a Jew himself and was ashamed of it. So he would come up and get me against a wall and say, 'Sheeny,' and hit me.

It was a school for boys only and the teachers had to be tough. Or rough. I can remember a master I had for a year there who was a shocker. He finally had to flee the country to escape some sort of charge. It was said that for one thing he was homosexual and for another that he had defaulted with the savings of the local football club, and that the police had finally closed in on both counts. He disliked me because I didn't respond to his emotional blackmail. One day he sang in class a sentimental Irish song about 'Mother' until gradually—and it was what he was after—he had almost every boy in tears. When he saw I wasn't crying he turned on me and deliberately tried to disturb me by stirring memories of my own mother. There were certainly one or two class teachers there who helped me, but I can't clearly remember them. It's a pity, but one can easily forget the steady good work some teachers put in, even though they never actually fire your imagination. The teacher I remember best at that school was the headmaster, who decided early on that I was bright. He had been to a training college, gone pupil teaching and then come to Hunslet and saw himself as in some way helping to civilize it. He could be as tough as anyone; yet he had the will and patience, if he saw some talent in a boy, to help it along. Without being soft, he helped me a lot. I never really knew this till later; it's remarkable how much you don't notice when you're a child (and how much you do notice, in other ways). I remember that when I had pneumonia and nearly died—I was about nine or ten years old—the headmaster came to the house to see me, which is unusual. I don't suppose I saw a great deal of him, but I knew he was in the background.

The morning I took the scholarship exam, I walked to Cockburn High School, which is a local L.E.A. 1902 grammar school, to sit the papers. As far as I know, nobody before had gone in for it from our school, though there may have been another one or two who went with me. Incidentally, I think it would do some of us good if we could go back to those slum schools and see how inadequate and ill-equipped much of the teaching was thirty or forty years ago. So many teachers were sweating it out, ill-paid; they hadn't been well trained themselves or had any refresher training. I'm sure it's better than that now in most schools, a good deal better. I was ill-prepared for the exam and, of course, failed it. But when you talk to people around my age about that exam you discover that many who are now reasonably successful failed to pass.

I was told that my headmaster then went down to the local education office and said to them, "Look at this boy's essay;

there's some talent here," and they decided to give me a place at Cockburn. I don't know whether they did actually re-read the essay. But I went to Cockburn. Cockburn was lavatory-tiled up to elbow height inside, a brick cube outside. There were several masters and mistresses—it was co-ed—who had a sense of 'mission' of one kind or another. There was a Latin master who was tough and effective; his sights were set on getting good School Certificates. He had a house nearby, in the Dewsbury Road area, and lived for his work. He would smile on all those boys who worked hard because he thought you could achieve anything by work. He would be very severe on others. I was hard-working so he was always helpful, and he taught me a lot about keeping your head down and going at it. There was a very nice English master—I see, now, rather sentimental but warm and friendly. There was a good French mistress too who tried to see through to the sort of person you might become.

Cockburn is a curious, interesting school. It's had a succession of quite well-known or successful alumni by now; I can think of three professors from the tiny arts sixth in my time alone. But, then, there'd been a lot of sifting. By the time you'd gone through all the hoops to get to Cockburn you were either very good indeed, or you had enormous staying-power or self-preservation or luck. You had been brought up in one of these streets, and in a bookless home—this was true of almost every boy or girl in that area, especially on the Hunslet side. The Dewsbury Road side, which the school also drew upon, was slightly posher. To have been at one of those elementary schools, to have sat the scholarship exam when the number of places, compared with those today, was tiny and to have got a place—all this was much harder than it is today. I sometimes have an imaginary aerial picture of a typical morning, at the time I started at Cockburn—of one door opening and a boy coming out with a new Cockburn cap, one boy contributed from a big range of streets and probably being called at by the other boys as he went; then another one from another street and so on. Then they began to make friendships from a wider range around.

The headmaster at Cockburn in my time, who didn't stay there long, was an odd character. He had been a master at Dulwich College. He left Cockburn to go into an Anglican monastery. He came to Cockburn because he wanted to try his hand at this type of school. He was a Southerner with a markedly middle-class southern voice. It's said that he was very forgetful and one year forgot to send off the completed matriculation papers. Many of the teachers seem to have thought him a poorish headmaster. But he wasn't for me. I'd never met anyone like him before. I remember once, when I was in the Upper Fifth, for some reason he marked or looked at a set of essays. I had written one on Hardy and had begun it, "Thomas Hardy was a truly cultured man . . ." He stopped me a day or two later, swung against the door of his study, and said, "What is 'a truly cultured man', Hoggart?" I was baffled. I thought he was playing me up, because if our headmaster didn't know what a truly cultured man was, if the phrase wasn't absolutely cast-iron, where were we? And he said ,"Am I one? I don't think so. I don't feel myself 'truly cultured'." This was my first sight of a mind speculating, of thought as something disinterested and free-playing, with yourself outside it. I usually thought of a master as somebody who said, "This is what the such-and-such a verb is, or this is what happened in 1762, and you have to learn it." That's one key person and later I had the good luck to be one of Bonamy Dobrée's students in the English Department at Leeds University. I have written about that elsewhere.* One of the things both my headmaster and professor did for me, and perhaps this is where my interest in cultural change starts, was to give me a feeling for cultural comparisons, between the cultures of the North and South in England, and between different social classes. They also helped me to get used to arguing and disagreeing, without taking it personally.

My grandmother was pleased and proud that I'd got to

* In 'Teaching with Style (on Bonamy Dobrée)', Vol. II of this collection.

grammar school, and she helped to make it easier to do homework, and in lots of other ways. There was still a sense in her of the old respect for learning. She used to tell me with great pride that 'poet Longfellow' and 'painter Hogarth' were both members of our family, and I think she was right. She read quite difficult books, which was unusual in a woman of her age and background. There were a handful of books in the house, because an uncle there also had some literary interest—one of her sons, the youngest. And we had the usual two or three volumes of Dickens given away by newspapers, a few woman's novelettes, of the sort that were presented at Chapel Anniversaries, but no great range. If there was a Bible it was never on show. I suspect there was one, but by and large there was little of the Bunyan-and-the-Bible tradition in the home. My grandmother was officially Church of England, but in an unexpectant, countrified way; she didn't make much of it. Certainly she had imagination and a latent capacity for intellectual excitement. I did my homework on the end of the table; obviously, there could be no heating in a bedroom. She always reminded me to do my homework and wouldn't let me go out to play till it was done. She would worry a bit if there was too much noise and say, "The lad's got to get on." It was recognized that it had to be done, but there were sharp limits to what they could physically make arrangements for. There were also what you might call imaginative limits, in that it would have been expecting too much of them to get everybody to hush up because I was doing my homework. There was no radio until quite late in the '20's or early '30's, when we could afford it.

I don't remember consciously getting the idea of going forward to higher education. I did what I was told to do, one step after the other. I didn't have a perspective, a vision of a goal. I enjoyed doing the work. I was in some ways timid and though I had a kind of quirky, urgent quality, I usually just went on. But I suppose I wouldn't have gone on if I hadn't enjoyed it at bottom. I did my four years to matriculation, during which time I had one nervous breakdown. That may have been a way of paying off a lot of strains that had been considerable before then; I've been able at least just to cope with my worst situations since. Then I took a very good matric. I hadn't even thought of a job, though I suppose I would have simply gone into town to a Labour Exchange or looked in the local paper. The headmaster put at the bottom of his report, "Should think of professional life." My grandmother didn't know quite what to make of that. She had an idea what professions were, but she didn't know exactly what it meant. So she asked the Board of Guardians' visitor, a lady called Miss Jubb who used to come from the Leeds Authority every so often and was very helpful and rather proud of me, because she didn't have many scholarship boys on her list. She said, "It means that he could well become, say, a doctor." Then she said, "Wait and see." If I've got my figures right, up to then the Guardians were paying 7s. 6d. a week for me, all in, and they increased it for my sixth-form work to about 15s. od.; and on this my grandmother felt she could go ahead, and was glad to do so.

So I worked for Higher School Certificate and after that there was talk of university, but there was never any suggestion of going to Oxbridge. The daughter of one of the senior masters went, I remember, to Oxford, but she'd had a special year's training. I didn't think much about making a choice of any particular university. The word seemed to get round that you went to Leeds University—instead of to a training college—if you did very well. I think the figure was then twenty Senior City scholarships; that is, twenty university scholarships from the Leeds L.E.A., every year, for the whole city of nearly half-a-million people. I don't remember being interviewed in advance at the University. I got a letter saying what I'd done in High School Certificate and it was good; and a letter saying I had been accepted by the English Department at Leeds University. I knew I wanted to do English and I imagine that my English master said, "You want to do English, don't you?" and I said, "Yes," and it went down on a form somewhere.

I was always a keen reader. I obviously had a respectable sort of mind, one that would have passed the eleven-plus scholarship exam with better training. For instance, I had the usual interest in working out abstract patterns. I got a Grade 1 at School Certificate in Maths, in spite of having failed Maths at eleven, so there was some ability there. As for imaginative excitement, the first instance I remember was when I was standing one day—I must have been about eleven at the time—in Hunslet Public Library. I picked up a complete Swinburne, read a lot of it and wanted to cry. That was the moment I first consciously felt the excitement of poetry. I can never scoff at Swinburne, though his faults are obvious, because he was making me respond to the wonder of words in their own right. But basically one went on, at Cockburn, doing the job. The literature work I loved, and became, as boys like me so often do, very mannered in my writing, mannered and poetic. The masters always said, "You're too elaborate." It takes a long time to work through that.

On going up to university I was in a mixed frame of mind. I was interested and eager; but I didn't go up feeling that this was to be the most wonderful period of my life. I knew I hadn't enough money to do anything very special. In my first year, when I'd paid for everything, I had left over for pocket money each week—that is, to pay for any books, fares, smoking, toothpaste and soap, fish and chips, cinemas and so on—1s. 6d.; and you couldn't cut a dash on that even in the '30's. I was not isolated because of this, since there were several others in that position. On the other hand, we felt a bit sniffy about students who took their pressed-cardboard attaché cases to the university each day from nine to five, and seemed to have settled for a subfusc routine. We had to create our own style on the cheap, so to speak. What pleased me about university life was, again, meeting people who were intellectually interested, who liked ideas and their relations to experience. Without that I would have gone on and done the work expected of me, but at the same time I would have felt detached from it. I could always hang from the chandelier with my alter ego. I think one of my basic qualities, and I suspect it comes partly from the whole working-class tradition, is a kind of dissident, ironic, micky-taking quality. I can remember how even at twelve or thirteen one side of me was very impressed by the grammar school masters, and I thought they lived lives of great comfort and luxury. But I also saw the long vista of what is often a kind of safe dreariness, and didn't like that at all.

Summing-up, I suppose there were several major turning-points in my childhood. The first was the move to my grandmother's home. Then, clearly, there was the scholarship exam at eleven. In terms of personalities: my grandmother, the headmaster of the elementary school, the headmaster of the secondary school and Bonamy Dobrée. Put another way, there was the change from that enclosed life with my mother in Potternewton into the big South Leeds slum school; then grammar school, and entry into the sixth form; and then the various moments of imaginative awakening, such as finding Swinburne's poems, and the discussion of essays by the headmaster. One of the strange things is how late it all seems to have been in my case.

I can recognize some characteristics, today, which I suppose are due to those experiences; though it's difficult to be sure. I often feel insecure and anxious to justify myself. I always feel guilty if I haven't 'done my homework', so to speak. I find it hard to relax sufficiently. Perhaps some of this is due to being an orphan, and changing homes. One of the obvious results of going to grammar school was that it gave you another world to live in, a different world from that of the streets of Hunslet. It had advantages, but I still sometimes feel I am working out this isolation. I react too quickly to hints that I am being cut out, rejected. On the credit side is the nonconformity and dissidence I've mentioned, a capacity, now and again, to say 'come off it'; and an ability to go on going on.

1966

A SENSE OF OCCASION

As I was thinking about this essay, a particular scene kept coming into my mind. It shows the classroom of a new secondary modern school on a municipal housing estate outside a provincial city. Almost all the large class of thirteen-years-olds look healthy and are well clothed; their young teacher wears what is almost a uniform—sports jacket and charcoal-grey flannels. A sense of vocation still gives some glow of idealism to his face, though it is shadowed with signs of strain. He is taking a poetry lesson and finding it at times rewarding, at times disillusioning. He knows most of his pupils go to the pictures at least once a week and watch television for two or three hours a night. They tell him about the programmes; they know he hasn't a TV set. He is an ex-scholarship boy, by choice committed to educating people whom he knows as deeply as one only knows those one was born among—and whom he yet feels he does not know.

Most of the cultural aspects of a complex social revolution can be seen there: the emerging Britain of a modest diffused prosperity, of a new kind of 'working class' and of the mass-media; a Britain which has superimposed on many other changes a stream of inter-class movements through educational opportunity; a Britain which has not yet learned to speak straight to its new self. If there is no war and no considerable economic breakdown it is likely that some social assumptions, and many forms and manners, will be very different by the end of the century from those we knew as children. My general assertion is that we are moving towards a sort of cultural classlessness; that if we understand these changes better the new society could be an improvement on the old; if we do not, it may be worse.

The present boundaries of the move towards cultural classlessness can be easily illustrated. British national morning newspapers are by tradition politically divided. As the popular press has become during the last few decades more and more a form of entertainment this political quality has weakened. But a typical resistance prevents the classless morning daily from emerging at present. The point so far reached can be seen in the *Daily Mirror* and the *Daily Express*, which between them account for more than half the total sales of daily national morning newspapers. There is some overlapping in readership, but substantially they appeal to two bodies of people who still like to think of themselves as distinct— say, to working-class with lower-middle and to middle-class people respectively. The two papers use different properties and forms of speech because these differences are still significant to their audiences. But the kinds of life each promotes are tending to merge; one sort of cultural classlessness can be seen in the making there, held at the moment from greater assimilation by a residual sense of difference.

In some respects television would be the best instance of emerging classless culture. Still, in one part of the field of popular publications the signs are greater, the culturally classless world is already here. The colonel's lady and Judy O'Grady are sisters under the skin and their reading—though previously class-divided (all the way from *Peg's Paper* to *The Lady*)—has never been much concerned with either politics or the arts. *Woman* is the first truly classless journal of the new Britain.

All classes are on the move but one class is most strikingly moving, emotionally and often physically. The great body of urban working-class people are at last beginning to leave the dark, dirty back streets and the imaginative horizons which the economics of life there encouraged. There is no need at this stage to look back in nostalgia. If we remember the physical conditions for these families—many of them our own families—fifty years ago, then we have a lot to thank our radical forefathers for. Our children ought to be healthier, and have more opportunities to develop their gifts, than our parents ever had.

*   *   *

What kinds of outlook will a technological, commercial, mass-communications society encourage? What qualities will the new class of consumers, embracing the large majority of the 37,000,000 adults in this compact and literate country, be urged to exemplify? Will they express a modern version of what we are used to thinking of as aspirant lower-middle-class attitudes? In some ways the pressures of a consumers' world do turn people away from traditional working-class attitudes towards those of the aspirant lower-middle-class; 'sticking together' tends to be replaced by 'keeping up with the Joneses'. But the prospects are both better and worse than this. Better, because the new society is likely to be more open and unaggressive. Worse, because it may become what the Americans call, speaking of trends in their own environment, 'bland'. 'Blandness', which is a sort of imaginative boiled milk, will be lying in wait for all classes, not only for those we are used to calling working people.

This situation is further complicated by two native characteristics: first, slowness to accept change (in working-class areas today there is little evident difference in the styles of emotional life from those of fifty years ago; and a conversation with a provincial lady Conservative usually illustrates how hard a sense of the importance of distinctions dies); second, the Establishment's power to maintain or remake itself by receptivity, flexibility and flair—its ability to absorb almost anyone into the British socio-cultural Happy Family. But though these qualities do make change slow, they do not finally prevent it; under the surface change is taking place all the time—in the life of that provincial town and housing estate, in that class of boys and their teacher.

If we look back to the activities of those who were concerned with social problems at the turn of the century, at the comparative sureness with which prospects were assessed and expressed—often in statements which are now classics of their kind, or in new social agencies—we are likely to decide that there must have been giants in those days, or that their problems were simpler. Perhaps it is easier to see a hole in a shoe than to assess the attitudes encouraged by television. No doubt those earlier documents got vigour from the more obvious relationships, to authors and audience, between evident needs and assumed values. But they remain memorable chiefly because of their intellectual and spiritual energy.

We could have a similar sense of occasion; the challenge today is in some respects finer. There is more dignity in questioning problems of choice than in opposing economic injustices. The present offers this challenge—to affect the future of a society which is now, because it is seeing some material improvements, in danger of losing its grip on its own strengths. A society can be bemused by its own slogans. A society which repeatedly tells itself that it is tired and second-rate will begin to act that way.

Changes of attitudes are needed generally; so are, more specifically, changes in some common attitudes on the Left. The British Left often exhibits a bull-headed parochialism towards artistic matters. At one extreme this is the brass-tacks insensitivity of many party and trade union officials, ready to associate anything artistic—or intellectual—with upper-class gentility; "Don't teach my boy about poetry; he's going to be a union boss", is their form of an old statement. At the other extreme is the narrowness of some intellectuals, a doctrinaire, anti-imaginative, single vision. Such people dismiss the evidence for an emerging classlessness by pointing out that, economically, the Insiders are still very much in control, or that only a minority of working-class families has so far left the dirty districts—and round matters off by calling the argument only another form of neo-Conservatism. They would like still to find visible villains—in the Establishment, in the Press, in the other media. Teasing out the interactions of greed, self-delusion and weakness all the way through workers, intellectuals and men of power is less satisfying. A tycoon is a more satisfactory enemy than an able, pleasant, amusingly disillusioned—and probably mildly Left-wing—advertising copywriter.

We are ignorant about many changes in depth. First, about

31

mass communications today. The basic facts of the situation are presumably well known: that during the last few decades the instruments for mass persuasion have undergone three main changes—a great absolute increase (e.g. in daily newspapers, which might have been expected to decline under the pressure from radio); a considerable centralization (chiefly because Britain is so small geographically); and an increasing concentration (we are reading fewer different publications). The pressures are mainly commercial. But the mass-media primarily reflect larger forces, and the event which did more than any other to encourage these three changes was the last war, when means of mass communication had to advance quickly if the common effort was to be improved. That immediate pressure is now relaxed (it will not disappear, though, and will probably gradually increase over the years unless we take steps to counter centralization). Still, to some extent we are back at a less publicly purposive society, but one with all the media available to it. That type of society will show certain tendencies in its use of the media.

These tendencies will not all be unfortunate; there are possible gains. It is right to remind ourselves of the strengths in traditional class-groups, the fidelity and gentleness of face-to-face working-class communities at their best, or the devotion and unself-seeking responsibility which the best upper-class training could produce. But there is room for a lot more light in the cramped places of the English imagination. We tend to be spiritually insulated and insufficiently flexible. We would do well to get rid of some of our emotional gaucherie, a prevailing half-light in the English soul at all levels of society. We need to adapt and find our own way, and not allow ourselves to be pushed in *their* way by the men from our version of Madison Avenue. We should be as capable of throwing up strengths relevant to our new situation as those working-class people who threw up new strengths so as to make life liveable in the harsh Victorian cities.

I do not think the mass-media of communication can do much to make any one of us think or feel the better. But they can to some extent widen our sense of other people's lives, irrigate our sense of humour, reduce our curtain-twitching narrowness, stimulate in a number of useful ways.

What of the other side of the coin? We know enough by now not to attack the mass-media on the grounds that they are crude, violent and sensational. Their temptations are not these. They are almost always on the side of the angels; their new society will be a very 'moral' one.

I have suggested that the mass-media must, whether consciously or not, work towards a culturally classless society. Stratification keeps the potential customers in separate groups. Mass sales are helped by suitable mass attitudes, and these the mass-media must encourage. They cannot move quickly, for they are bound to reflect what most people will accept at any one time; and this means they have to express what most people thought yesterday or this morning, not what some of them might move towards thinking tomorrow. They must roughly show us as we at present are or, more important, as we like to think we are. But their mirror-image progressively distorts. Clever shifts of angle and deceptions of lighting can slowly bring about a change; we begin to believe what the mirror says and do not notice its subtle alterations.

At present attempts to win consumers are a mixture of appeals to old attitudes (many common to all groups, though their forms still differ), and appeals to the popular philosophy of democracy in a debased form. Traditional working-class values such as group loyalty, tolerance and idiosyncratic non-conformity can change into the gang sense, 'anything goes' and 'no flies on Charlie'. Basic democratic ideas such as freedom, equality and progress can change into the notion of freedom from rather than freedom for anything, a lowbrow levelling and bandwagoning progressivism.

The writer who wishes to appeal across class divisions still has a difficult problem, since physical properties and manners are heavy with the overtones of class (from the posh to the low in almost every aspect of life). He has to find forms which will not arouse the irritations of unconscious class prejudice. Separated from the ability to draw upon local and particular situations, whether in Camberley or Hunslet, he has to invent a world acceptable to the greatest number in which his characters can move. So there emerges the copywriters', illustrators' and storytellers' bright unreal world, a smart-young-wife-dominated world of young couples moving among contemporary splay-legged furniture to prepare a modish meal out of a modernistic can. Oddly enough, the old class-defined way of life had advantages. We knew where we were and this allowed us—unless we belonged to the aspirant minority—not to waste much time being anxious about status and identity. We usually knew in our bones how to behave: that this was an occasion for bringing out a special bottle of wine, or getting the three-shilling tin of Grade 1 salmon off the kitchen top-shelf. There will be no gain if we are to be constantly running to the latest issue of *Good Housekeeping* to find out what 'place-setting' goes with what guests at this 'stage' in our career.

The process proliferates and feeds on itself. Compare the glossy narrow fragmentation of *Reveille* with the bitty but comparatively wide curiosity one used to find in *Tit-Bits*; or think of the hypocritical double-eye of the newer kind of Sunday sex papers; or of the way in which the old sense of the personal is graduating from the backyard fence to the larger-than-life personalisation of the soap-operas or of the 'national personalities' thrown up as a classless substitute—Royalty as it is treated today, the ubiquitous TV pals and all the other friendly persuaders. When local detail is no longer usable you are thrown on to the artificially projected.

But the main dangers are stereotyping, the pseudo and narcissism. If we think head-counting is all-important, we play for safety and are pushed towards simpler and bolder generalities. We dare not introduce many complexities and qualifications, even though most of us can sense these complexities without necessarily being able to articulate them. The *Daily Express*'s stage-stereotypes include the nice little semi, the small car, those dreadful teenagers earning £15 a week and the workers with TV in practically every room: the *Daily Mirror* has the pools, the push-bike, the honest pint. I hope the middle classes are not one and all such acidulous relatives of Mrs. Dale as the *Express* suggests: I *know* the *Mirror*'s working man is not true to life. As the *Mirror* insists, working-class people do often show gusto, tolerance, big-heartedness and scorn for pomposity. But they are also— and this the *Mirror* does not illustrate—sometimes very discriminating, often cautious and canny, and altogether more phlegmatic than the *Mirror*'s intermittent hysteria would lead an outsider to suspect. We are presented with a simplified inflation of some undeniable working-class virtues—but they are only meaningful when seen in relation to a great number of other virtues and vices. The *Mirror*'s stereotype is no more like the body of English working people than a stage cockney is like a real cockney.

The movement towards prefabricated responses is general. Recently I saw both a Conservative and a Labour Party political broadcast. Each exhibited the same stereotyped assumptions as the commercial mass-providers about the people they were so strongly claiming to speak for—standardized bright new interiors with bright new families; an unctuousness in the interviewer asking the father what he wanted from life (and turning the answer to his party's profit), a phoney toughness in the journalist put up to challenge the Minister in the name of the common man.

Behind all mass communication is an inhibiting condition: nervous awareness of the audience. The pressures begin with questions of sex and go on to almost anything which might shock anyone who happens to be in the audience. They all tend towards holding the limits of response at what is already acceptable; whatever is, is right. The mass-media insensibly encourage conservatism and conformity in both their providers and consumers.

But the competitive need to attract more consumers generates a pressure to find excitements, a constant tendency towards pseudo-sensationalism, towards the shadow-boxing 'radicalism' of the popular press when it goes on a 'crusade', towards the idiosyncrasy of characters who, going through the motions of nonconformity, produce an unrooted bloodymind-edness—the non-significant nonconformity of professional public grumblers. All this leads to a narcissism of the emotions. I spoke earlier of the way the older and class-based popular art was able to root itself in local and particular detail. So may highbrow art, because highbrows are or should be classless whilst reading, disinterested. A sensitive working-class youth can read *La Chartreuse de Parme* with the same sort of attention as he reads *The Loneliness of the Long-Distance Runner*, whereas the *Daily Sketch* or some popular middlebrow and middle-class novel would irritate him.

Moral values become meaningful in concrete situations; we come to know what tolerance means by living through to it in a succession of demanding situations. Good art, whether highbrow or popular, embodies its moral sense in specific details. The modern mass-media, inspired by the desire to reach across all classes and by their undervaluing of what people are capable of appreciating, are led towards a cracker-motto celebrating of certain values *in themselves*. Some television programmes exist chiefly to exhibit this narcissistic indulgence in emotions in and for themselves ('aren't we nice people—we are so tolerant—or kind to the aged'; not 'life is such and such . . . so tolerance is necessary'). Such programmes are not simple extensions of the occasions when Gracie Fields sang about tolerance, very sentimentally, to a Northern audience, for whom a sense of the virtue of tolerance had been forged in the business of day-to-day life.

This process is more developed here than most of us wish to realize. Americans are shocked by our popular press whilst we still tell ourselves that the worst features in modern mass-media are all American, that it can't happen here. We point to our checks and balances; the Trust quality-press; the Third Programme; the public libraries—forgetting that the adver-tisements on television are more symptomatic of middle-

twentieth-century trends. We tell ourselves that the 'intelligent minority' has increased from about 2 per cent to about 4
per cent of the population in the last fifty years and fail to
assess the centralization and concentration in the provision
for almost everyone else. We might inquire how many local
councils have increased the library rate to meet this increase
in the proportions of the 'intelligent minority'. We might say
to ourselves at intervals: in the fifties commercial television
was introduced, several quite good journals died and the
British Museum library continued to close at five o'clock because the country 'couldn't afford' to keep it open. Though
we are scarcely even maintaining our checks and balances we
use them as illustrations of our continuing cultural health—
like a man who refers to his maintained membership in a good
club to suppress the thought that all but one floor in his house
is let off to non-U tenants.

We show an open-mindedness which looks superficially like
mature tolerance but can be a weakness, fed by unease towards the mass audience and guilt about being 'highbrows'
at bottom. This is a knowing treason of the clerks which supports itself by not getting close to the reality of recent developments. I think here of M.P.s, dons and other writers for
intellectual journals who confess that they enjoy *Reveille*;
it is not as stuffy, they say, as the clever publications they
write for: they talk about *Reveille*'s roots in the full-blooded
tradition of British popular art.

Or there is that reaction to the advertisements on ITV
which takes the form of saying that, far from objecting to
them, one quite enjoys them; they are amusing. Of course
they are amusing; this is a gimmick of self-conscious mass-
persuasion. Amused intellectual patronage of this sort is a
long way from the laughter which expresses a nonconformist
refusal to buy an obvious line.

Or there are the people who admit they have a soft spot
for the *Daily Mirror*; 'it's got gusto', they say, and when it
speaks out is in the direct line of the old Radical tradition.
One does not need to deny that the *Mirror* is pleasanter than

the *Express*, or, of course, the *Sketch*; or that it expresses a kind of generosity: but it also fails totally to express the fullness of working-class life and of radicalism. Intellectuals who make this mistake are as crude in their judgments as the stockbrokers who enjoyed a vicarious thrill during the Suez adventure because the old lion was showing its teeth again.

It all helps consolidate a situation in which one group of graduates produces the mass goods and another excuses itself for dealing in a more highbrow brand—and compensatingly hastens to defend the first group. Or occasionally someone attacks mass-entertainments with an irrelevance to the real cultural issues which suggests that he is inspired by pique because he has not found either the wealth or fame which mass success brings. I suggested earlier that it could be a mistake to look for 'villains'. Yet the refusal to face issues can cover many peculiar activities, and it is a fact that today old Etonians and Wykehamists often direct mass-entertainments.

We shall not assess the possible effects of this process unless we have a firmer knowledge of 'ordinary' people's lives, of the interaction of family, neighbourhood and workplace relationships, of older and newer attitudes, in those local areas now being flooded with centralized goods and ideas. Life in those areas did not provide ways of meeting all emotional situations; but it provided for a great many and provided surprisingly well, by a kind of unconscious absorption. On balance it evolved an unexpectedly mature pattern of sanctions, responsibilities and freedoms, out of the exigencies of a life predominantly hard and unendowed. Behind its dull appearances it had a quality of melodrama, of the histrionic and heroic which—so middle- and upper-class is our predominant literary culture—one rarely finds accurately reflected in, for example, the English novel during the last half-century.

To realize this can lead to sentimental over-valuing; but that danger has to be met if we are to get away from the self-flattering attitude which thinks of working-class people as almost blank slates, with none of the rich manners of the middle and upper classes. The clichés of intellectuals can be as powerful as those of copywriters: the dulled automata of the mass-media or the upright workers waiting only to be turned into tidy lower-middle-class figures are as unreal as the hearty boozers of the advertisements.

If we do not gain this closer knowledge we shall fail to allow for the most hopeful group of elements in older attitudes—the power of resistance and resilience, of scepticism, nonconformity and irony; and the fund of decency which these support when they combine with traditional charity and tolerance. We have heard a great deal during the last few decades about 'the decline of family life'. If we look more closely we shall see that in fact the family holds together well. Similarly we shall gain a better sense of resilience, of the power to remake or to assimilate new elements in their own way, if we look without patronage at working-class amusements today. It is easier, because they have an antique music-hall flavour, to admit some of the strengths in working-men's club singing than to see the signs of life in skiffle and teddy-boy clothes. These elements may not amount to a great deal but they can show a kind of independence, vitality and choice. And even as one says this one realizes that such a widening of view only increases the need for sharp distinctions. Instances of vitality are usually taken over quickly by the mass-media, wrapped in cellophane, and then presented as the real thing. It's important not to confuse a more flexible view with cultural slumming or with a highbrow's anti-highbrow nostalgia.

Irony, scepticism and nonconformity; these and other elements make up a life of such body that most assessments seem thin by comparison. British people still exhibit a capacity to ignore the emotional changes expected of them, to laugh in the wrong places, to go on with their complicated human routines whilst the electronic computers and the electronically-transmitted persuaders buzz all round them. We shall meet better the change which is nevertheless going on all the time if understanding is based on unsentimental respect, on humane feeling which draws on as much as we can encompass of the realities of people's lives, so that we do not mistake the material now fathered on them for their true character.

The problem is further complicated by understandable difficulty in assessing what—if not a consumers' glossy culture —is to succeed a culture which was, in places of power, predominantly high bourgeois in tone. To assume that it is possible to spread widely the traditional kind of European high culture leads only to an impasse; which is why Ortega's *Revolt of the Masses*, once pondered, should be seen as the last fine statement of a position now largely irrelevant.

More of a nuisance, because more widespread, is the assumption that one is really seeking to develop a sort of middle-class culture-vulturedom. Group excursions of selected scholarship boys to Arts Council exhibitions may be valuable; but they are not the only nor even necessarily the best successors to working-men's club concerts or Frankie Vaughan. Jude the Obscure will not really have done more than get out of one trap and into another if he becomes a middlebrow semi-intellectual, specializing in opinionation rather than fragmentation, graduating from *Tit-Bits* or the *Weekend Mail* to the *Reader's Digest* and *Any Questions*.

When this uncertainty goes with that lack of knowledge of and slight guilt towards 'the people' which I have described it produces a peculiar deference in intellectuals when they speak or write before a mass audience. So on the one hand there is the Intrusive You ('you too can . . .') or Wot Abart it Chums of the popular mass-media; on the other hand, the 'I'm sure viewers will agree . . . a good argument even though no questions were settled . . . ventilation . . . friendly exchange . . . etc.' of intellectuals who also are hesitant at the thought of the Great Public outside, who smile and smile in a way they never smile at their undergraduate students in seminars. It is a strained desire to be accepted which reminds one of a colonel advised by his adjutant that he really must have a drink in the men's mess at Christmas. And every day is becoming Christmas now, what with the quizzes and the forums and the brains trusts. We mitigate such force as our convictions have as much as the fighting men of the popular Press. If we would dare to risk being dull or intransigent, we might become interesting in a new way.

After all, there does exist the waiting group I indicated at the beginning of this essay, in the figure of the young uprooted teacher. Here we may be thinking of small numbers, and my own illustration may lead to the suspicion that I am going to talk about some small and dissident cult. This is not so, and two considerations should make clear why. First, the dissident or concerned (no word is entirely satisfactory here) exist in all classes and have a variety of backgrounds and intellectual equipment. One of the best fruits of the educational and cultural changes of the last few decades has been that increase in the informed minority in all parts of society which I mentioned earlier.

Second, and more important, we need to realize that many people at some time, with some part of their experience, belong to this group. There is no firm or final division into the eggheads and the rest. We are all in some ways more discriminating than the image of us which the mass-media put out; we are all at intervals among the dissident, the concerned, the serious. No thought can do more to discourage us from timidly flattering that abstraction 'the people'—than this: that it *is* possible, even among all the noise, now and again to make contact with people other than through the simplified generalities of the mass-media.

For all that, the peculiar problems of those who can be described as an uprooted minority do throw into relief some complexities of emerging classlessness and some possibilities for growth. One of the most difficult feats for an Englishman from below the upper-middle-classes is simply to become educated or an intellectual. In seeking to be so he is pushed towards a whole new set of social forms, a new range of ways to speak, write, laugh and cry. In the degree to which he is sensitive he is likely to be carrying on throughout a love-hate duel with social manners. This is not altogether a bad thing.

One of the advantages of the culture-and-class mixture is that we are not strongly tempted to think of ourselves—simply because we have cultural or intellectual leanings—as the bearers of a sort of Cain's brand, creatures whom the power-groups or money-groups in our society are quite unused to accommodating. We are not greatly pushed towards the heroics of alienation and despair, towards becoming self-consciously esoteric or towards a sense of separation from practically all of society's everyday life.

Still, the disadvantages are considerable, especially in a society changing as comprehensively as this. So far this challenge has not been appreciated. Why are the sixth forms in grammar schools not bursting with a special energy at this time? Why are provincial universities, which have greatly developed during the last thirty years, still generally regarded —for all the public assertions to the contrary—as inferior imitations of Oxford and Cambridge? Or recall the recent U and non-U controversy. It had its amusing side, and one might seem over-solemn to regret it. Yet how parochial it was. The fact that it roused so much interest indicates that this kind of frozen irrelevance matters far more in English life than it should. No doubt we all know local authority schools where the junior mistresses, scholarship girls from local training colleges, spend a lot of time teaching the children to say that they want to go to the 'toilet'. On the other hand, I used to think that American and Irish voices were popular on the radio because they sounded tough or folksy; I now think they are liked because they are free of class over-tones. Eamonn Andrews can speak to English children in a voice with an aura quite different from that of the prosperous Sussex uncles we hear on the B.B.C. But most people still type-cast regional accents by class or comedy (every Lanca-shire man his own George Formby); and don't recognize that the genteel Oxford drawl is as much a form of lazy speech as the urban working-glass glottal stop.

These are only instances of factors which lead many people who might have become informed and active to stay in a cultural no-man's land, suspecting the 'fancy' forms which seem to be concomitant with the condition of being 'cultured', suspecting also the imaginative inadequacy of the more activist Left wing which claims to speak to their condition. We are not short of sources of information and intellectual stimulation: we are short of people who try to choose and discriminate consistently, and here might be a good point to start. If we learn to speak relevantly to such listeners, we might also express ourselves more satisfactorily when we try to communicate more widely. We have nothing to lose but our fear of 'the masses' and the mass-media. We can afford to be more highbrow; we can hardly afford not to be, at the risk of losing what small virtue we have. When a society reaches the point where some of its most successful citizens can speak of 'the faith of a salesman' its language has become blurred and so has its hold on its own life. In this part of the problem we are committed to increasing the area of consciousness. We have to think harder of ways to keep open that decent middle range in communication which is truer to the talents of most of us than the 'wotcher-cock' populars. The distribution of readers for the more serious publications suggests that, for the first time in our history, cultural and intellectual matters need no longer be associated almost entirely with selected social groups. Here is a particular and fairly precise point at which one good kind of classlessness might begin to emerge, a classlessness neither that of outsiders nor that of massed consumers.

The ideals of the young teacher described at the beginning of this essay, though now somewhat inhibited, are strong and well-rooted in the tradition of British nonconformist idealism. At the moment he has been led into a sandy delta. Luckily, he usually has a saving irony towards himself—his own type of scepticism—which should prevent him from becoming an amateur Cassandra and, if he does begin to act, could save him from the callower progressivisms in much progressive social thought.

My argument has been that we need to think more firmly in

three main areas: about the use and misuse of the mass-media; about persistent old strengths; and about the whole business of change in class formulations, its strains and its promise. It is a matter of reassessing our own view of ourselves, our false formulations or irrelevant romanticisms. Between the grey Britain often conjured up by depressed intellectuals and the export-Britain of Elstree, the British Travel and Holidays' Association, the British Council (too much Galsworthy and clubmen), or the artificial heroics of *The Bridge on the River Kwai*, there already exists in part, and there could grow stronger, another Britain, not at all so grey and limited, and a great deal tougher.

This period is full of exacting and potentially fruitful tensions. If we still have some belief in the ideals which were partly responsible for bringing us to this point of change then we have no cause to be alarmed. We are likely to become in a certain sense classless. It need not be left to the free operation of blind forces to encourage a classless conformity of consumers. By a close discipline of thought and feeling, working from the grounds outwards, we shall be better able to take stock of the lines for growth. We often accuse the Americans of false democratic *bonhomie*. To me the most chastening aspect of life over there is the realization that people at all levels of wealth and power really can, at times, look at each other face-to-face, that they can believe that each is as good as the next man. When two Englishmen meet for the first time, by contrast, one can almost hear the built-in fruit-machines of class-assessment whirring. Yet we could find a decent classlessness, one fed not by the admirable American dream but by a fusing of the lived-into virtues still to be found in all our classes.

1958

CHANGES IN WORKING-CLASS LIFE

I SHOULD guess that it is a long time since British people as a whole, and working-class people in particular, felt so sharply the sense of change in their lives. This conversation was recorded in a public-house in a Northern working-class district at the beginning of the 1960s. I do not think one would have heard it five years before. It indicates with economy, and vividly, the main cause and effect of the changes in British life today. The speaker is a middle-aged working-man:

> "Everyone's bloody-upside-down if you ask me," said Freddy. "They're bound to be happier," went on Owd Jem, "because they've got a bit of cash to play with!" He stared at us to let his words sink in. "Before the war money was that tight every penny was spoken for! But today folk have a bit of choice. And they feel better for it. You go out and you can see it on their faces. They're no longer frightened. They feel freer. It stands to reason!"*

Prosperity—to make generalizations out of what he is saying —removes old fears and increases confidence; it increases the power to make choices of one's own, because the straitjacket of poverty has been loosened. It increases the feeling of individuality, of being a person with idiosyncratic wishes and decisions. Of course, to feel more of an individual is not necessarily to be more of an individual; there are plenty of agencies which aim to take money from working people by encouraging their feelings of individuality whilst, in fact, encouraging them to think and choose exactly like millions of others.

You can begin to see the main physical changes by making a simple tour through, for instance, one of those massive working-class districts—in the North, the Midlands or London—which are monuments to the energy and toughness of

* Quoted in *Britain Revisited* by Tom Harrison, Gollancz, (1961).

45

the Industrial Revolution. Most of them were established in the early and middle years of the nineteenth century. It has always surprised me that they remained so little changed for so long. I was a working-class boy in the 1920's and '30's and my physical setting was substantially late-Victorian. Nonconformist chapels, battered pubs, tiny corner-shops, cheap little houses, even the uneven cobble-stones in the road, all had been there since about 1870 and framed a way of life which, in many of its essentials, had not greatly changed. Look at those districts today or, if they have been cleared, go outside to the new municipal housing areas. Many of the old areas still do exist, because rehousing is slow; but the late-twentieth century is emerging in a thousand details: in the wider range of goods in the corner-shop's window (the shop itself may well have become a small supermarket), in the forests of television aerials, in the scatter of cars—usually second-hand —outside the doors. You can see it in people's clothes, and especially in the clothes of younger people. The clothing which identified a class, the clothing which says that you are and expect to remain a worker, has almost gone. In Lancashire 25 years ago clogs were still often worn and the women draped black shawls round their heads and shoulders; today they can hardly be found and in their place are a variety of relatively cheap and usually attractive clothes. Some day a study will be written about the contribution of one firm— Marks and Spencer's—to this change. Women's drinking cannot now be identified by the old music-hall jokes about stout and port-and-lemon. The new drinks look sophisticated, are not heavy or befuddling and are reasonably cheap. Showerings of Somerset estimated this need precisely a few years ago and produced Babycham, perry (pear cider) which has been aerated and vaguely suggests champagne. Packed so as to increase this suggestion, it sells enormously. Even the fish-and-chip shops sell roast chicken and chips; and Chinese restaurants exist in towns so solidly Northern working-class that the conjunction seems at first against nature. Recreations are becoming more glossy, streamlined and centralized—bigger

Bingo saloons open week after week and indoor bowling alleys on the American pattern, large and bright and electronic, are taking hold.

Leicester, where I used to live, is basically what used to be called a 'respectable-working-class' town. Its population is about three-hundred thousand and they tend to work in medium-sized industries (making knitted woollen goods, typewriters, shoes, printing machinery, polishes). It has always needed a lot of female labour, so its married women are used to going out to work. It has been a centre of Nonconformity and must have more unusual small sects than most cities of its size; it is the birthplace and a strong centre of the working-men's club movement (when these began they had an educational and philanthropic side). It is a cautious, undramatic, hard-working town, full of streets of small and quite tidy houses; and it has never had a real centre. There is practically nothing monumentally civic in the whole place, nothing which says with the voice of the City Fathers—this expresses the corporate being of Leicester.

Today there are plans for a large and probably attractive city centre, though it will not appear for many years. But the new, centralized society is in fact arriving very quickly. It is arriving through the inevitable movement of commerce, for Leicester claims to be the most prosperous—or sometimes the second most prosperous—city in Europe. This is based on its per capita income; Leicester's money is spread unusually evenly over its thousands of individual families. So it is moving quickly into the consumer-families' world of the 1970's and '80's. In the space of a few months it opened, in the middle of town, one of the biggest car-park structures in Europe with, on its ground-floor, the largest supermarket in Britain and on its forecourt the largest petrol-filling station in Britain.

But these are surface details, physical changes which are only pointers. The important questions have to do with the way in which habits, manners of life and attitudes, are changing under the new pressures. It is easy to name the main agents of change and some have been mentioned already. Prosperity is clearly the most important. To a quick or biased observer prosperity may seem to encourage chiefly 'materialism', by which is meant the wish to have certain large consumer goods. More important, as we saw earlier, prosperity can increase the sense of individual choice; and it can lengthen perspectives. It not only gives immediate opportunities but, since work is more secure, encourages a longer view, the ability to plan ahead. If you fear unemployment without warning you will not, when extra money becomes available, be likely to plough it into some future project; you will be more likely to spend it at once and enjoy a brief liberation from the grind of week after week. Now working people can begin to plan ahead and, inevitably, younger people are leading the way—especially young married couples. Such an adjustment is not easy; it requires a point by point change in old outlooks, old habits, old customs.

Then there are the changes in housing. Those tightly-packed working-class communities—'the barracks of industry', the Hammonds called them—are being cleared. But they were not simply row upon row of shabby dwellings for masses of workers. They were more like interlocking villages, with their own close and embracing ways of life. They had developed these ways partly—perhaps primarily—in response to the social and economic situation of their inhabitants. You were, for example, a 'neighbourly' person and hoped those around you were good neighbours too. This neighbourliness was fed by your Christian background (which was probably Nonconformist) and by your feeling that, if you did not help one another, no one outside in the larger and more prosperous world would much help you. Nor could you, as the middle classes could, often buy service for money. A particular economic situation helped nurture a specific way of life.

Now those districts are being cleared. More and more people are moving into the architect-designed new towns, or on to suburban housing-estates on the far outskirts of the cities. These estates are improving but many of them look inorganic and are inorganic; they have no natural centres and their layout does not encourage the emergence of centres for social life—'a graveyard with lights' said a teenager of the main street in one such brick and concrete estate. Or people are moving back into the old districts after they have been cleared, and after towering blocks of flats have risen on the ground which before contained hundreds of two-storied little houses in a horizontal vista for as far as one could see. Again, people have to learn to live in their new settings, to find contacts, to establish habitual routines, to identify their relationships with their neighbours, their estate, the larger town life—and with themselves as a family, since that too changes as its setting changes. It is not easy now to maintain, for instance, one of the strongest characteristics of the old districts: the extraordinarily complicated interweaving of visits between members of the 'extended families'. Grandmother was likely to be around the corner in the next street, available to help and be helped; whatever they may have lacked, children grew up with a sense of the interdependence and continuity of generations within a family. Cousins, aunts, uncles, all were likely to be within hailing distance and to be constantly 'bobbing in' for a word.

Even more, people are becoming readier to move as the locations of work change. In my childhood a man belonged first to a district and if his job came to an end he—being probably a general labourer—looked for another job in another works in the same area. He hardly thought of moving from that area. Today his son is likely to pack his suitcase and move where new work and bigger money are to be found —to the Midlands and the complex of motor-car industries; or to the outskirts of London and one of the new electronics factories. Similarly, the nature of work is itself changing and will go on changing. The Lancashire cotton-belt is, as a cotton-belt, almost dead. But the big mills are not all of them silent. Some are on new kinds of work, which their skilled men can do as well as anyone. But the old 'general labourer' seems likely to be less and less in demand; training of some kind is more and more needed. The pattern of relationships at work itself is changing—the old pattern of men-on-the-bench, with the foreman between them and the lower echelons of management, is giving way to more elaborate, more professionally 'lubricated' forms of industrial relationship. Functions are defined in more complex ways. More married women are appearing in the factories as work becomes physically less heavy and increasingly demands precision and patience. All these industrial changes challenge older habits and assumptions.

As the changes increase the style of life has to alter or absorb. It is difficult to live in a society which is changing so quickly, and perhaps especially difficult if much in your way of life was previously decided by the customs of the group, if the range of deliberate, planned, conscious, individual decisions was limited by custom as well as by lack of cash. Here a whole new feature of British life comes in strongly: mass communications. Mass communications—advertising, the press, television, magazines (especially women's magazines, which are flourishing since women decide on major purchases and lead the movement towards new social styles)—all these do more than pass idle hours. They are helping people to come to terms with, to live with, their new world and new opportunities. Older working-class habits are being eroded and working people—whatever some observers may say to the contrary—do not on the whole wish to imitate the manners of the traditionally 'higher' groups: they want a new style, a new picture of life. The new men, the classless men—the advertisers, their artists and copywriters, television personalities, magazine columnists—are creating an image of a new way of life which does not belong to the old class-defined society of the past. All these are socially educative forces. Their aims are not usually disinterested and we may suspect the sort of life they promote. But we must recognize that they are social teachers, are replying to an unspoken but powerful need for directions within a more open society. As one of their spokesmen has said, grand as ever: "Advertising may play a large part, perhaps a leading part, in teaching the art of living."

But this is going ahead too quickly, claiming too much change too soon. In some important respects working-class life is still much as it always was. I remember noting this power in the middle-fifties—the power not only to resist change but to assimilate, modify and adapt to traditional ends, things which looked at first like major agents of change. Professor Zweig makes the same point in the early sixties, and will not be the last to do so. There is a strong thrust, or drag, to keep things recognizably as they have usually been, especially in those parts of life which are most personal and near to us. Of course, change is going on even here; but it will be a long time before major breaches are made in some areas.

Supporting this capacity is the assumption that home and family life are the most important things in life. In some sense this may be true of working people in other countries, but comparisons like that would not have much point in this essay. In some sense this may be true of other classes in England, but a working-man's feeling for home and for his family life is not quite the same as that of a man from another class. Home means both a refuge and a place of free-standing independence against an outside world which is rough or which holds you of little account. Here you can 'go your own way' once the door is shut; and here there should be, it is felt, love and affection. One gets above all, listening to people talking about their ideal of 'a good home', the impression of a warm and cherishing security. The ideal is not always attained, of course, but ideals are illuminating. Behind this assumption one can see again, as behind the belief in 'neighbourliness', a creative response to economic and social hardships.

Is the sense of family, then, unaffected by the new movements in society? Not quite. Leaving aside metaphysical relationships, a sense of powers outside man, we can say that all of us have to try to establish working relationships in four areas: with our own personality, with our family, with our immediate neighbours and locality and—last—with some larger groups. Traditionally, working-class people put most emphasis on establishing relationships in the second and third categories; and most of all in the second category, in relationships within the family.

By the first area, 'personality', I'm thinking of the extent to which the assumptions of one's group encourage one to be individualistic, to think of oneself as a separate personality. These distinctions are bound to be rough, but one may say that the older forms of working-class life did not much encourage the development of strong individual 'personality'; to have done so would have worked against the emphasis on the importance of the family and the neighbourhood-group. It may well be that 'personality' in this sense becomes stronger as you move into the middle classes or aspire to do so (e.g. the individual desire to 'get on' in life, or the individual acceptance of larger social responsibilities—the self-made business man or the devoted colonial official). It seems likely that the sense of 'personality', of individuality, will appear to become stronger among working people—partly because it will be encouraged in its own right, partly because it will grow as the sense of neighbourhood weakens. Yet it will have to co-exist with strong pressures towards mass conformity. So it may actually not be stronger at all. One might see emerging a massive pseudo-individualism.

As to our second area of relationships, those within the family: here the power to adapt and assimilate the objects of the early sixties is remarkably illustrated. The two most obvious products are the television set and the motor-car. Most working-class families now have a television set; many have a car and within a decade most are likely to own one. The television set is quite obviously keeping the family together. It cuts down attendance at cinemas and even at public-houses. It dominates the living-room, as a sort of substitute-hearth; and the family group around it. It can, we always tell ourselves, suggest wider horizons, different ways of life, new ranges of outside activities. But primarily it is a cohesive force. Most working-class families have it on for three to four hours a night, as a sort of unifying noise and moving picture, whatever the actual content of individual programmes. It does not much appeal to teenagers; it is too enclosed, too much of the family hearth, for them; they are beginning to find their own way, in the town's coffee-bars. They are moving into the almost autonomous and classless world of the European teenager. More, the circle round the television set tends to keep out odd members of the 'extended family' who used to drop in for a gossip. All in all, we may say, the set encloses the single family more and more within itself, the family of father, mother and the younger children. Here, it co-operates with the new forms of housing, which tend to isolate individual family-units.

So some people say that television reinforces the family. But what does this mean? The old family hearth was a gregarious and garrulous place (as any studious scholarship-boy knew better than most; it was all-embracing and assumed that people hardly ever wanted to be alone or silent. You heard all night the gossip of work and neighbourhood and school, with the chirp of a pet-bird or the yawning of a family cat in the background. Is watching television—though it is often broken by talk—really strengthening the same sort of relationship as existed round the living-room fire? In many respects that life goes on; people can carry on the traditional life of the family against the most persistent background. But for how long? It is likely that as the years pass the relationships within such family groups will change. Visions of the future tend always to project at unreal speed and without enough checks and balances; but the tendency is towards holding millions of disparate individuals each umbilically linked to the one quasi-personal centre.

By contrast with the television set, the motor-car might seem likely to break up the cohesion of the family. It takes people away from the hearth, introduces them to new areas and new ways of behaving. There is some evidence that working-class people with motor-cars are beginning to desert their local 'pubs' and go out to different kinds of public-houses, houses not so identified with one social class and its manners. But in spite of such exceptions the most striking characteristic of the working-class adoption of the motor-car is that they have assimilated it to their own uses, their own older values and attitudes. Middle-class observers have remarked, with regret or amusement, that most working-class people do not know how to take advantage of a car. When they get to the countryside or the sea-front they do not always go for a good walk or a swim. They are just as likely to sit in the crowded and fuggy machine, surrounded by food and newspapers, with the window steamed-up and a transistor blaring out the Light Programme. But this, as Dr. Mark Abrams was the first to point out, is one form of adaptation; the car has been taken over, made to fit, made into an extension of the family living-room. It has become for many people 'a mobile living-room'.

Old habits die hard. Hobbies, for example, have always been a major interest of working-men. Some of them, such as fishing or pigeon-fancying, may take men outside the home. Many more keep them pottering about in the house or yard. There seems no evidence that this interest has weakened, in spite of the attraction of television. Here, prosperity is bringing the sophistications of technology into old routines; many working-class handymen get sets of home-power-tools for Christmas from their wives.

It is increasingly common among young married couples for the wives to stay at work for a few years. Both husband and wife tend to accept overtime willingly, and to put their spare money into purchases which will help establish their new style, that style so often taught by the women's magazines.

A subtler change lies behind this, a change in the relative positions of the father and mother within the family. Traditionally, the father was the boss whether he was in or out of work. This is not to say that the mother was necessarily a drudge and feeble creature. She had her sources of power and authority and, to the children (as many a novel by an ex-working-class boy shows), was the heart and centre of the hearth. Still, the husband was regarded as and referred to as 'the master' and enjoyed a kind of deference or respect. He was the one who every day and for long hours toiled in a not particularly friendly outside world and brought back the money which gave shelter and food to the mother and children. In both father and mother this relationship produced strengths and weaknesses, both in quite large measure —at the extremes the domineering but careless father and the protective but smothering mother. Now the trend seems to be towards a more even balance of power and responsibility between the parents. Two purses, two people going out daily into the outside world, make as much difference to the internal relations of a family as they do to its capacity to buy goods. At the moment women seem to work until children begin to appear, to start again when the last child (probably of two or three) has begun to go to school, and to give up finally at about the age of fifty. As the nature of work changes, so men's work is not so often heavy, back-breaking; his wife may be doing a job physically no less demanding than his and perhaps more demanding in skill. So the tired-out husband sitting at his sacred seat by the fire, plied with mugs of tea by his home-bound wife, is becoming less and less typical. We are more likely to come upon a husband and wife, each quite tired, but each doing a share of that work about the house which has had to wait until they both returned from work. More and more husbands help with the occasional chores such as washing-up; more and more take shares with the basic housework. Among younger couples, more and more make joint decisions about the spending of the family's spare money; and more and more young husbands can be seen pushing prams around the streets on shopping expeditions.

The third area of relationships I suggested is the immediately social: relationships within the locality or neighbourhood. These are 'face-to-face' relationships outside the family. Here, I think, the trend is towards a weakening. We have seen that the old form of life—in its physical setting and economic background—helped encourage a remarkably strong sense of neighbourliness. Wives talked regularly over backyard fences, slipped into one another's houses, helped one another in times of stress (childbirth, illness and so on). Husbands did not take so active or pervasive a part in maintaining the neighbourly network; but they lived within it through listening to their wives and contributed to it at the local pub or working-men's club, and by helping one another with odd jobs at nights and weekends (two men would decorate a room or put up a hen-hut). Much of this still goes on, naturally, even in the most individualized-looking suburban estate. But it is easy to see how some present tendencies are combining to weaken the sense of belonging to one's immediate neighbourhood. One can buy things or services which hitherto one had to rely on neighbours to lend or give. Wives are not so likely to be at home all day and, when they do get back from work at night, are too busy cleaning the house to have much time for gossip. When a wife and her husband relax they are likely not to go out but to stay in watching television. So the older sense of neighbourliness is likely to be transformed. New groupings will emerge; young wives with babies, for instance, do need help from each other and the reassurance of one another, and on even the most unpromisingly agoraphobic estate they will create ways of satisfying these needs—at the Clinics or Launderettes, for a start. But they will have to act, to take thought, to learn some of the arts of social intercourse to do so; they will not be immersed within a neighbourhood and an extended family like fish in a deep pool.

The last of the four areas of relationship was the largest and most varied; it covers larger, public groups, relationships wider and less immediately intimate than those of a neighbourhood or locality. (But not, in this essay, relationships at work. They are very important but I'm not qualified to talk about them.) They can cover a wide range—from clubs and societies which people join because they have common interests, not simply because they happen to live in the same street or area (e.g. advanced hobby clubs, cultural clubs), to those which imply a larger than local sense of one's rights and responsibilities (local government or party political activities, for instance). Understandably, this kind of activity has not hitherto attracted more than a tiny minority of working-class people (though that minority has exercised an influence out of proportion to its numbers). But for most the character of their lives and especially of their assumed relation to the public world outside did not encourage this 'civic' awareness. Just as certainly, more working-class people need to acquire this sense or we could end with a society which would look freer than the old but would really be less free (since most of its citizens would be sitting, mildly content, among their possessions in the enclosed family lounge). Working people are likely to begin to move outwards, but rather slowly. I do not think mixed or general-purpose social clubs in the new areas will be the main sources of strength here. Working people will probably move outwards by means of those specialist skills and hobbies which prosperity is encouraging them to develop even further. Most British hobbies and recreations have been identified by social class (our kind of people do this kind of thing, not that kind of thing); but these divisions are crumbling. In one town, for example, the local education authority claims to have some of the most successful classless groups in Britain—of teenagers bound together by common specialist interests in such pursuits as advanced photography and boat-building. As that generation marries and sets up its homes it is more likely to want to retain centres of association for these specialist or 'highbrow' interests than to feel drawn to recreating neighbourhood centres of the old general kind.

Some people are content to sum up all this change in the phrase: "The working classes are becoming middle class." What does that mean?

If it means that many working people, being rather more prosperous and secure, are acquiring the longer perspectives described earlier, the statement might seem partially true. The fact that previously most working people did not dream of buying their own homes was not usually due to indolence or a desire to live for the day. They knew enough about their lack of prospects, the uncertainty of their jobs, their incapacity to obtain credit from a Building Society, not to cry for the moon. But now they are beginning to look forward longer, are taking out bank accounts (often in the Post Office Savings Bank which seems 'homely'—the main banks still look formidable though they are now making big efforts to convince newly affluent groups, especially young married couples, that a cheque book is as much part of a normal man's equipment as is the key to his front door); or people are planning their children's education as a long-term matter; and they are becoming more ready to think of buying their own houses. To buy a house is an act of confidence, based on a long steady look down a vista of twenty years. It is only within the last year or two that more than an occasional member of my family—those of us who became teachers, chiefly—have made this considerable imaginative leap. This sort of thing may be called middle class. But it does not necessarily indicate that working people wish to assume the mores of the middle class; it is a form of parallelism, a sign that more and more working people have reached that stage of security at which they too can adopt some of the more useful practical arrangements long common to middle-class people.

And of course most working people are anxious to own more of the larger consumer goods. Many of them are keen to work overtime; they have a lot of leeway to make up. As more goods come on to the market and as wage-rates rise rather more quickly than the prices of many of the more attractive mass-produced consumer goods, so extra money is spent on things man and wife jointly want. If you put in the extra hours the goods are available, are within reach.

Will all this and much else—increased eating in restaurants, the spread of wine-drinking, the increase in telephone installations, foreign holidays—make working-class people middle-class? Not in any useful sense of the words. The essence of belonging to the middle class was to hold a certain range of attitudes, attitudes chiefly decided by that class's sense of its own position within society, and its relation to the other classes within it. From this its characteristics—its snobberies as much as its sense of responsibilities—flowed. These attitudes are not brought into play merely by possessing certain objects or adopting some practical notions from the middle class.

New kinds of social stratification may be developing, but they will not correlate exactly with the old social orders and gradings. And they will have to mesh, somehow, with a partial classlessness. Here one comes back to the world of mass communications, to those agencies which are helping to educate people socially for life in a changing society. The voices from the older order—the public and 'establishment' voices, the voices of the Guardians—find it increasingly difficult to make themselves heard. The new voices of the mass persuaders are more friendly and gregarious and consumer-conscious; in many respects they are more attractive than the old, slightly hierarchical voices. They are also, very often, callow and cheap. But they have their ears to the ground and are likely to register major successes for years ahead. In a puzzlingly open society the voices of popular mass communications are bound to be ingratiating. In all this teenagers are, as usual, the best barometers. They have taken over much of the new commercial world (after all, it isn't drab); but many of them make their own criticism of this world. They know when they are being 'got at' and make themselves some space for living in their own way. As they marry they are beginning to constitute the first generation of working-class families which has not known economic distress and insecurity. They belong to a more prosperous world and have either assimilated themselves to its persuasions or—whilst taking advantage of its opportunities—have learned how to make their own choices. They have then become more self-aware as individuals, more used to making decisions, than their parents were usually required to be.

So there is a tension between the movement towards a kind of openness and the movement towards a narrowing or stratifying. The openness I have already sufficiently described, and its origins in increased prosperity and security, in industrial changes and the erosion of older class-forms. And I have suggested that to live in so much more open a society requires a degree of self-awareness, of critical choice-making, greater than we have been accustomed to, and from many more people. The narrowing and stratifying is being assisted by two groups of forces not naturally allied, since one is commercial and the other a product of social good intentions.

The commercially-inspired movement towards narrowing is a result of the tendency of a prosperous commercial democracy to weld its consumers—its customers; its readers—into large single blocks. This process of concentration can be seen in any technologically advanced country but is particularly well advanced in Britain. Look at the press. In the last twenty years we have taken to reading more and more newspapers. Yet—and this is the evidence of concentration—we publish fewer different newspapers today than we published twenty years ago. More and more of us are reading the same newspaper. This is economically more profitable to those newspapers which remain; it can be a convenience to advertisers; it can be assisted by persuasion. Look also at the energy and skill which are used every week to make teenagers turn their attention only to a very few popular songs on gramophone records, buy them in great numbers and forget them as soon as the next batch has appeared. Or look at the tendency in television—a tendency aggravated by the existence of only two channels—to settle not for the programmes which stimulate (and so divide) but for those which keep the largest possible number quiet for night after night.

The educational system, oddly enough, seems at the moment as much to be encouraging this tendency as to be working against it. It can more easily encourage stratification than educate people to live in an open society. One could argue that within such a society the primary aim of education should be to help people to live intelligently; to live not by the routine habits of a class nor according to the wishes of commerce nor of one's self-regarding ego. One might argue that education should be taking a longer view of that peculiarly pressing need for personal and social education which is now being answered, in their own way, by many of the commercial mass-persuaders.

There are places where teachers try to do this. But the main trend is in another direction. It is towards a stratification remarkably like that cultural concentration and centralization described above. Scholarships and a wide range of other arrangements are making it easier for a boy of any class to receive training to the limits of his capabilities. On the face of it, this is a plain gain. The difficulty is that, unless we at the same time take more thought about the aims of education, we shall encourage the appearance of a society in which, though the old gradings by birth have been removed, a new grading, a new hierarchy, a new stratification by function, has appeared. No doubt the traditional British feeling that, do what you will, there are always three basic types of human being (the high, the middle and the low) will help this trend. We are still too ready to think, though often unconsciously, that about 70 per cent of the population are the ineducable remnant. They are a very large remnant.

We commonly underestimate the capacities of working people. It was easy to think in this way when workers looked —and probably sounded, since British speech is so much defined by class—like members of a 'lower order'. Yet a kind of contempt for people can be found in the friendly but condescendingly shallow approach of many 'democratic' mass persuaders today. It would be better if we could combine some of the strengths of the old life (tolerance, nonconformity, neighbourliness, responsibility) and some of the new (flexibility, greater emotional and intellectual disinterestedness). Otherwise, we could move from the inarticulate 'lower classes' to the conformist classless mass in one easy stage. It really depends, at bottom, on how we look at one another. What sort of people do we think we are? What sort of people do we think 'they', the body of other people, are?

1961

THE 'CONDITION OF ENGLAND' QUESTION

I WAS struck by an American friend's reaction to Britain when he came here recently, after a long absence. He is a Renaissance scholar and an anglophile, in particular a respecter of the dense inherited textures of British social life. I wondered whether—when he first saw a Britain of skyscraper office-blocks and flats, three-channel television, pullulating motor-cars, weekend colour supplements, frozen food —he would react in the same way as most of his scholarly countrymen. "My God! You've gone American," they gasp and set off, head down, for the British Museum Reading Room.

This man has read the current 'condition of England' debate steadily, so he knew the arguments in advance. But his first few days of walking and listening gave him an unexpected impression. He said England seemed rather exciting to live in just now, seemed livelier and freer. The feeling that society's base was formed by a large, immobile and unexpectant working-class—whether regarded as the salt of the earth or as a surly threat—was surely going? Young people in particular seemed even to hold themselves and move differently, to have a more fluid style.

He could see plenty that was only an adaptation of American models, plenty that belonged to the common consumers' culture which is now spreading throughout the technically-advanced world. But what most interested him was the extent to which the British, in taking up the opportunities of a more open society, seem to have been able to use them, rather than be used by them, had married new styles to older.

He was exaggerating, since this was the honeymoon phase of his visit. But his early response seems to me important in two ways. First, it is not at all the same as the attitude

63

which claims we've never had it so good; it does not belong to the same world as the advertisers' 'Mrs. 1970s' or the political P.R.O.'s happy families. It is more subtle and better based. Second, it is a more honest response than that made by many British intellectuals; in particular, literary intellectuals. No less than them, the American opposed simple progressivism. But, if he saw good cause for it, he was not afraid to say something reasonably cheerful.

By the end of his stay he had, of course, made many adjustments. He had seen that the loosening of some habitual forms of social relationship and the difficulty of identifying oneself within new ones can lead also to aggressive insecurity, ranging from offhandedness and bad temper to brutality. But he was not led to deny his first response, only to put it into a fuller context.

He did leave in a mood of great disappointment. He was bewildered at the state of British intellectual opinion, at what seemed to him its almost complete failure to analyse British life today. In place of this analysis intellectuals usually put, he suggested, a self-indulgent nostalgia or a brash band-waggoning. For the direct and responsive observation of the changing life around them they seemed disabled by their own prior positions, which were either élitist or merito-cratic (and the two have a lot in common). So there was a thinness in social debate, a failure to appreciate the imaginative dimensions of the social changes British society is now experiencing. He noted some exceptions, but felt in general that a people with a long tradition of self-inquiry—not muck-raking nor social masochism, but sharply observed explora-tions of its own condition—that this people had lost its sense of itself and so lost the capacity to analyse itself effectively.

I think he was right. As he said, there are a few exceptions; but, on the whole, debate about Britain today operates from routine positions and uses inadequate models. Whichever side is talking, one does not often get the sense of freshly considered, irrigated thinking.

*　　　*　　　*

THE 'CONDITION OF ENGLAND' QUESTION

Of all the changes in British society today surely the most evident—since it increases the clamour of persuasion, over-crowds the roads and resorts, determines the general programming of mass communications, puts extreme pressure on higher education—is the 'entry into society' (to borrow a phrase from a sociologist) of whole classes of people who were previously too poor to be able to make themselves felt. Now they have some money and often even some sense of security; they are making their own choices more, rather than following the economically determined customs of their class; and their horizons are lengthening. Other people are having to move over to make room for them.

This is bound to be a shock. It demands that we reconsider our ideas about class, order and status; and reconsider also our ideas about culture, education, taste and brows. Most difficult of all, it requires us to think again about the relations we assume between class and culture. Reconsiderations like these cannot be easy: most of us make do by settling in one or other of two main blocks of opinion.

On the one hand are those who, often unconsciously, wish it had all never happened. In mood they range from the nostalgic to the resentful and tend to think of themselves as the last lights of civilization winking before the advance of the barbarian flood. A deep fear of anarchy and disorder easily becomes a fear of diversity, pluralism and variety. They equate 'working class' with 'lowbrow', and do not appreciate the inadequacy of that link or recent changes in both its main terms. They sometimes acquire the ghetto-mentality and, especially if they are 'Arts men' feeling their occupation in danger, begin to hold on to 'tradition' in an over-stiff and uncreative way. They either do not have television or, if they do, use it only as an occasional transmitter of pasteurized 'high culture'. On higher education they talk about 'scraping the barrel' and reject the Robbins Report virtually whole-sale. They suspect sociologists, social psychologists and all their relations. They moralize too quickly and on too little evidence, scientific or imaginative.

Members of the opposed group show cheerfulness and confidence as against the doubt and self-doubt of the first group. I do not mean to include in this second group those whose welcome to the new forms of society is founded in their professional advantage, is humbug glossing-over a determination to cash in. One does not meet advertisers who drag their heels at 'progress' or disc-jockeys who are not 'with it'. Still, two things are worth saying about them; that their position is made more comfortable, and their humbug easier, by the confused state of the whole debate; and that if we look carefully at even their appeals to their audiences, we shall see further into the nature of change, good and bad, than we have seen so far.

The second group proper is also optimistic and energetic but in more respectable ways. When we are in this group we welcome the 'entry into society' of people who were before largely submerged. A man stands a bit more upright, we are likely to say, if he is making his own choices, even though those choices (transistor sets, crawls to Brighton by car, package tours to the Costa Brava, James Bond films) are not those we would make ourselves. And if a man now feels secure enough to buy a house over 20 years, or plan on higher education for his children, surely this perspective is an advance on the week-by-week horizon of his parents? In this group we are anxious not to dictate a style of life to anyone else. We wince at phrases like 'public service' or 'values'. We have some good reasons for doing so.

Or we insist that Britain must become more 'forward-looking' if she is to survive, must use all available talent, capitalize on skill and develop more trained manpower. We are strongly in favour of increased higher education. But we do not often discuss education as a means to a more alert whole life for many more people. Usually we talk about education as a form of training, an accretion; hence our vocabulary, when we are talking about education, becomes mechanical and manipulative. We accept Robbins (and Crowther) completely, in tone and substance. C. P. Snow's

lecture on the two cultures seems to us a fundamental statement about the nature of life, education and culture rather
than a provocative shot from camp two to camp one in the
local British dispute. We are technocratic and meritocratic
rather than traditional and hierarchic: but we sometimes
suspect diversity, pluralism and fluidity as much as group one.
We welcome the erosion of old stratifications so as to erect
new—'more efficient'—ones.

Naturally, few people belong to one camp completely. Most
of us have a base in one but move to the other from time
to time. Meanwhile, intellectual exchanges at all 'levels' grow
odder and odder. It would be difficult to name a single
publication in which one can be reasonably sure of finding
nourished and disciplined discussion about cultural change.
Increasingly, gimmicks take the place of intelligence and
free-wheeling fancy is valued more than imagination. Stance
and camera-angle are substituted, because they are more
superficially striking, for the patient defining of a position.
The illustrated supplement to one of the 'serious' Sunday
papers (*The Observer*), can give generous space to the 'way
out' sets for *Goldfinger* while critical analysis of Fleming's
writing is dismissed as the solemn irrelevance of literary
moralizers. Or one of the few programmes on television
devoted to the arts, apparently anxious to silence the critics
who said its earlier version was class-bound and 'culture-
vulture', becomes frenetically fashionable.

So some intellectuals take refuge in a scholarly reserved
area, for whose value they make unreasonably high claims (its
just claims are high enough) but from which they freely
make observations about the life around them which are
usually ill-informed and often ungenerous.

Other intellectuals, tired of the loose rhetoric of their
colleagues, move towards what they call a 'value-free position'. This is essential in some areas of inquiry; and as a first
test of academic disinterestedness, even in areas where it is
not sufficient, it can be therapeutic. But when critics like
these reach the point at which choices have to be made they

are without tools. They have thrown away the old ones and been disinclined, for complicated reasons, to forge new ones. So they begin to say that new forms—new techniques, new kinds of communications, new physical patterns of living—make their own justification. This is quite different from saying that the peculiar characteristics of new forms—television, for example—have to be understood before we can assess them. This substitutes acceptance for assessment; 'whatever is, is right' and it is necessary only to respond to technique rather than consider meaning; style is more important than substance and manner than matter. They are usually, of course, inseparable. But these critics have rebounded from the old 'moralism' only to land themselves in a new aestheticism—an aestheticism or relativism which makes them feel less stuffy.

Anyone who tries to define the present cultural situation better, without recourse to the citadels on either side, is bound to be attacked by both sides. The first group will say that he is finding smooth words for the usual betrayal, the second that this is the old rhetoric in a new form. But it is important, and difficult, neither to regret for the wrong reasons that society is more open nor to accept it uncritically. We have to look and listen more closely for ourselves, trying to get rid of the imaginative myopia that our *a priori* formulations so often induce.

1965

IMAGES OF THE PROVINCES

I T would be easy to write about the wild permissiveness of city life in the provinces. The right selection of anecdotes could make Leeds seem more exotic than London. It would be just as easy to retail stories which showed that the provinces are still comically conventional. Either approach would be sympathetically received. The first, because it's smart to say that the provinces, led by Liverpool, are setting the pace today; the second, because it would reinforce an older myth—that the provinces are always good for a giggle, but not for much else. Can any intellectual journalist in a national paper report on provincial life, especially provincial local government, without having his tongue somewhere in his cheek?

The truth is a good deal less melodramatic or clear. Some people know some aspects of provincial life well. I know no one who has an overall grasp of the changes now going on, and don't claim to have that grasp myself. But this is plain: the homogeneity so dear to leader writers is little more than an appearance. Urban provincial life is more varied, has more different subcultures, than is usually recognized; and some subcultures have gained strength during the past couple of decades. Greater prosperity, immigration and the new travelling-student population have seen to that. It follows that the common stereotypes about provincial life (and about metropolitan life, since they are Siamese-twin stereotypes) are preventing people from seeing what is really interesting and complex in provincial life today.

Still, it's not surprising that from provincial towns there should come public utterances which express a sense of a single, corporate identity. "Manchester will not tolerate . . ."; "In Leicester we believe . . . "; "Let it not be thought that in the Second City . . ." You couldn't speak like that about London. By comparison, the Lord Mayor's Procession –

Mansion House Dinners – City of London pageantry and protocol are inorganic ritualistic gestures. At this level the big provincial cities *are* entities. They have their own governments, and their Lord Mayors are given the trappings and consequence of minor royalty. They have local establishments composed of the more powerful aldermen and councillors and a range of other 'leading figures in the community'—senior clergymen, a few headmasters, some of the more public-spirited industrialists and professional men. Such people can still think of themselves, fairly unaffectedly, as able to 'speak for their city'.

More often than not they speak stuffily. The 'We don't like that kind of thing in Rouen' spirit lives on. But this is not surprising. It is in the nature of things that local councils will attract some people who are bossy and opinionated. It is in the nature of things that the local evening newspaper, which is traditionally the voice of the home-centred citizen, will give a lot of space to the doings of local leaders, and will more often than not echo their outlook in its editorials. It is in the nature of things that on matters of morality most of the important clergymen will present a common front with the council and the Bench. With the Roman Catholic clergy this has a special edge, since they are characteristically unintellectual if not actually anti-intellectual and keep as tight a hold as they can, often by authoritarian methods, on their flock. Finally, it is in the nature of things that the less liberal statements of all such people should be picked up by the national press, since they support their prior picture of provincial life as a whole. From this angle, it's all a self-selective and self-perpetuating cycle.

About Birmingham, for example, we are likely to read, if we look through the national press for the past year or two: that it can be heavy-handed with books of which it disapproves, that its film censorship committee gives some odd judgments, that its Recorder has particularly strong views on drugs, that the Clean-up TV Campaign (and, now, the Viewers and Listeners Association) tend to have their big meetings in the town and that some councillors and leading clergy support them, that it had a Swizzlewick-style meeting about local radio and an even odder debate about prostitution. In the face of all this it looks as though that large metal bull which decorates the main walls of the new Bull Ring, looking like the city's presiding genius, is a proper Ferdinand.

There seem to be more such incidents than there used to be. Provincial establishments, feeling themselves 'charged with the good name' of their cities, also feel themselves besieged by rapid and increasingly unintelligible social changes. It is up to them, they decide, to defend 'our traditional values' against the anarchy of what looks like total permissiveness. This fear finds a focus in worrying about the effects of mass communications (especially the 'boldness' of television), or about the ways of immigrants or—and here everything comes together in a generalized whole—about the habits of young people. The main recurrent elements are: too much money to spend, vandalism and other forms of delinquency, pop music, 'working-class louts', coffee bars, drugs, long hair, and short skirts.

One minor irony is that the prosperity of the sixties has produced in all the big provincial cities a rash of clubs—gambling clubs, cabaret clubs, strip clubs—which for brassiness and vulgarity would take some beating. I'm not suggesting that the aldermen or the Clean-up TV Campaigners turn their attention to these new versions of the traditional pleasures of middle-aged entrepreneurs. Or that they should scrutinize the habits of the gilded executive youth of the town, blarting at high speed from pub and club to party in their souped-up Minis and Spitfires. They might, though, notice the gap between their virtual ignoring of these things and the toughness with which they try to remove from public buildings anyone who looks like a 'beatnik layabout'. I'm not saying, either, that concern about drug-taking or vandalism or the effects of television isn't necessary. It is, but ought to be better informed.

But what effect does all this have within the life of the

city as a whole? Less than is assumed. Subcultures of the
kind I mentioned earlier go their own way, or at least take
their tone from outside, not from the city leaders nor from
the local Home Service nor from the local press. Working-
class adolescents have always been free spenders, when they
could be; today they spend more freely than ever, and that
spending goes in the search for a style. Their images are not
municipal. Nor are those of the students who, since the introduction of maintenance grants freed them from home and
the local university, have created pocket Left Banks in all
the big cities. Both groups take their styles (which overlap
but are not the same) from the trend- and taste-leaders in
their peer-groups.

One stage further back, styles are mediated through pop
programmes on radio and television, through magazines and
records. Still further back, the styles are not only national
but international though there is still some time-lag in taking
up a trend, as you get farther from London or a really big
city. Of course, none of this tells us anything about the centres
of intellectual life or its quality; that would need a different
essay. About the nature and meanings of styles of the sort
I've mentioned we have only hints, chiefly in scattered essays.
Some of these are perceptive (see Colin MacInnes or George
Melly); but I don't know of any extensive description and
analysis. We need some. For instance, the description I've
given makes the process sound too much like one-way
exploitation, downwards to the audiences; but we can guess,
without knowing how the process works, that it is more
elaborate and two-way.

So the image of the provinces as monolithic and uniformly
behind-the-times needs a lot of qualifying. As do common
images of London. That part of London which is popularly
regarded as the heart of swinging Britain is a small stage-set
with a floating population, most of which changes daily. It
is given, by its local municipalities, that raffish, rootless licence
allowed to the entertainment centres of most capital cities. It
is fed by provincials on the spree but, no less importantly,

by the illusions of thousands and thousands of courtesy
'Londoners' who are pleased to feel they belong to the pace-
setting capital, and come in at nights or weekends from homes
or bed-sitters in places like Croydon or Surbiton or Penge,
places themselves just as provincial—using the word, now,
in its conventional pejorative sense—as King's Heath or
Roundhay. If the comic aldermen are representative voices
of the provinces then Peter Simple is the representative voice
of these London suburbs.

But, to turn the argument right round, there is a sense in
which the provinces can seem more involved with what
social change really means than the areas of licensed permissiveness in the West End. Many traditional values *are* being
shaken, and we haven't much idea which need to be dis-
carded, which modified and which held on to. If you live in
the provinces and get mixed up with public arguments about
film censorship or play selection you can, if that is what
you want, maintain a spirit of superiority; and every encounter will give you new funny stories for your next visit to
London. Or you can acknowledge that though some councillors are buffoons others are more intelligent than you;
and that the sense of local and domestic values is not always
illiterate parochialism but can be a considered strength.

Of course, one reads the national weeklies. They discuss
questions about changing attitudes at greater length and
with greater intellectual reference than is usually found in
provincial publications. But they speak to closed, monolithic
audiences, to the converted (or they spar with their favourite
stock-figures among the unconverted, such as Robert Pitman).

At the best you can have something different but just as
important in the provinces. You can gain a much fuller sense
of the conditions within which change has to take place. If
you are arguing the case for a new theatre, most of which has
to be paid for from the rates, you can't for long—unless you
are incorrigibly romantic—satisfy yourself with general
statements about society's duty to the arts. You have to recognize that there are many other genuine demands on the

money available and that not all those who vote against you are thick-necked philistines. Similarly, it is useful to have to justify the place of experimental plays in your repertoire, in the light of its obvious effect on the size and spirit of your audiences. You don't end by avoiding experiments; but neither can you kid yourself that you are the one artistically enlightened man in a crowd of lowbrows and middlebrows. Your belief in the need for the community to pay for a theatre, and for that theatre to have an intelligent and imaginative programme, isn't weakened; it becomes much better rooted in social realities—and this helps to humanize it.

I could add many similar experiences from committees and other kinds of public confrontation. There are occasions in provincial life when you feel yourself unusually close to the varied texture of change in British attitudes today. Depending on how you look at it, 'provincialism' is either a regrettable state of mind (which you can find anywhere) or the recognition of historical and structural complexities which the yearning for 'metropolitanism' can obscure.

1967

EDUCATION IN THE NEXT
FEW DECADES

O NE prediction seems sure: we shall have much more education. Since we already have universal education to the age of fifteen, this is another way of saying that more people will go on to higher education. The demand has increased phenomenally in the last two or three decades. Greater prosperity and greater security of employment make more people feel able to let their children have higher education, since they can manage without the additional wage-packets. They recognize also the increasing vocational importance of educational qualifications. And to some extent they respect education in its own right, as a civilizing force which they want their children to have. Last, as automation increases, higher education is likely to become here, as it is already in the United States, an unintended device for keeping excess labour off the market.

Britain is likely to respond to the increased demand, though with much stress and strain. Not just economic strain (can we really afford it?), but psychic strain. Expansion on this scale should challenge our whole social thinking, but so far our response to the demand has been due less to re-thinking on our part than to pressure from outside. We hear more about the need to educate because we must preserve our competitive place in the world than because we have consistently underestimated the intellectual potentialities of a large section of the population. So we have the odd situation in which people recognize that we must educate more people—so as to survive—and yet shake their heads about the way we are 'scraping the barrel of ability nowadays'. They sound as though we are being driven to educate the basically not-very-educable. This attitude has its roots in inter-connections between privilege and educational opportunity which lie deep in British history.

75

On these grounds the pressure for education will continue, to adapt an American's terms, to be one of 'pull' rather than 'push'; the demand for more people with higher education will tend to set the pace in the earlier stages. There is a big public demand for higher education; there is so far much less for comprehensive education.

Higher education will also become more varied and more specialist. But this change can only be properly brought about if we are less hierarchical in thinking about structures. Most universities in what is now called 'the independent sector' (those who receive their public funds through the Universities Grants Committee) are, of course, academically very good. But their great cachet with intending students does not arise only from their academic merits; social snobbery comes into play too. Hence, other good institutions of higher education receive less than their due. Recent changes are not as great as Lord Robbins hoped but they have begun, and the next few decades should see a more mixed economy. A lot is possible, if we think well. For instance, as several people have suggested, there could be more inter-action between the various institutions of higher education within one city or area, including the traditional university. If we don't think well, we shall create new forms of separatism.

If we need more and more specialized training we shall also need more retraining. Refresher training and retraining are likely to become normal stages in the working life of many professionals. It follows that in education before working-life begins more stress will have to be put on training students in those basic principles of thought which can be applied to new situations as well as on bringing the student to the frontier in whatever branch he is studying. As the horizontal spread of that frontier narrows, so the strategic sense of what is involved in moving out from it must be made stronger. It is at this point that we are often told that today's administrators must have at least a general grasp of the scientific outlook. That seems indisputable. But before we enjoy a ritual laugh at senior civil servants trained only in the Classics we ought to reflect—as we will if we have worked closely with some of these men—that, whatever its limits, Greats did give the best men the ability to consider issues broadly and disinterestedly. This is not merely a wry comment. That kind of grasp is not automatically acquired along with a knowledge of the language of each of the Two Cultures; it needs to be specifically helped to develop.

It is from this perspective that we can look at education in schools. Though before doing that we need to take note of a development which is likely to affect education at all levels. I mean what is coming to be called 'the necessary revolution in education', the revolution which could be brought about by 'educational technology'. Its proponents regard the sophisticated equipment which is now becoming available and will be increasingly available in the coming decades—radio and television, programmed instruction, all kinds of electronic developments—not just as aids to existing forms of education but as necessary means to transforming the structure and methods of education itself. The enormous demands made by the great increase in numbers and in types of skill cannot be met, they claim, by a simple extension of traditional methods. There will not be enough teachers to maintain the accustomed teacher-pupil ratios; nor, if there were, would the country be willing to pay for them. Only the fullest use of the new technology, they continue, will give the necessary power and flexibility. The old model of one-classroom-one-teacher is as out of date as a horse-and-buggy. The new system must be much more fluid. And it will not demote the teacher, but will release him for more effective educational activity at the crucial points in the whole process. So far the battle—and it will be a battle—between the new enthusiasts and the defenders of the older styles is only just joined. But there can be little doubt that by the end of the century technology will have brought about major changes in the educational landscape.

To return to the wider background to education in schools. Presumably the basic leaving-age will, not as soon as we may

77

have hoped but well before the nineties, be raised to sixteen. That will put yet more pressure behind the demand for education from sixteen to eighteen, in response to what I called earlier the 'pull' from beyond there. So that by the nineties we may well have a basic leaving-age of seventeen or eighteen, or at least a majority staying on voluntarily till seventeen or eighteen.

In turn, education even earlier will be affected. Here the picture becomes more complex and even more disturbing to our assumptions. I assume that we wish as far as possible to develop all available talent and that we approve of equal educational opportunity. Yet it is easy to agree if we also have the quiet assurance that our own children have a head-start. We can accept a notional equality which doesn't interfere with our devices for maintaining privilege. Why, for instance, is there such pressure for places at public schools today? Happy the couple who find they can move easily from the protected middle-class privilege of their generation to similar protected status for their children in an emerging technocratic meritocracy.

Everything favours them. They may be intelligent themselves, of course, and this may ensure that their children too are intelligent. One can hardly object to that. There are books in the home and articulate conversation; again, one cannot object. But one begins to think of those children, just as bright, who are in bookless and not very articulate homes; already they are relatively at a disadvantage. Then there is the steady encouragement to get on, and the provision of a warm, well-lighted room for work; here, too, the potentially bright child from a small working-class home is hampered. Or there is the buying of private education, to ensure a public-school place or at least one at the best maintained grammar school in the district. By this point the dice begin to be really loaded. At public school there are smaller classes, probably better science laboratories (sometimes donated by large private companies), guided training for Oxbridge places and the rest. Then university and then—though this

78

is always hotly denied—the mid-twentieth century version of the old boy network. If you have that kind of accent, that confidence, that school background it is much easier to get into a whole range of professions. The chances for a working-class child are by now very much reduced. Many get through, but the casualties are heavy. The full implications of 'equality of opportunity' would frighten most of us if we really faced them. To give every child an equal chance to develop to the best of his ability (which means much more than developing his 'brain') must mean that some of us are not permitted to buy educational privileges since they are, in the long run, bought at the expense of others.

In the next few years, two areas will most test our intentions; the public schools and comprehensive education. No one knows what the present commission on the public schools will decide, or whether the Government will act on their recommendations. In my view, any plan ought to meet these two main needs: to feed back into the whole community as many as possible of the adventitious advantages now enjoyed by those schools, and to break the more general links between public schools and social privilege. Of all the divisive influences in British society this, the sense of privileged position which almost all these schools produce, is the worst. On that ground alone I hope the solution is a radical one; that the public schools, in anything like their present form, go.

Then comprehensive education. Some people argue, quite cleverly, that the country must be schizophrenic—in higher education to be stressing excellence, but earlier to be willing to damage the best grammar schools by introducing comprehensive education. But the paradox is a false one. Of course, no one wants to advocate a form of education which will dilute the training of the best minds. Yet what we know by now of comprehensive education suggests that the training of existing excellence need not suffer, and that potential ability can be better developed. We know that present systems of selection and segregation can have an inhibiting effect on good minds which, largely through social accident or late develop-

ment, are not ready for transfer at eleven. We know that
minds just below the top level can close down and take the
colour of the group to which they have been assigned. We
know that large comprehensive schools can develop, better
than segregated schools, other abilities than the strictly intellectual (which is what good public schools claim to have been
doing for years). If good comprehensive education can produce these gains without loss of excellence then to go
comprehensive is as important a task for the coming years as
the revolution in primary education which has taken place
since the war, and one we should try to effect successfully.
It will take time, but this is the way the tide is flowing and
public opinion will increasingly recognize the fact.

So far I have been arguing in fairly objective terms, chiefly
about education as intellectual training and about the most
efficient development of the intellectual capacities of many
more people. But the really difficult problems have hardly
been touched. Education is not simply a matter of training
students to fit their country's economic needs (and so, presumably, largely to accept its basic ideology). It ought to
encourage a fuller, more self-deciding life; and so, by clear
implication, should prompt judgment on the aims of whatever society the student happens to live in. Again, one can
isolate some typical points of pressure during the coming
decades.

The remark a couple of paragraphs back about educational
'schizophrenia' highlights one aspect. The comprehensive-
versus-grammar school debate bears on the argument about
specialization versus general education; about the best
training of future experts as compared with the giving of a
wider background and range of experiences to as many as
possible in the next generation of individual citizens. It seems
likely that comprehensive education will tend to stress the
importance of general education and so to delay specialization
(as will the presence of a majority staying on at school till
seventeen or eighteen). But the pressure of new knowledge
is likely to increase the demand for early specialization from,

for example, the universities. If we assume that the comprehensives have some success, that they enforce their more fluid educational ideas, the universities will probably meet their own special needs in the new situation by lengthening the first degree to four years and by making post-graduate work longer and more elaborately controlled.

We need to think more about education as a humane discipline at all levels, precisely because the tendency today is towards a narrower compartmentalization of knowledge. This does not only mean making sure that budding scientists have some knowledge of the humanities, and students of the humanities some sense of the way science sees the world. It is not a matter of science *versus* the arts, of trying to 'talk across frontiers'. It is much more a matter of continuous and, as it were, organic relationships. It means that all subjects and all forms of training have to be seen in the light of larger human meanings, that students of engineering as much as arts men need some sense of historical change, of relative cultures, of the nature of political decision and of the questioning of human values. They need some introduction to the problems of understanding, planning and acting in the light of purposes outside their discipline itself.

In the schools there are some encouraging signs. In higher education there is less discernible movement. At the worst, one finds scientists arrogantly in the saddle and Arts Faculties defensively tending their gardens. At the best, discussion and experiment are going on; in, for instance, the syllabuses of some of the new universities, but also—though we tend to forget—elsewhere. One can make no reasonable guess at the outcome except to say that if we are to make a material difference in the next few decades, we shall have to look more seriously at this whole question than we have done so far.

The other test of our grasp on the ends of education occurs in the current debate about leisure. In the next few decades automation, we are frequently told, will produce much more spare time; 'we must educate for leisure'. There seems little doubt that provision for adult education, further education and recreational activities of all kinds will increase enormously in the next quarter-century; and that subventions from public funds, local and national, will be more than proportionately increased. One can easily imagine (it has been outlined more than once) a typical Centre in the nineties—something like a French Maison de Culture or an Israeli Community Centre, but with specifically British characteristics—containing a range of provisions for all ages: discussion rooms, cinema, theatre, art rooms, work rooms, exhibition hall, games rooms, coffee bar and restaurant, public library and radio station.

Then the doubts begin. Much of today's discussion sounds as though the aim is to keep people docile by providing opiates—for the routine worker who might otherwise become dissident, or for those retired early who might otherwise slide unhappily to the grave. Today, that old-style liberal adult education, in which Temple and Tawney played such a great part, is often said to be too earnest and solemn. But it had hold of an important idea: that the best education you can offer a man in his spare time is that which challenges him as a whole man, not one which treats him like a battery-hen.

It may be that we will look at all these issues and their implications and then move out to a more flexible, a more democratic and so a more efficient and humane view of education. Or we may not. Not long ago I visited Russia, for the first time. I admired much in Russian educational achievement, of course. But I was struck by the evidence that a self-perpetuating managerial élite is emerging. Speaking of ways in which the new functionaries provide special opportunities for their own children, one British official told me: "Of course, no one is going to let his child suffer for want of a leg-up". He seemed pleased with the development, since it made the Russian bureaucrats 'more like us', less awkwardly after some idealistic will-o'-the-wisp. On the journey back home I met three or four senior men from a large British corporation. They were in their fifties or sixties and had been over there doing business. They chatted about the public schools their children attended, the wines they liked and so on. They talked with a mixture of admiration and superiority about their Russian opposite numbers, rather as though they were a little backward in some ways, but still "coming alone all right; learning to talk our language". When I mentioned the difficulty of squaring the changes within Russian education with egalitarian principles they were amused. Later, I discovered that three of them were from working-class families and had been to maintained schools. They were, however, scientists, and it is easier for scientists to break into this managerial world; accent and contacts count less. But the system was flexible enough to accept them and they to conform to it. Certainly, they seemed not to have questioned it. True, such a group would hardly have existed in the thirties, and to that extent we are selecting brilliant men better from all social classes. But if such a group, one with quite such a self-enclosed self-confidence, were to be found in the nineties that would, I think, be a sign that we had failed to understand the most important issues before British education in the coming thirty years.

1967

HIGHER EDUCATION AND
CULTURAL CHANGE

I T is probably best to begin by looking at expansion rather than at large educational purposes, because expansion is what most obviously affects us in the day-to-day business of teaching and because almost all discussion about other aspects of education is coloured by the fact of expansion. Consciously or unconsciously, almost all educational debates today are really debates about expansion. If the pressure to expand fell away so would most of the arguments, even those which seem most freely philosophic. On the whole, British teachers mistrust general discussions about 'education'. Perhaps a healthy attitude, to begin with. But when we are forced, as now by expansion, to start debating, our debates look thin, the manipulating of a few reach-me-down concepts, supported neither by considered analysis nor by first-hand reflection.

Whether we teach in sixth forms or in universities we are all having to accommodate ourselves to the notion that far more people will seek higher education than we have been used to assuming. Most of us will say that by now we know where we stand: either that, given proper safeguards for standards, we are in favour of a large increase; or that, with the best will in the world, it won't work and can only wreck standards.

I am in favour of expansion. I think it need not lower standards; indeed I think that, properly managed, it can have educational advantages. I believe that the human and social case for it (not the meritocratic or technocratic case) is strong. And I remember that even the Robbins proposals do not, by international standards, propose a very large expansion; and that—all social considerations apart—universities are bound to grow as knowledge proliferates and subdivides.

The immediate causes of the increased demand are fairly obvious: for many parents, more spare money and greater security of employment; for students, better government grants and an increasing range of jobs, many of them quite new, which require some advanced training. It is thus possible for many more people to think of giving their children the opportunity of higher education. This opportunity is one they may have wanted themselves, back in the thirties, but couldn't have because their parents could not afford it. I am in my middle-forties and like many another came through elementary school and grammar school to university, leaving behind at each stage the great majority of my peers, some of whom were in some ways better equipped than I was. It is their children who are now filling in the U.C.C.A. forms, who are making up the great number of today's first-generation university students.

To give them this chance still often means sacrifice on their parents' part, since they are losing the wages their teenage children would have brought into the house. It was this period which Rowntree isolated many years ago as one of the short prosperous patches in the map of a typical working-class family's life. In spite of increased prosperity, Rowntree's map still to some extent holds good.

But why do parents think it worth while to choose higher education for their children rather than extra money? Is it, as we are often told, chiefly because they want them to move into the comfort and security of professional life; is it an instance of ill-considered 'status-seeking'; or of jumping on the meritocratic band-wagon? Impressionistic explanations of this kind are usually given dryly, as though the parents and children concerned had been found out in something slightly discreditable, as though the idealism of the nineteenth-century fighters for popular education had been betrayed. Certainly, if the demand were predominantly a hard certificate-bagging for the sake of material gain one might well feel rueful. Though one would have to remember that, through the public-school system, the English middle

classes have for long had an educational structure well geared
to functional purposes, to perpetuating the professional
succession, to ensuring that even the weaker sons didn't, so
far as could be managed, become what George Bernard Shaw
called 'downstarts'. That system had a public conscience, it
is true, and at its best nurtured generations of public-
spirited men who put personal status and reward below service to the country. But we have heard about that for a
century. It is as well, when the debate about expansion takes
the particular turn I am describing, to remember those
schools' sheer practical effectiveness as maintainers of status
and income expectation.

Or again we should remember that in most working-class
families no one has ever had other than a weekly wage, that
memories of the thirties are often memories of the whole
family laid off and somehow managing on the dole, that for
such families it is still slightly surprising to have money left
over at the end of the week, and surprising that jobs do seem
to be going on, rather than disappearing without warning.
Against such a background one ought to hesitate before
accusing working-class parents of materialism, status-seeking
and the rest. One should remember too that, whatever the
attitudes of the parents, most grammar schools exert a strong
pressure to make children wish to follow the traditional route
to professional life.

Many hundreds of years ago an Egyptian father counselled
his son: "I have seen him that is beaten, him that is beaten;
set thine heart after letters." He was not advocating retreat
to an ivory tower but emphasizing that knowledge is power,
that book knowledge could ensure that his son was not a
labourer and so beaten. Even today many British working-
class parents would understand that expression well.

They would also understand, even if they did not make it
explicit, Francis Bacon's phrase about 'the power and *virtue*
of knowledge'. True, some people mistrust 'brains' and mock
them where they can. But also one traditional working-class
characteristic, especially among what used to be called the

'respectable' working class, has been a regard for the virtue of knowledge. In the thirties, to speak from my own experience, the attitude towards the occasional boy (or girl) who had passed through training college or university to become a teacher was not decided only by a realization that he had got through to comparative security and a higher income; there was also a respect for the idea of learning in itself, for 'letters'. A man who 'spoke well', who had a 'good tongue', who could manage a much larger than usual vocabulary, was held in regard. One of the more colourful elements contributing to this regard for fluency was probably the tradition of lay-preaching in chapels. Knowledge was felt to be associated not only with power but also with wisdom. There are many other even longer roots. Why should it be simply assumed that this desire for knowledge 'for its own sake' has disappeared suddenly, just at the time when it might be more easily realized?

I am deliberately stressing the idea that there can be a more idealistic impetus behind the demand for higher education—as against talk of status-seeking—because it is so much ignored today. But it could be replied that, though what I have said so far may tell something about parents' attitudes, it tells us nothing about those of students. Why are they willing to go to university and forgo good wages? Surely only because they (I am quoting) 'demand a qualification or a good time, or both'. You can't, some teachers say, seriously look at your students and see budding members of Arnold's 'aliens' or Coleridge's clerisy; a typical students' common room looks more like a dump for lay-abouts and bums. Of course, if we look for nineteenth-century earnest laymen we won't find them; but we may find their successors. Today's situations have today's languages, today's styles. There are—and I'm again weighting the scale against the tendency of most discussion today—elements in student life which assume that a university is a place which should do more than train people for a good professional billet. This notion may affect directly only a small proportion of students; but this has always been so, and the influence of such people is out of proportion to their numbers. More, this attitude seems now, to a greater extent than before, to over-ride considerations of social class. It challenges both the assertion that students are almost wholly meritocratic in outlook and its companion-assertion—that they have practically no intellectual curiosity.

The sub-culture which provides the most sought-after style in student life nowadays is vaguely 'beat'. Its whole mode is casual and at its best elegant—fluid, unstratified and semi-bohemian. One can't make absolute distinctions, but in my experience the students who most authoritatively embody this style express, more than others, the intellectual and imaginative undergraduate life of their universities.

In view of all the discussion about the Second—or the Third—culture we might have expected that the desired life-style would be that of the 'new men', of those who 'have the future in their bones', of technology and science. In fact, the most attractive mode for the more intellectual students, whether they are reading arts or sciences, is off-beat, extremely oblique to society and to power. To some extent this has always been so. But to say only that doesn't much help; we need to define its peculiar contemporary stance and feel. Today's style leans a lot on American experience. A few years ago, in the early days of this mode, one of its texts was Salinger's *The Catcher in the Rye*, a book which nicely appealed to a moral criticism of society (though in a very free-wheeling way) as well as to human charity (which it didn't always distinguish from sentimentality). Since then, various kinds of specifically beat writing have been popular, especially American beat poetry (again, one can see a mixture of idealism and emotional luxuriating). Saul Bellow's novel *Herzog* has something of the same mood, though it is trying to make closer connections again with the everyday life of society, and is probably too middle-aged a book to be taken up by students. It would be easy to name other elements—C.N.D., folksong, anti-apartheid—but I have said enough to indicate the general area.

Why should this sort of style appeal? Chiefly because it embodies a rhetoric of protest. Partly, the protest is easy—generous emotional judgments without responsibility (about colour, the Bomb, and so on), and undifferentiated sentimentality. Yet it can't be brushed off as simply as that; there is a real social criticism here which makes some adult adjustments look over-comfortable. However, the point I want to make at this moment is more limited: that for imaginative students this style is one way, perhaps seems to them the best available way, of living out their sense of the virtue of knowledge, and of universities as places in which that virtue is recognized and given play. It is surely very curious that when so many other images are offered by society—sexual, technocratic, commercial; smooth, glossy, bossy—the image which most attracts has this direct connection with the imaginative life—is one which, in no matter how unfinished and often unaware a way, respects the critical mind and the creative imagination.

Both my counter-arguments in this debate about expansion are meant to weigh against popular talk about status-seeking and the like. The first claimed that many parents still have a regard for the idea of learning in itself; the second that some students—from all classes and all Faculties—expect universities to introduce them to the life of the mind, humanistically understood. An important impulse of long-standing has been translated into contemporary terms but is still recognizably there, linking parents and students. (There is a danger of sentimentality here; I have tried to avoid it.) If there is any truth in my two points, and even more if there is any truth in the suggested link between the two, this alone should powerfully affect our attitudes to the demand for higher education.

Even if all I have said so far is true, it has to do only with the 'temper' of demand, with people's expectations, not necessarily with their abilities to live up to those expectations. It would not follow that there has not been or will not be, as a result of expansion, some decline in standards. Some people base their opposition just here; they say that, though they have no social objection to expansion, professional experience tells them that it necessarily lowers standards. One sometimes wonders, listening to the way they phrase their case, whether their social and educational judgments are as cleanly separated as they claim. If they are themselves from the middle classes they sometimes sound obscurely resentful, as though a preserve has been encroached upon; if they are migrants from the working classes they are likely to say that 'all the really good people' got through in the old days, and that the larger proportion who get through nowadays must be of poorer calibre—mid to lower seconds at best.

But suppose we assume that people who speak like this do separate their social from their educational judgments. We are, they say, scraping the barrel; more means worse.

But we have hardly any objective evidence either way. We usually rely, or say we rely, on the accumulated experience of long years. Rather more people seem to assert that standards have gone down than that they have stayed still or gone up. But some do claim that there has been an advance, and the fact that more deny it may be an instance of the innate conservatism of university life. One might have expected that the Robbins Report would do some ground-clearing in people's minds here, and to some extent it did. But by a great many people the Robbins Report has by now been comfortably absorbed and cut down to size.

One can remind those who speak of a decline about methods of recruitment to universities in the 1930's, and ask whether they are seriously claiming that those methods promoted better overall standards than today's more rigorous selection. If they face that argument, they may be ready to agree that what they are really arguing for is not to preserve an earlier standard from debasement, but to establish a new higher overall standard, taking advantage of the opportunity provided by a glut of potential students. This position has at least the merit of not mixing its categories.

Still, more might be done to clarify—if not resolve—the

disagreement. One might compare answer papers in the same subjects at the same universities from the mid-1930's, mid-1940's, mid-1950's and mid-1960's, to see whether any alteration in standards could be detected. Perhaps it would be possible to do something similar for School Certificate and O-level papers, because evidently many more are passing those examinations than ever before. Has the slope wound downhill all the way? Is this the secret reason why some university departments steadily notch up their requirements for entry, in terms of A-level standards?

Until we know more, it seems fair to assume that better nurture, greater economic security and better schooling have all played a part in allowing us to bring more children to the point at which they are respectable candidates for university, that there has been no general decline in university standards. There certainly has been a steady increase in what is expected from undergraduates in some subjects, and this—as much as any other factor, such as a shortage of talent—may explain why the number of first-class degrees has remained roughly the same in these subjects. Given our present staff-student ratio or even one slightly less favourable, we can probably cope with greater numbers, do well by them and benefit from them. No doubt there is a ceiling but we have not hit it yet. The life of a large department, if it has a mixture of lectures, seminars and tutorials, of graduate and undergraduate work, can be more variously nourishing than that of a small one; it need not inhibit the brilliant but can considerably enrich the middle range of students.

Our attitude towards educational opportunity has been habitually mean. It little becomes us to talk about 'going American', as though that were a dirty phrase, or about 'throwing out the baby with the bath water' when we at last begin to provide rather more opportunities. One opponent of Robbins, in a fairly long review, made his case chiefly by quoting Vance Packard on the scattier fringes of American higher education; that is a discreditable procedure, but not uncommon. In this part of our social thinking, we are only just beginning to lift our heads, and to make irrelevant comparisons with American experience will not help. Our case is different. And we are our own generation, not that of our fathers, for whom educational opportunity was too closely connected with social class. We have to find the right way for ourselves, in this place, at this time.

Many things are wrong with our educational system today, and I do not mean to minimize them. But in some parts we have come a long way, and more talent has been revealed than most of us would have thought likely a few decades ago. Little of this change was inevitable; if everyone had talked then as some are talking now we would have remained educationally in much the same position as we were then. Here is Samuel Butler describing mid-nineteenth-century rural labourers:

> The row of stolid, dull, vacant plough-boys, ungainly in build, uncomely in face, lifeless, apathetic, a race a good deal more like the pre-Revolution French peasant as described by Carlyle than is pleasant to reflect upon—a race now supplanted. (*The Way of all Flesh*)

Those 'hinds' were supplanted by the 'hands' of the Industrial Revolution; we have to go on from there. Another instance: not long ago we had in Birmingham an exhibition of photographs of the district from seventy or eighty years ago. The old sepia prints had a nostalgic appeal—like long late-Victorian Sunday afternoons in damp, deserted, panoramic streets. But the print which most interested me—and a local journalist who pointed it out—had a quite different effect. It showed hundreds of workers from a Black Country foundry, lined up in such best clothes as they had, ready to go off on their annual works outing—apparently the one week-day of the year they had off. One has to allow for the ambiguities of photography. But it was shocking to see the lumpish, beaten-down quality of the faces. Those people looked like beasts of burden; that was their life.

This seems so obvious as not to need saying. Yet it does need saying—and feeling on the pulses—again and again.

Otherwise, more teachers—in schools of all kinds and in universities—will settle for the view that 'that lot' or 'that shower' are dead losses, congenitally ineducable, wasters of public money. I don't think one needs to give examples of this attitude, but if you think it rare you will find many instances in such books as Josephine Klein's *Samples from English Cultures* and Mary Morse's *The Unattached*. Some pupils—especially in tough schools—are incredibly difficult, a few are virtually ineducable, and teaching of this sort can be deeply disheartening and overtaxing. But the fact we must hold on to, unless we are going to make our profession a meaningless treadmill, is that most 'stupid' pupils are chiefly the victims of their background and of the inadequacy even now of our social provision.

Sometimes we criticize those who are handicapped by their background in a way that reveals how much we are ourselves prisoners to the assumptions of our own class. Surely enough is known by now about the educational disadvantages which poorer children experience from the start, and the ways in which the educational system can widen the gap between them and middle-class children. Only recently we have had evidence to this effect from Douglas and from Jackson, and they are not the first. More particularly, there is such evidence as Trenaman's about the relation between background and the readiness to assimilate knowledge (this was done in the course of inquiries into broadcasting); and there is Bernstein's important work on language and class.

Above all, it is essential to keep looking and listening rather than to settle for comfortable half-true generalizations, to remain open to the changes going on around us, and to the need sometimes for changes in our own attitudes. Not long ago we had as a visiting teacher at Birmingham a man who had written against university expansion. He was not a professional teacher but a well-informed commentator on political and social affairs, and had what seemed to him good intellectual grounds for his position. He wasn't with us long but when he left he wrote an interesting letter in which, he said, he 'cried peccavi'. I think he would have felt the same if he had been at any other university. He had been impressed by the challenge of university teaching and by the responsiveness of the students. It had convinced him, he went on, of "the absolute necessity of providing education for boys and girls coming along to university level . . . one feels a human categorical imperative."

We all get tired and our enthusiasm fades; or, since we are anxious to avoid seeming soft, we hide concern for our students behind a dour exterior. It is a pity that more of us don't occasionally bring to the surface, as this man did, our recognition of the 'human categorical imperative'. It might reduce the gloom induced by looking in too claustrophobic a way at our profession. From here we could go on to discuss better the more practical matters, such as how much higher education we can afford at any given moment, or the need for greater variety in types of higher education, or ways in which we can reduce the pecking-order among universities, and so on. On that last matter my own view is that the best aim is to cultivate our own plots better rather than snipe at the older universities. A decline in the pecking-order among universities will first and best come about through good graduate schools, so that this man will not be put off by social considerations from going to Manchester for graduate work, or that man from going to Newcastle. This process has already begun and ought eventually to filter through to undergraduate work too. At present, our knowledge of the quality of the work done elsewhere in our subjects—I mean among university staffs—is often, as a recent report by the Advisory Centre for Education showed, a mixture of decaying snobbery, folklore and tourism.

I am not being optimistic for optimism's sake, nor easily progressive. I know of the trivializing elements in the consumers' culture emerging around us. But at least people now have to be wooed, not ordered or kept quiet with cheap gin. We ought to be able to move on from this point.

If we do not keep this balance right we shall not be alive

to the important questions raised in modern society for us as teachers. Even if we believe that most students and parents seek higher education for status-seeking reasons, shouldn't this make us ask questions as much about the society which encourages this view of higher education as about the students who are influenced by it? Shouldn't it raise questions about our own responsibilities, since we train young people for the service of that society? But I have argued that some of our students come to university because they think it is precisely a place where such questions—questions about the quality of our lives—are asked. All the more reason for us to be aware of the nature of social change today.

Here we come to tricky ground. What is the function of university teaching? Are those students right who expect a university to concern itself with inquiry about the values of a society and the quality of life that society assumes (I am not talking about what may take place indirectly, when like-minded young people are thrown together)? Or do those university staffs act most wisely who ignore this wish and concentrate on the purely 'professional' aspects of their job?

Obviously, there is no simple answer; it is a matter of emphases within a complex and shifting pattern. And the emphases will differ at different times. Still, we should be more involved, more informed and involved, than is commonly thought nowadays. We need to remind ourselves that universities are places for education as well as for the prosecution of research and for professional training; with rare exceptions, where this view has not gone by default today it is held in too crude a form.

But universities are indeed research institutions, advancing knowledge for its own sake, in all their various Faculties, and transmitting it at a suitably high level. An institution which did not do that, no matter how large its undergraduate population, could not properly be called a university. Universities are also places for practical professional training, chiefly by means of first degree courses—for lawyers, doctors, parsons, teachers and so on. Recently this direct professional function has greatly widened, especially by including the training of a great range of applied scientists and technologists. All universities have a difficult job in keeping this growth in reasonable balance with their other activities. When we are inclined to object to this development on the grounds that 'it is making universities into nothing more than schools of higher instruction' we might remember that universities have for centuries been professional schools. More important, we might also ask ourselves whether the professional training element, especially in its modern form, does not give something valuable to the life of universities.

What would be lost if this element were taken away? It is easy to think of two kinds of institution for higher education which would have no truck with professional or applied training: a purely graduate research institution, and a 'pure' liberal arts college (that is, one which didn't even train teachers). Whatever their merits I think these places would lose by not being married to, in a more direct relation to, the life of their society. The first might contribute to knowledge and the knowledge be used later, for good or ill, by society—out there. The other might train minds and, if it trained them well, the experience would no doubt be of use to their students' later work in society—out there. But in both cases an enfeebling dissociation from society would be likely. Lively-minded students who couldn't afford three years of liberal studies before taking up professional training would go to professional schools which would then be even more narrowly professional. Members of a great range of professions now catered for by universities would not have such a good chance to set their professions' ethos against a fuller view of individual and social needs. University staffs, whether on graduate or undergraduate work, would not be close enough to the life of their society (and by 'close enough' I do not mean so close that they trim their intellectual sails to fit society's wind, but close enough to let the life of ideas be properly tested against the life of choice and decision). One of the virtues of the university, then, has been its impurity. Here, in Britain, this has meant a continuing concern with the responsible conduct of society and a readiness to serve it. We all know that we do not always manage to make this relationship arise in the way we wish. But it is important that a university, for both its senior and its junior members, remains committed to the idea of itself as a mixed community in the sense I have outlined.

That last argument will only weigh with those who think that a university should be a place of education as well as of instruction, that it is committed not only to the training of intelligence but to the maintenance of intellectual life, and that these two things are neither the same nor necessarily found together.

Just what this commitment means is difficult to define satisfactorily; and it is denied, explicitly or through default, by a great number of university teachers. Or it is accepted in too narrow and socially-limited a sense. In the face of such people—who still talk easily about 'educating the whole man' or 'education for life'—others (from the arts as well as from the sciences) turn back more firmly to their professionalism.

But that is only one element in a general turning-away from discussion about extra-academic relationships, most strikingly within Arts Faculties. Other elements include the wish to match scientists in the 'objective' pursuit of one's own subject of study. Another, especially in my own field of English literature, springs from the uneasy feeling that too much is often claimed for the 'civilizing' power of our subject. Another is suspicion of any talk about 'values', a fear of seeming authoritarian, to the point at which we become indifferentist or relativist. Yet another is the fear of intellectual sloppiness (of mixed courses which look like half-cooked omelettes), a fortified desire to maintain standards, a holding fast to the 'straight' argument that undergraduates should learn to study a single subject hard and deep, that relations, connections, applications can come after they have been properly trained in that single discipline. This is an argument one naturally respects; though one has to add that some of its supporters have made mean-spirited attacks on the efforts of the new universities to alter the boundaries of subjects.

Still, all these reactions from what no doubt seem like other people's excesses do not give sufficient grounds for rejecting a crucial relationship. The humanities *are* about values, about men trying to make sense of—to find meanings within—their individual and social lives, and we cannot keep all that in separate boxes marked 'scholarly and specialist only'. If we try to do so we will, when we are asked to make a direct decision about something which concerns society here and now and concerns also the intellectual independence of our university, be more likely to make it superficially.

There has recently been talk of founding at a British university a School of Journalism, probably based on the Department of English, to give full professional training and presumably attract financial support from the newspaper industry. Quite a number of university teachers seem happy with the idea. I am interested in journalism and know it is an important profession with some distinguished practitioners and publications. If my students want to go into journalism I do not deter them, so long as they are talented and know the stakes. But if I were asked to say whether a School of Journalism should come to Birmingham—and this does not contradict what I have already said in favour of professional training within universities, but reinforces it— I would first have to resolve this question: how, given those economic forces which increasingly affect newspapers, could a Department of English help its students to understand the functions of journalism, and so analyse the degree to which the present situation inhibits these functions, without causing the students not to want the kind of success which the profession rewards today—I am speaking chiefly of the big national newspapers—or without making employers suspicious of the School? The same sort of argument can be applied, but with more force, to advertising, public relations, and some parts of broadcasting.

But all that is negative comment on the relation between

universities and their society. It is more difficult to be positive. This is not the kind of problem for which there can be a neatly programmed solution. Nor can it be much advanced by discussion about the Two Cultures. In their relation to questions of value it is obvious that there is in some cases a division between arts and sciences. Some subjects cannot be studied without direct reference to values, e.g. Philosophy, English, History, Sociology; some can, e.g. Chemistry or Physics. But to talk about direct reference of that kind doesn't take us far. I am concerned with the attitudes of members of staff, and here the division is not between Faculties.

It is more important to think harder about our basic attitudes towards the educational function of universities than to worry about precise formulations of what might be done to 'bridge gaps'—about general lectures, arts for science men or vice versa. Such efforts are not always useless; but if the groundwork is done properly they will be better informed. Most of us are more involved with the educational function of universities than we realize. If we say that this aspect does not interest us we are taking part in it by default. We are free to choose which way to put our weight in this educational process; we are not free not to choose because, if we say we have not chosen, that choice will not prevent our intervention but define its nature.

In this situation, two ironies are obvious: first, many arrangements with a clear socially-educative purpose do exist in universities, even in Redbrick universities, and are accepted by almost everyone. One would have thought that those who denied the relevance of this function to universities would have been more vocal in attacking such arrangements, on grounds of principle; but they sit happily on, say, old-fashioned Halls of Residence Committees. I suspect some of these arrangements myself; not on principle, but because the social assumptions behind them are too narrow. At the extreme one sees in the same person a refusal to consider the larger relevance of his particular specialism together with a bland acceptance of these tagged-on fragments of social education.

99

The second irony is this: some people do not realize that, though they may say they have no concern with other than the professional education of their students, they are in fact educating them socially all the time, by inspiring either imitation or reaction. They might avoid this if they disciplined themselves so rigidly that nothing which was not part of their professional *persona* got through to their students. But who does this?

We need never make a specific social comment or value-judgment to our students. In the inner quality of our concern or insolence, in the timbre of our rebukes or praise, in our omissions and ignorance, in our stamina, in the patterns of our lives as the students see them, in our use of leisure and in much else we are educating our students to see the life of a university teacher and 'the life of the mind' as *this* rather than *that*, as having this weight and density and commitment.

So if we mistrust this other-than-professional relationship and want to protect ourselves against it, we ought to have a fair idea of its ramifications; or our positions will not be tenable positions but half-considered postures. But if we think this relationship is a proper part of a university teacher's life, it is just as important that we do not over-simplify or settle for a narrow view. Without trying to be 'with it', we need to know more about the world our students live in and their efforts to come to terms with that world and the one we seem to represent. One of the more depressing experiences of university life is to sit in on typical S.C.R. conversations about student culture or social class or mass communications.

Some people are understandably suspicious of this line of argument. They fear they are being asked to become 'committed' in an intellectually discreditable way, to choose a crude kind of contemporary involvement. It's at this point that members of Arts Faculties are likely to mention 'the lust for contemporaneity' and to insist that a full study of Chaucer or Shakespeare or Milton can expose and challenge more— can give a better perspective . . . and so on.

It is not difficult to agree in principle. Such people are not making solely scholarly claims for the study of literature but are accepting its involvement with matters of value—and then making a strategic decision about the best way of exposing that involvement and increasing understanding of it.

But to be consistent they ought to accept certain implications of their position. First, a person who believes that only the reflective study—in perspective and depth—of great literature separated from topical muddle and the enticements of the contemporary, can adequately feed and develop one's sense of life, should be hesitant about making snap *ex cathedra* statements of mere opinion about contemporary life. This rule would halve the duration of many Departmental meetings. More important, a 'full reading' of Chaucer or Shakespeare or Milton involves a determined effort to understand issues in our own day. It requires this effort both for understanding Chaucer or Shakespeare or Milton themselves—through whom the movements of their age flowed— and for making those connections between the life of that literature and the life of today about whose value both sides agree. We have to seek relevant comments of the right depth, not manipulate second-hand dichotomies such as 'the organic versus the atomized society', or even more inadequate models.

We do not all have to be members of a political party, or to take up a public position on immigration or apartheid. There are different ways for different people. Many, perhaps most, may take practically no direct social action. It's at bottom a matter of relevant understanding, of the determination to aim at that in one's own way. The dangers of crude involvement are plain and need to be guarded against. But what is one to make of a medieval historian or classicist who finds nothing odd—that is, nothing to be made sense of, at the least, if not opposed—in the sight of one of his new graduates going without second thoughts into, say, advertising; or of a sociologist or statistician who will undertake consultant work without much questioning the implications of the uses to which his work is put?

As I have said more than once, I am talking first and foremost about attitudes, about understanding the relevance of our subjects as fully as we can. The rest is likely to follow, in terms of connections and analogies; but it does little good to strain after connections. So we are right to be suspicious of those proffered 'bridges between disciplines' which have a large attractiveness. Otherwise, we are likely to see the kind of scientist who has a particularly dry vocational attitude to his work being swept off his feet by a general lecture from an arts man who has an easy rhetoric. This, as W. H. Auden said in another context, is as odd a sight as the tycoon who is sentimental about animals. It helps neither the links universities should make between subjects, nor the understanding of the place of the arts within universities. Best, wherever possible, to start from one's own subject and make links as they are demanded by it, but always under the pressure of realizing the importance and relevance of such links. A quotation from I. A. Richards' brilliant and not sufficiently known book *Interpretation in Teaching* is useful here:

> It is easy to talk eloquently about freedom in the pursuit of truth and the democratic method. But what we need is to induce the struggle between the rival forces repeatedly on a small controllable scale so that the different outcomes of the choices shall become apparent.

To sum up so far: the debate about expansion is too thin; it needs a greater sense of social and cultural complexity. In particular, we ought to improve our sense of the mixture of motives behind the demand for higher education. One important element, especially among the more lively students, is still the sense that there is something special about a university; that they are not simply seeking status or a certificate but feel that a university is a place where the relationships between an individual's sense of value and the outlook of his society can be examined. This should make us—university teachers—think more about where we ourselves stand in this relationship because, whether we will or no, universities are in a significant relationship with their society. If we thought about this better we would not talk, as some happily do, in almost purely technocratic or meritocratic terms about the function of universities today. Conversely, we would not, in attacking technocratic or meritocratic attitudes, offer as an alternative a narrow, too socially-decided view of what constitutes a cultivated person and a good life. Culture in this sense is not something one can ensure by acquiring certain 'manners'. It has to do with the growth of the responsive and responsible imagination.

There is a harder issue. Some people believe strongly that universities do have a direct relationship with the quality of the life of their society, yet oppose expansion. They do so on the grounds that to spread culture (in the Faculty of Arts sense) widely is necessarily to dilute it, that good things are always thinned out as they spread. One can see reasons for this view. The processes of mass communications in a techno-logical society more and more make a great many things into objects of consumption, even cultural objects—egg-head paperbacks, prints for one's walls, ideas. This process does tend to keep the 'image' but take the life out of the objects. It is part of the drive of a mass-production society, and we need to understand it better. Here the analogy of diluting and thinning does hold.

It does not hold at a more important level. We have to distinguish between cultural objects—artifacts—and culture as 'cultivation', as a process, a training of the intellectual and imaginative life. If we try to make sure that what is done is well done, then I cannot see how the fact that ten people have had this opportunity instead of only one in itself makes the slightest difference to the quality of the training they have all received. The physical analogy is false: culture *is* divisible and infinitely self-recreating; you cannot use up the life of the mind simply by making it more available. Nor, of course, is the training of the original one, or of the other nine, necessarily better. It will be just as possible and just as difficult for each one of them to inch himself to a position of intellectual and imaginative independence as ever it was. It will finally depend, as always, on qualities of character.

A related argument suggests that it is false egalitarianism to think a great many people can benefit from higher education, and asks us to recognize that most people neither want to think for themselves nor are capable of doing so; that since the old, oral, rural, folk-culture which once sustained them has gone, we must organize things not on the assumption that we are all capable of becoming self-sustaining intelligences but so as to allow for the emergence of a twentieth-century urban folk-culture.

From this one can take fair warning about not claiming too much at this or any time. For the rest, the mind boggles at the implications. Leave aside the begged questions in the claims about an earlier organic community and look only at the situation today. In the face of mass communications, between the commercial people and the old Establishments—between Lew Grade and Sir William Haley—what conceivable kind of urban folk-culture would really be likely to emerge? What chance would any other kind of culture have against the new persuaders and what they stand for, working at that solar-plexus level? Why, in fact, shouldn't an urban folk-culture prove to be simply a mindless, soporific, 'togetherness' culture?

So my own working hypotheses are: that, given better conditions, more people are capable of more than we usually imagine; that, since we no longer live in closed societies with high, dense, local textures, no unselfconscious folk-culture is possible; that, since we are all under a centralized pressure towards what I called mindless togetherness, we must commit ourselves to the increase of individual knowledge and self-consciousness, to greater self-awareness (in which is naturally included the development of the imaginative life). We all seek this for our own children; why should we seek less for the children of other people? Without these linked hypotheses we shall speed that process by which the Gutenberg revolution could come to seem only an interim period, a pause of a few centuries between a rural oral culture for the peasants and an urban oral culture for the masses—George Orwell's machines for making popular songs in place of dances around the maypole. "An institution," said Emerson, "is the lengthened shadow of one man." Such a man is standing upright. It is always difficult to stand upright, and today there are many pressures which would like to make great masses of us bend this way and that by turns. We should suspect any educational thinking which did not begin with the necessity of helping every human being to stand more nearly upright on his own.

I have tried to avoid the rhetoric of either alienation or progressivism. I have a deep suspicion, which seems both natural and acquired, of easy progressives. I have on the other hand a natural leaning towards alienationists and apocalyptics, and have sometimes indulged it. It is time—for all of us—to take stock better: not to strike attitudes from either side of the cultural fence, nor to fence-sit; but to make the hard and necessary distinctions which can lead, not to 'a middle position'—since to call it that might imply trimming —but to a new position.

Such a position could inform a criticism of our society and of the life it offers just as sharp as any alienationist's critique —perhaps sharper, since it would be more humanely close to the realities of our life today, to its mixture of weakness and strength (though it will then be accused, by the apocalyptics, of compromise). Such a position could give at least as good a sense of the real gains within modern, technologically-advanced societies as that of the progressives—perhaps better, since it would not be led astray by the merely new and become relativist and successive (though it will be accused by progressives of being dull, earnest and, worst of all, 'moralistic'). We have to start by remembering our own history; we have to consider as carefully and freshly as we can where we really are today, and what kind of people we really are. We have to let our imaginations be informed not by minatory rhetoric nor by smart acceptance, but by charity, irony and hope in about equal proportions.

1965

TWO WAYS OF LOOKING

IN face of the enormous technological changes now going on some people cheerfully invoke a kind of technological necessity. Others think about costs in more traditional terms. Usually the two groups don't seem to be talking the same language, or to be capable of learning each other's language. But this is not new. John Stuart Mill noted the division in his essay on Coleridge of 1840:

> Both sides were in the right in what they affirmed, but wrong in what they denied . . . take for instance the question how far mankind has gained by civilisation. One man is forcibly struck by the multiplication of physical comforts; the advancement and diffusion of knowledge; the decay of superstition; the facilities of mutual intercourse; the softening of manners . . . the great works accomplished . . . and he becomes that very common character, the worshipper of 'our enlightened age'. Another fixes his attention, not upon the value of these advantages, but upon the high price which is paid for them; the relaxation of individual energy and courage, the loss of proud and self-relying independence; the slavery of so large a portion of mankind to artificial wants . . . the dull unexciting monotony of their lives, and the passionless insipidity, and absence of any marked individuality in their characters . . .

Fundamentally, the difference may be one of disposition. So, though both may be partly right, it's not easy, Mill continues, to reach an agreed position:

> How easy it would be to choose one's path, if either half of the truth were the whole of it, and how great may be the difficulty of framing, as it is necessary to do, a set of practical maxims which combine both.

Students in the humanities who want to point to dangers in the way the world is going might at least reduce their rhetoric.

What we are saying is important. But we often say it in a way which makes the most literate technologists think we have stopped looking. This writer is predicting the situation of the arts in 1984:

> Passive entertainment will fill ever-expanding periods of non-employment. Bigger and better stadia will be built to accommodate vaster and vaster crowds of football fans. Cinemas will have disappeared because it requires less effort to view the same kind of programme on the television screen. But driven out by boredom and satiation the younger people will crowd into dives where they can expend their unused energies in dancing like dervishes to the jazz bands . . .
> Meanwhile the arts, in any historical meaning of the word, will have disappeared. Already in 1964 few people read books for pleasure; they 'use' them, or even 'view' them (books will have more and more pictures and less and less text). Poetry, already an arcane activity, will have totally disappeared. Fiction, even now a dwindling form of entertainment, will fade out and the only writers will be script-writers for the television screen. . . . The lighter forms of opera will survive because they are entertaining but composers like Beethoven, Wagner and Stravinsky will be forgotten . . .
> It is not a cheerful prospect for the arts, though there will be more and more artists in the sense of the word used by the entertainment industry. It will be a gay world. There will be lights everywhere except in the mind of man, and the fall of the last civilisation will not be heard above the incessant din.*

There may be much that is right, in Mill's sense, in that passage. But it is too out-and-out. It hasn't looked round closely enough.

The other side, the cheer-leaders of technological society, assume that an increase in knowledge of the way things work (including our own minds) will automatically bring an increase in rationality. They revive one of the simpler forms of eighteenth-century perfectionism:

* Herbert Read, 'Atrophied Muscles and Empty Art', in N. Calder (ed.), *The World in 1984*, Penguin (1965), Vol. II, pp. 91-2.

Through a better understanding of his fellow men, which can rapidly come about through available information, instantaneous communication, and fast travel, mankind can be released from fears based on ignorance, and the suspicions and hatreds those fears bring about. Accordingly, if his mind and spirit can be directed toward a constructive application of leisure and resources at hand, then what has been said here is just a preview of more wonderful things to come.*

"And if wishes were horses. . . ." What questions are begged in that 'constructive' and in 'more wonderful things to come'; how tinny is the rhetoric compared with Herbert Read's resonance. Worse, how simple is the assumed sequence of effects. Here is a channel for communication; we all want a more 'constructive' and 'wonderful' life; the channel must bring about good because we wish it; so it will be used in that way. Has such a man, one wonders, ever had a single political thought? Has he never—since he is American— looked at the wealth of television channels available in his country and reflected on what they might do, in relation to the country's needs and diversity, in comparison with what they in fact do:

> The ability to create environmental conditions which can maintain ideal climate, pure air, and freedom from noise will make available to the average home dweller the seclusion and comfort once limited to those who could afford the luxury of travel to nature's resort spots . . . with the possibilities of greater leisure . . . interest should turn to cultural development and creative hobbies . . .†

Again, all the difficult questions are left begged within the unplumbed meanings of such phrases as 'cultural development' and 'creative hobbies'. Again there is the old simple sequence of assumed effects. Would that it were so straightforward and that, once we'd all read the best that had been thought and said and been individually psycho-analysed, we were ready for Shangri La. When such a man talks about

---

* E. Finley Carter, 'Homes of the Future', in Calder, *op. cit.*, Vol. II, p. 39.
† Carter, *op. cit.*, pp. 37-8.

TWO WAYS OF LOOKING

'creative hobbies' one wants in reaction to talk about the
loneliness required by the practice and appreciation of art,
about the effort involved, about art as a form of taxing engagement, not as something to be absorbed subcutaneously.
One suspects that when this man talks about 'community',
he is really thinking of public bonhomie. There seems no
room in such a condition for art as the exploration of experience, as the celebration of the strangeness of life, or as pure
play. Herbert Marcuse's remarks in *One-Dimensional Man*,
about the way modern society can be hospitable to art, are
apposite: that, though a society's impetus may be basically
behaviouristic, it can find room for some oddity, for a small
amount of artistic roughage: "They are the ceremonial part
of practical behaviourism, its harmless negation, and are
quickly digested by the status quo as part of its healthy diet."
   This isn't an unfair inference from Finley Carter's claims.
The latter also says:

> The home equipped with facilities for lightening housework,
> the availability of fully or semi-prepared foods with ready
> facilities for warming them or cooking them, as the case
> may be, will allow more time for engagement in study or
> hobbies which can be both entertaining and creative. Con-
> versation pieces or even status symbols may well be art work,
> literary compositions, collections of rare books or rare objects,
> or ingenious devices developed in the studio, library, hobby
> room or shop.*

And there it is, in the open: art, not as a criticism or celebration of life nor as a form of play, but as a source of status
symbols and 'conversation pieces'. If one had to choose between such a position and that of the alienationists one would
have to choose the alienationists; they make better human
sense.
   Self-evidently, there have been great gains in man's power
to control his environment; many people have more opportunities for growth of many kinds than they would have had

* Carter, *op. cit.*, p. 38.

in a pre-industrial society. A humanist isn't, or shouldn't be, denying that. But he will often seem minatory because he is warning against the tendency to have an over-simple view of man. A subtle and sophisticated 'scientific' approach to the study of man can live happily with a basically simple imaginative sense. Behind all the complications of the approach, the complexity of human beings is not realized:

> Two fistfuls of tissue, the colour and something of the consistency of porridge, contain more information than all the computers and libraries in the world stacked together . . . Even the smaller, simpler, more primitive brain of the rat, the octopus, snail or cockroach is substantially more complex than any human artifact yet produced.*

That is about intellectual complexity only. Human experience—knowledge—is also affective, moves through space and time in always shifting patterns of relationships, and is all the time weighted with values.

The area of freedom within which choices can be made, in spite of all the conditions which limit those choices, is easily undervalued. This increases the tendency to see people chiefly in terms of role-playing, as objects who can be manipulated (and hence increases the tendency to arrange, through social machinery, for people to be more and more manipulated). Language is strikingly manipulative too, as it moves out to match these attitudes. Such a phrase as 'scientific management' is accepted quite readily today though, looked at carefully, it's foolish and patronizing. But it's not as gross as 'human engineering'. 'Social engineers'—if that expression isn't already coined it is just around the corner—talk more about 'adjustment to' than about the rightness of the 'what' to which people are supposed to be being adjusted, more about 'deviation from' than about the merits of the 'what' from which people are rebuked for having deviated.

* Steven Rose, 'The Brain in Outline', *The Listener*, 1 February 1968, p. 141.

TWO WAYS OF LOOKING

In the American sociological journal *Trans-Action* Professor Irving L. Horowitz once discussed the enormous socialscientific operation called Project Camelot. With millions of dollars available, a group of social scientists were to examine the origins of revolution in modern societies. They produced some intricate and interesting possible causes. But Professor Horowitz points out the question they never really asked themselves: was something so rotten in the state of the societies in which rebellions took place as to make it right for men to rise up and oppose them? They started by assuming the rightness of 'adjustment to' the society and were led to regard all dissidence as aberration.

There is a great deal of talk about the technological society of a kind which implies that it contains not only a functional morality (if it works it is, within its own field, good) but also a substantial morality (it can define goals outside itself, or define the goals of a society by reference to itself). We have been told recently that there is such a thing as 'technological rationality' which cannot be contained within established institutions. Technology, it is claimed, brings its own lifepattern, values and morality. The tone in which this is said suggests that if we don't get on to this particular band-waggon quickly we will be at the best badly left behind or at the worst liquidated. The implication is that technology can tell us how to live as once revealed religion was said to do. The people who claim this with such unexamined fervour are in spirit the heirs of the religious absolutists of a century ago. Perhaps it's people who will accept neither of these absolutes who are 'the new men', if anyone is.

If the claims, or even only a part of the claims, made by such technological absolutists are true then it is up to them to show us, to make the connections between facts and values. They might begin by teasing out this problem: we are told that as technology advances it is bringing with it a relative or even absolute decline in the standard of living of what, with unconscious irony, we call 'the developing countries' in comparison with the advanced West. Is this an instance of the process of 'technological rationality', which has to be accepted as good in itself?

Until the advocates of technological rationality make their case better that case will seem to have one hidden assumption and one plain consequence. The assumption is that at bottom their statements are modern forms of 'whatever is, is right'. Here, the form is 'whatever serves and suits the machine is right'; and this is no more than a philosophy of the expediency of mechanics. The consequence is harder. The consequence is not only a neutral serving of the machines. Extreme technological rationalists are innocent people, more academic than most students of the humanities; it is they who are the descendants of the medieval scholastics, without a sense of the irremediably political nature of social life. For the consequence of their position is that they become the servants of whichever party happens to be in power. Those parties will make their decisions about the use of technological knowledge according to their assumptions and ideology. So the use of technological advances will tell you less, in any society, about the new 'technological rationality' than about the continuance of the old Adam.

Until the technological rationalists tell us more, we are left having to assume that technological change does not within itself produce other than expedient answers. Outside this area, and you are soon outside it, you are in the area of value-judgments. This is inherently so, even when you seem to be following the logic of the machines. Every choice made opens *that* possibility to human beings or closes *that* one, makes *that* more likely or *that other* less likely. It incorporates a judgment, no matter how unconsciously, about the nature of a worthwhile human life.

So the people who claim to be neutral technological rationalists are more like modern moral Vicars of Bray, subservient either to the machine itself, or, more likely, to the main drift of their society. The drift of their society needn't show us anything melodramatic, needn't be totalitarian or even sharply political. It can be something within the 'feel' of the whole culture, in its unexamined sense of desirable life. But technological rationalists are automatically and positively engaged with it; here, there are no neutrals.

It is true that many people who claim to speak for the humanities are scientifically and technologically illiterate, and we have often been reminded of this in the last few years. It is also true that some scientists and technologists are imaginatively illiterate. People who claim to speak for the humanities are suspicious because they think technologists often ride rough-shod over questions of value; and this is sometimes true. Technologists are suspicious because they think some students of the humanities cling desperately to moth-eaten myths; and this too is sometimes true. Clearly, many old values are being called in question by scientific and technological change. Some need to be called in question. On the one side, the humanist's outlook can be obscurantist, crippled by historical and social conditioning. On the other side, there can be a crude kind of technological utilitarianism.

It won't do to suggest that this is a split between two 'cultures'. It is not. It is the difference between two ways of looking, and tends to cut horizontally across both the 'cultures'; you can find those who see and those who do not see on each side. The same questions are before each. How do you assess the quality of life assumed and offered within a society? What are the grounds for judgment? Is the individual to be made to fit large man-made purposes, political or technological? The trouble today is not that we haven't answered these huge questions. It is that we have not asked them in a responsible way.

1965

ON CULTURAL ANALYSIS

Marshall McLuhan and Making Choices

What will be the new configurations of mechanisms and of literacy as these older forms of perception and judgment are interpenetrated by the new electric age?*

IMMENSELY wide-ranging, synoptic, histrionic, and eccentric, McLuhan is exhorting us to understand better the psychic effects of those new media which are electronic 'extensions' of the central nervous system, to recognize that they alter the psychic balance and pattern of attention, develop or over-develop certain kinds of sense-life, with very different results in different cultures.

The forms of the new media, he argues, just as much as, if not rather more than, the 'content' for which they are channels, give the media a life of their own, make them alter what they transmit. To read a newspaper is psychically different from reading a book; to hear news on the radio is different from reading a newspaper; a television news bulletin is psychically a different thing from one on the radio. The older, Gutenberg-dominated attitudes on which our civilizations are largely founded are private, individualistic, specialist, detached, exclusive, linear, sharply defined, successive, and categorizing. The newer media tend to make us once again, as before Gutenberg, oral communities. They are communal, collective, participant, involved, inclusive, amorphous, and tactile; they immerse us in undifferentiated sense-experience and make us move towards a 'general cosmic consciousness'. They substitute depth of involvement for 'point of view'.

Naturally the argument is less cut-and-dried than that précis makes it seem; and it is rich in unusual insights. But it isn't a fully-developed argument. McLuhan's 'mosaic' approach

* Marshall McLuhan, *Understanding Media* (1964). Routledge and McGraw Hill.

114

sometimes has great cumulative force, sometimes fruitlessly yokes things together, sometimes is repetitive. Still, in this kind of free-ranging thinking about communications, McLuhan stands on his own. You don't simply learn something new from each of his books; you see certain things differently ever after.

So, to choose a few items almost at random: he throws new light on the fluid, 'cool' style of teenagers; he reinforces the view that discussions about the use of the mass-media for persuasion which don't get below the literal level—is it true or false?—are not of much use; he turns attention to the peculiar nature of television, its 'statement without syntax', without understanding which we shall not use it better, whether for information, education, or entertainment.

Reading McLuhan is like being on a big-dipper operated by an imaginative but scatty intellectual. There is a continuous heady swing and swoop, an epigrammatic snap-crackle-and-pop, an enormous and fascinated hospitality to the multitudinous phenomena of the contemporary world. He carries on a continuous battle with 'the men of print culture', 'the book oriented', 'the earnest moralizers', for their ignorance of the true nature and tendencies of the new forms of communication: "To lament . . . is to miss most of the game. It is to make value judgments with *fixed* reference to the fragmentary perspective of literary culture [his italics]." We do need to know more about the inherent nature of the new media. But this won't solve any problems; it will only define better the point at which they begin to be argued about. McLuhan himself can say that the new media "give new patterns to our lives by acceleration of older patterns . . . all media exist to invest our lives with artificial perception and arbitrary values."

Later still the pendulum swings back again: "a moral point of view too often serves as a substitute for understanding in technological matters". This is true: but what then? Are 'technological matters' self-validating? Do we succumb to their flux, getting what kicks we can from charting the complexities of the currents? We may do well to reject the extremer rigidities of 'point of view', but are we then left with no more than 'involvement in process' for its own sake? Years ago, in *The Mechanical Bride*, McLuhan could say:

> Freedom, like taste, is an *activity of perception and judgment* based on a great range of particular acts and experiences. Whatever fosters mere *passivity and submission* is the enemy of this vital activity [his italics].

That slightly Arnoldian note is not heard now; indeed, it is specifically disowned. This is odd, for more than once, in arguing that the new media lead towards total social involvement, McLuhan mentions (merely mentions) 'responsibility' and 'commitment', speaks of the need to be 'informed and aware' and—most surprising of all—of his hope that we may soon "be able *to program consciousness* in such wise that it cannot be numbed or distracted by the Narcissus illusions of the entertainment world" [my italics]. But we are given no adequate outer reference for any of these large value-words.

Many other questions are left hanging. If we really are moving towards 'a single cosmic consciousness', why is this not likely, within present systems, to be a drift towards a shared mindlessness? How explosive will be the clash between the new movement towards amorphous fusion and the fissile, categorizing consciousness which sustains the superstructures of our present societies?

In the end we all choose, even when we refuse to choose; and our tone shows first the nature of our commitment. McLuhan's 'get with it' tone—increasingly now—is a product of the electronic age as he himself defines it: 'cool', disconnected, free-floating, flux-like, sometimes as brittle as *Time/Life* prose, excited by the flow of multitudinous sense-impressions and by the opportunities for intellectual fireworks which his mass of untraditional data offers. He ought to give his own tone as much critical attention as he has given that of the 'earnest literary moralizers'.

1964

ON CULTURAL ANALYSIS

Professor Bantock and Authority

Some of the worst writing by British academics has come from Departments of Education. I mean a kind of general and generalized writing about 'aims and purposes', about 'moral education', about 'education and the good life' and so on. More often than not it has been orotund and woolly. It has regretted 'the passing of traditional values', but has so little considered what those values were that it has been able to make a liaison with the looser forms of progressivism; and the result has been a very skittish hybrid.

It was inevitable that there should be a reaction by a younger generation. Shocked by the shortage of objective knowledge about education, about its relation to the social structure or to the national economy, some became social psychologists or sociologists of education, or specialists on the economics of education; and we already have a lot to thank them for. On the extreme other end of that line, with its practical bias, others have settled for minute-scale empirical research. Again, this can be useful. At its worst, it demonstrates an absolute faith in 'scientific procedures' which would be admirable if the research workers were studying rats under clinical conditions; since they are talking about children in schools, however, it suggests a failure of imagination.

For questions about values remain, as importantly as they ever did, and we cannot escape them by pretending they don't exist. To react from Christian uplift to Watsonian behaviourism is no gain. Against this background one sees why G. H. Bantock is a valuable writer. Since *Freedom and Authority in Education*, in the early fifties, he has challenged what he regards as sloppy thinking in the educational world, especially that progressivism which doesn't recognize the need for any distinctions and is prepared to let standards of excellence collapse for the sake of its egalitarian ideology. At his best he is direct, intelligent and deeply concerned.

But, though I have a lot of sympathy with Bantock's initial

premises, I think the position into which he has led himself
in the late sixties unjustified. In *Education, Culture and the
Emotions** his attitudes seem increasingly olympian. "Anger
has a place when the object is anger-worthy," Bantock says;
and this is true. Nor need an author seek to be ingratiating.
Most of the time, too, Bantock is perfectly polite in the usual
academic way. Yet the prevailing undertone of his writing
is rather choleric. And where an event or attitude may be
interpreted in more than one way, he is likely to stress that
explanation which suggests self-indulgence on the part of
other people. The popularity of *Catcher in the Rye* among
adolescents can be partly interpreted in such a way; from
another angle, it can suggest aspiration and the search for
love.

One gets the impression that Bantock sees himself as an
isolated figure, insisting on the truths which a vulgar generation persists in disregarding. There must be times when
isolation is the only honest position, and none of us can say
unthinkingly that today is not such a time. Just as surely a
man who finds himself being led into taking up that position
has a big responsibility, towards himself and his subject, to
check all the time on the reality and relevance of his responses.

Bantock's method is essentially bookish. It draws exten-
sively on other books, but in a special way. He has a strong
set of ideas or frame of convictions. He does qualify them
from his reading: but the qualifications I have noticed are
small, and the possibility of adjustment to the main pattern
seems slight. He is now ready to recognize 'discrimination
within the world of "pop" itself'—chiefly, it appears, from
reading Stuart Hall's and Paddy Whannel's *The Popular
Arts*. But he doesn't engage directly with Hall's and Whannel's own thesis, which runs contrary to his. Rather, he enlists
the insight I quoted above in the service of his own unchanged
major thesis.

Even more striking, Bantock has made some use of Marshall

* Except where otherwise noted, all passages by Professor Bantock quoted
in this essay are from *Education, Culture and the Emotions*, Faber, (1967).

McLuhan's argument about the emergence of a new oral culture. It becomes part of his own general case about the need to give 'the folk', 'the comparatively unreflective', the kind of cultural experience they can cope with. But this is to use a bit of McLuhan that seems to fit, and to ignore the major part. Certainly a footnote of Bantock's suggests some disagreement with McLuhan. Yet anyone with Bantock's views should be fighting the McLuhan of the last few years hard. One could say much the same about others from the great number of authors from whom he habitually quotes, authors greatly mixed in type and stature. The point is: does this way of writing sufficiently advance an argument? Couldn't someone else, using a different selective frame, produce a book supported by quotations from at least as large a range of authors but running in quite the opposite direction?

Bantock needs to make two changes of approach at this time. He should look again at adolescents and at their forms of popular culture. I don't claim that these are easy to understand, or that I understand them. But when one reads Bantock one seems to be meeting stereotypes that haven't recently enough been tested against experience. He says we need to know more about 'inner images' and the way the mass media promote them. Surely this is where to start.

Second, he should define more thoroughly his own special position on the main concepts used in this debate. He is challenging some current views on what we mean, or should mean, by 'culture' and its relations to class and education. Some of us who don't share his views are trying to improve the argument too, and we can't engage better with him unless he analyses more closely. At present he leans too heavily on Eliot's *Notes Towards the Definition of Culture*.

Eliot's book is one of the most formidable modern statements of the conservative case about culture and can't be cavalierly answered. It is also, when you look at it critically, highly idiosyncratic and culturally conditioned itself. It has its place, but also demands to be 'placed'. One shouldn't simply quote from it for supporting evidence;

its own assumptions and concepts need questioning too. Worse, Bantock quotes H. L. Wilensky in support of his own defence of minority culture against mass culture. That is, he quotes Wilensky's digest of his findings published by *New Society* in 1964.* But that article, and certainly Wilensky's fuller material, contain assumptions about what constitutes 'high culture' and 'low culture' which themselves simply have to be challenged before we can decide what the findings signify.

One could say much the same about Bantock's use of the word 'authority'. We might agree that standards of excellence have to be defined and maintained, that they have their own 'authority'; and that schools and universities must recognize this, if they are to do their proper job of intellectual training. Once we look wider, the problems multiply and Bantock's continuing assurance becomes surprising.

> Basically, the adult world here has lost its nerve, in the sense that it cannot feel deeply about what is passed on or consider sternly the means by which this can be done. It fears to be thought authoritarian—and it fears this more than it fears the helplessness of the young.

I think 'the adult world' fears a great deal more. It fears authoritarian personalities and authoritarian institutions, from hard experience. To reduce these fears Bantock will have to define better those élites who will "stand as a bulwark against the enveloping tides of vulgarity from the community outside". He criticizes sharply the extent to which people insist on individual freedom to set their own standards, and regards this chiefly as a form of moral evasion. It can be evasion. Can it not also be a reaction against real pressures? Centralized mass societies like ours exercise powerful and constant hidden pressures; from this angle we can well feel that we are already subjected to far too much authority. Bantock would probably reply that this is not the kind of authority he respects. But it needs to be taken into account

* 14 May 1964.

in an analysis of prevailing attitudes towards freedom and authority. Otherwise he could seem to be saying this is an almost totally 'free' society; we can fairly easily define the authority it needs; and we can find the sort of people who could enforce this authority. But I think he would, in fact, agree that all three of those statements are false; and that their implications are appalling.

1967

Professor Marcus and Cultural Reading

Professor Marcus claims that its sexuality can uniquely illustrate a culture. At one point he describes his book, *The Other Victorians*,* as a set of 'related studies in the sexual sub-culture of Victorian England' through its sub-literature. It is that, but more: it is a demonstration of what can be involved in the 'cultural reading' of literature, whether of sub-literature or recognized literature, and whether or not that literature is about sex.

He found his material in the collection of Victoriana at the Institute for Sex Research at Indiana University, and was highly selective in choosing it. Two-thirds of the book discusses only three authors: William Acton, in his time a well-known medical writer, particularly on prostitution and on the reproductive organs; Pisanus Fraxi, the pseudonym of Henry Spencer Ashbee, the first considerable bibliographer of pornography; and the anonymous author of the 11-volume sexual autobiography *My Secret Life*.

Marcus sees Acton as the bearer of the official views of sexuality held by Victorian society. This means more than it seems. It means embodying and confirming the prevailing 'ideology'. In this sense, an 'ideology' expresses itself in direct ethical precepts only on the surface; deeper down it works as much through shared fantasies as by a grasp on reality—in this case, say, through fantasies about fundamental differences in the sexual responsiveness of men and women or

* By Steven Marcus. Weidenfeld & Nicolson and Basic Books, (1967).

about the appalling effects of masturbation. These fantasies are the unconscious underpinning of the ideology. But Acton was also humane and intelligent and his intelligence sometimes contradicted the official ideology. He could not break out of it; that would have needed a more self-aware man. His double consciousness reveals more about Victorian sexuality and so about Victorian culture than he knew or than we might guess from a surface reading.

This, roughly, is the burden of the first chapter of Marcus's argument and he does something similar in his study of Ashbee. These two chapters are rather like preliminaries to the heart of the book, first shots at his method. That method is primarily to look closely at the texts themselves and work out their cultural meanings, the degree to which they express the consciousness of the age below the explicit level, at the level where the strains show. "The instruments which I could hope to bring to bear on the material I was about to study," he says, "were those of literary criticism, of the historical method, something of applied psycho-analysis and something of social theory." Certainly he is well acquainted with social history, social theory, and (particularly) psycho-analysis, though I cannot judge how accurately he knows all these areas. But I think he describes the problem of method, and his own procedure, in too compartmentalized a way.

At its best, his book, notably in the chapters on *My Secret Life*, shows brilliantly how by rooting yourself first in literary critical method, by reading the texts 'in themselves', you may begin to release wider cultural meanings. Even that describes the problem in too mechanical and successive a way. You won't get far with the texts unless you have considerable knowledge in other than literary fields. But you won't get anywhere unless you 'read' them first in the sense understood by literary critics. Yet literary critics themselves are not always effective in this kind of cultural reading. This is the way we should, but don't often, try to read even recognized literature if we want to understand its cultural meanings. Incidentally, Marcus makes some comparisons between his texts and classic Victorian literature which reveal how, though the public literature could not refer explicitly to many murky areas of life, it nevertheless carried at its best the strong emotional sense that that life did exist.

With sub-literature, most literary critics fall down. Since it is outside the accepted pale we find difficulty in believing that it justifies detailed textual attention and so deal with it in large bundles, looking (say) for the main recurrent patterns and little else. But by analysing it closely, its language, its tone, its stresses and evasions, its omissions, its total rhetoric, we may bring out cultural meanings beyond what we would have expected. We are making, in a sense very difficult to define satisfactorily, a reading for values; one which brings to the surface the complex pattern of values embodied in, carried by, the prose.

Perhaps not in all works. One has to choose that sub-literature which is most likely to be fruitful. Fruitful can mean two things: either that which most nearly approximates to the 'ideal type' of the genre in the Weberian sense, or that which has inherent qualities which make it 'representative'. The author of *My Secret Life* is a considerable writer, both as a Mayhew of street sexual experience and as a man 'faithful to his unconscious', 'a representative consciousness'. But by then we are using 'representative' in the sense used by critics of recognized literature, so at this point the usual categories have collapsed. Which is all to the good in this instance.

The approach by 'ideal types' occupies most of the last third of Marcus's book; the second approach occupies the first two-thirds, and is especially effective in the discussion of *My Secret Life*. The 'representativeness' he finds from his close reading leads him out into social theory, pre-eminently into illuminating how "the workings of class here can be seen as penetrating virtually to one's organs of sense and as conditioning fundamental mental structures". Class, cash, and sex are linked deep within the consciousness. Here, Marcus makes a link with Mannheim's theory of the sociology of knowledge. He is also trying, as he says, to add another dimension to Weber's work on "the relation between modern forms of economic and social organization and the kind of character that was necessary to create those forms and to perpetuate them". It is interesting to recall that Weber in, for example, *The Protestant Ethic and the Spirit of Capitalism* often made his points emerge from a close reading of literary texts.

There are big problems in work of this kind and we have not yet taken the measure of them. Professor Marcus is on thin ice with some and doesn't always seem to recognize how thin it is, especially in the assurance of some of his psycho-analytic connections. Still, at its very good best his book is a most helpful pointer down a road more literary critics will have to travel, if we are going to be able to justify the claim that literature illuminates society.

1967

Mr. Gorer and Attitudes to Death

Mr. Geoffrey Gorer believes that the rituals associated with death, grief and mourning have greatly declined in Britain during the last few decades; that we need such rituals to express our grief fully and publicly instead of keeping it to ourselves and so perhaps falling into neurosis; that the contemporary lack of these rituals has, in fact, increased neurosis among the bereaved.

He argues* that the falling away of ritual is a sign of a deeper refusal: a refusal to face the fact of death at all; and this refusal he associates with the decline of religious belief. He finally claims that there is a relationship between the loss of a public ritual for coping with death and some of the most discussed phenomena of modern society (vandalism, horror films, and so on).

This is an interesting theme though not new. In this century's literature it has inspired many kinds of book, from

* In *Death, Grief and Mourning*, Cresset Press and Doubleday, (1965).

the ironic to the darkly allegorical. One thinks of Huxley's *After Many a Summer*, of Waugh's *The Loved One*, of much of Eliot's poetry (especially of Sweeney reminding Doris: "Birth, and copulation, and death. That's all the facts when you come to brass tacks"), and of Golding's novels. On the other hand, as Mr. Gorer points out in his essay 'The Pornography of Death', deathbed scenes (and I would add burial scenes) seem much less common in contemporary literature than they were in Victorian. I say 'seem' because one is relying on strong impressions; I do not know that anyone has done an analysis.

Still, assuming it to be true, what does it prove? The answer is complex since it has to do with secular changes in our attitudes towards ourselves, our relationships with others, our sense of society and our ideas about the function of art. Literary criticism can help in this inquiry. By comparing crucial moments in Victorian and contemporary literature, one can detect complicated shifts in the emotional pressure behind different elements of experience. Think, for example, of the differences in tone in deathbed or burial scenes by Dickens, George Moore, Arnold Bennett and Joyce.

Later the deathbed scene, if it appears at all, is likely to be in double focus: seen both as a harsh fact (a character has, after all, died) and as a commentary on a society's wish not to accept that harshness or at the least to mitigate it. The burial scene in Lionel Trilling's *The Middle of the Journey* is a good instance.

Yet contemporary fiction, as Mr. Gorer also remarks, is full of extended scenes of copulation. They are its major set pieces, as deathbed scenes were for the Victorians. Why is this? To reply that it is because we are 'freer' (or even that we are 'more immoral') is only to argue in circles. To say that the stress on sex, together with the lack of attention to the experience of death, reinforces the argument that we are running away from 'the harsh facts of life' into immediate sensual experience—to say this is to make over-crude conjunctions. Sex, after all, is as much a fact of life as death, and copulation in modern fiction is as likely to be a harsh testing and a challenge as a pleasure.

Perhaps each generation, in confronting its own mental climate and trying to find a sense of personal reality within it, turns again and again to those particular elements in human experience which expose its deepest insecurity and so most put to the test its search for meaning and identity; and perhaps today the act of sex—a man and a woman at their most exposed, and outside society—rather than the fact of death, best provides this arena.

One could go on to suggest that we talk less about death not because we are running away from it but because, in the light of recent experience, we have all too fully accepted it—as massively impersonal, imminent and immanent, and perhaps as meaningless: that we are not so much evasive as dourly stoic.

I cannot prove either of these ideas. I am throwing them in to underline that the shape and process of attitude changes are intricate. Several kinds of scholar could each spend several useful years writing books about Mr. Gorer's theme. A literary critic would probably work outwards from the textures of the prose itself to all the other characteristics of, say, fiction at different periods and so to their authors' sense of human experience, of their relations to their audience, of their cultural climates. Other scholars have their own ways; but all of them will be involved in a difficult exploration of material irradiated with human commitments and, most difficult of all, with those values constantly but slowly undergoing change.

Mr. Gorer's particular field is social psychology. For his inquiry into death, grief and mourning 359 people answered a questionnaire and of these 80 later had an extended interview with Mr. Gorer or his assistant. On working-class life, in particular, the detail is quite rich. One remembers again the widows in solid black hurrying off to spiritualist meetings, or all the business of laying out, 'paying respects', drawing blinds along the street until it was judged that the funeral was over, the regular visits to the cemetery and the annual In Memoriam notices in the local newspaper. Or the phrases: 'Isn't he lovely' or 'Well, he's at peace now' when you went to see the body. Or, to quote one of Mr. Gorer's respondents: "We were in the hospital when she *drew her last breath*" [my italics—there is nothing evasive there].

The last funeral I attended was a cremation, in a Leeds working-class district. I was told that cremation was becoming much more common, chiefly because it was cheaper and more 'convenient' than the business of finding a grave. But otherwise the pattern was much as I have always known it; the new elements had, as so often, been grafted on to the old. Mr. Gorer's evidence does suggest, not surprisingly, that rituals like these remain strongest among working-class groups, among the unskilled and comparatively immobile, among people who have lived for several generations in one poor area and have built up—where life does not offer much public dignity—a way of giving some public dignity at least to death. Mr Gorer's inquiry suggests also, again not surprisingly, that the social rituals of death decline more quickly as people become more mobile. There is no longer standing neighbourhood tradition for coping with burial, grief and mourning.

One has to say that Mr. Gorer 'suggests' rather than proves these things for a number of reasons: because, whatever its accuracy as a representative sample, his group is so small that the case lacks a consonant texture and weight; because he has not provided, within his own social scientific discipline, any comparison in time (comparable with that provided by the literary critical comparisons I described earlier); because, in so far as there is such a comparison in time, it is provided by the contrast between the material in the main text and the reminiscences in an autobiographical introduction . . . and this is to mix approaches so different in kind that one risks proving nothing at all.

The emotional sense of the rituals associated with death can best be presented through one kind or other of creative writing (which can include autobiography). The objective analysis of these rituals, as they are today and, even more, as they have changed over the decades, can only be carried out by another discipline, of a social scientific kind. Each has something to learn from the other and they can, on the right terms, be put side by side to advantage. Mr. Gorer seems to have thought this conjunction was easier to make than it really is. One is left with a dilute mixture. He argues that despair after the loss of a loved one is linked today with the loss of a public ritual for grief, with attempts to "deny the psychological reality of grief and mourning". But in the ritualistic working-class society I grew up in I saw despair which seemed much like that Mr. Gorer describes, and seemed as common. He may be right in saying that there has been a change, but he gives neither enough spread of evidence nor enough penetration into the relevant psychic pattern to cause someone with a fair body of first hand experience to be willing to reinterpret it substantially.

Similarly, he may be right in saying that there are links between the flight from the fact of death (if that *is* what is taking place) and the appetite for horror comics and X films; but it will take some proving. If such links are simply asserted, we are in the world of intellectual impressionism, which is even trickier than imaginative impressionism.

1965

Mrs. Leavis and the Dangers of Narrowness

To anyone interested in the relations between literature and the general culture Mrs. Leavis's *Fiction and the Reading Public** has for many years been one of the half-dozen most important texts.

It is an exceptionally forceful book—for its unremitting seriousness (which is bracing, since much talk about popular culture and mass culture is insecure in tone), for its single-ness of purpose, for the force and detail of its critical com-

* Q. D. Leavis, *Fiction and the Reading Public* (reissued 1965). Chatto.

parisons, for its effort to define and trace the links between 'the quality of life' in a society and literature of all types, and for its refusal to let literary studies stay in a comfortable reserve—"To be interested in cultural questions is necessarily to set out from the contemporary situation."

All this comes up fresh on a re-reading. So does a sense of the need to meet the major criticisms of this approach, since these are criticisms not only of Mrs. Leavis's book (though inevitably they often start there) but of the work of many of us who combine teaching literature with an interest in cultural change. These seem the main problems:

Selective history: J. H. Plumb is only one of the more recent of several historians who have charged literary-cultural critics with the partial use of historical material, with—for instance—idealizing the life of the eighteenth-century peasantry. Graham Hough, unfairly, has called all such critics 'happy peasants' themselves. But the accusations have a point. It is important not to raid history selectively in the service of another discipline. The distinctive contribution of literary criticism to the discussion of cultural change is its attempt to define what is meant, in the fullest sense we can reach, by 'changes in the quality of life' of a society. It is a pity to tempt historians and others to dismiss this contribution as nostalgia for an Arcadia that never was.

Ill-supported comparisons: Miss Dalziel criticizes, I think fairly, some of the comparisons used by Mrs. Leavis to illustrate a decline in popular literary taste since the early nineteenth century. She adds, "But in spite of the fact that the evidence for the conclusion is poor, the conclusion may still be right."* Since Mrs. Leavis wrote there have been a good many useful background studies: R. D. Altick's *The English Common Reader*, Louis James's *Fiction for the Working Man* (especially the material on Dickens and his imitators), and Margaret Dalziel's own *Popular Fiction 100 Years Ago*. But most literary-cultural critics have continued to lay themselves open to Miss Dalziel's criticism.

* In *Popular Fiction 100 Years Ago* (1957). London: Cohen; N.Y.: Dufour.

Literary insularity: This has several branches. We often claim too much, too single-mindedly, and too quickly, for the influence of literature on individuals and on society. That influence can hardly be 'scientifically' proved, but it can be argued and expounded more connectedly. Our view of what constitutes 'cultivation' and 'maturity' is more historically and socially conditioned than we realize. Some of our guiding assumptions (about 'brows', 'levels', 'cultivated taste') have become rigid, and obscure the cultural complexities. We are led to underestimate the other-than-literary ways in which human beings can express the quality of their lives, and so we infer too much from changes in popular literary taste. Raymond Williams's examination, in *Culture and Society*, of nineteenth-century working-class institutions as creative expressions of a whole view of life is a useful corrective. Or, if we think that irony and anti-sentimentality did not figure in English working-class entertainments after the eighteenth century, we should listen to 'Cushie Butterfield' from the North-east coast, or the Cockney 'The 'Ouses in Between', or any of a hundred other nineteenth and early-twentieth century songs. It is easy to enthuse patronizingly over the popular arts, and we have instances of this every day: it is easy to show that they have little that will 'nourish a culti-vated taste'. But to understand their appeal, and so under-stand what they really signify about the changes in a society's life, requires a more difficult relationship.

1965

CULTURE: DEAD AND ALIVE

I N one part of his Fabian pamphlet, *Socialism and Culture*, Mr. Richard Wollheim remarks that judgments about 'mass culture' are often vitiated by false assumptions. We condemn 'mass culture' out of hand by assuming that it is no more than a watered-down form of that 'high culture' we implicitly seek to defend. We do not distinguish between, for instance, sex-and-violence pulp literature and 'skiffle'. Both are enjoyed by 'them', 'the masses'; therefore both are low and uncultured.

I agree with Mr. Wollheim, and would go further. To think in the way he criticizes is convenient and self-flattering. It carries into new and confused areas of cultural activity the old, comfortable grading by height of brow. It can be reinforced, as it has often been reinforced in the past, by an implied social or educational grading. 'Lowbrow' culture was that enjoyed by 'the lower orders'; 'mass culture' is that enjoyed by the 80 per cent who have not been to a grammar school.

Any analysis, by social class or educational background, of the audiences for some of the more successful forms of 'mass culture' (the most popular newspapers, certain television programmes) makes this distinction untenable. More important, such a distinction prevents us from understanding the peculiar problems of cultural change today. In using it, most 'highbrows' show themselves out of touch with cultural change, and as much deceived as the 'lowbrows' they feel sorry for.

The crucial distinctions today are not those between the *News of the World* and *The Observer*, between the Third Programme and the Light Programme, between sex-and-violence paperbacks and 'egghead' paperbacks, between Bootsie and Snudge and the Alan Taylor lectures, between the Billy Cotton Band Show and the Brains Trust, between the Top Ten and a celebrity concert, or between 'skiffle' and chamber music. The distinctions we should be making are those between the *News of the World* and the *Sunday Pictorial*, between 'skiffle' and the Top Ten; and, for 'highbrows', between *The Observer* and the *Sunday Times*, or, in 'egghead' paperbacks, between Peter Townsend and Vance Packard.

This is to make distinctions between the quality of life in each thing of its own kind—distinctions which require an active discrimination, not the application of a fixed 'brow' or educational scale. We are required to judge the quality of the response being shown or implied in each instance. We have to distinguish between life, creative life, and death, a mechanically-twitching death. 'Life' may show itself in 'serious' or 'light' programmes, as scepticism and irony or as broad emotion or firm intelligence—but will always be disinterested and honest. 'Death' may show itself as trivial and slick (even though it may be purporting to be serious), cynical, against the mind and afraid of the heart—but will always be interested and out to persuade. We have to ask: Is this really a comedy? Or documentary? Or variety show? Or discussion? Or religious programme? Or is it going through the motions, a well-packaged emptiness?

Perhaps we should stop talking about 'mass culture', since the phrase invites us to stick to the old categories. Perhaps we should speak about 'synthetic culture' or 'processed culture'—and then remind ourselves that our job is to separate the Processed from the Living at (to use the old grading) all 'levels'.

Processed culture never imagines an individual—only masses, typical audiences, status groups. Living culture, even if many people are enjoying it at the same time, speaks to individuals or to genuine communities, and cuts across boundaries of age or class or status. Processed culture has its eye always on the audience, the consumers, the customers. Living culture has its eye on the subject, the material. It expects the same attention to the subject from the members of its audience. Processed culture asks: "What will they take? Will this get most of them?" Living culture asks: "What is the truth of this experience and how can I capture it?"

Processed culture rapes its material, consumes it in deference to the assumed needs of its block-audiences, and is thus led to put its products into such uniformly glossy packages that a comedy show and a political discussion look and feel alike. Living culture recognizes the diversity, the particularity, of all experience. It sits down before its material, and does not fear being clumsy or gauche so long as it is in touch with that material. It can sometimes go on too long or fail to 'take tricks'; but it does not let virtuosity take over from virtue, presentation from substance, the 'way' of saying from the 'what' is being said.

We have to learn to make these distinctions not only because they are proper distinctions at any time, but because one further characteristic of mass society has shown itself in the last few decades. We have often told ourselves that a mass society would be culturally all one, a homogenized mish-mash; there would be no place for 'high culture'. It is now clear that technological competence and marketing pressures will ensure that differences are retained; we shall have a culturally varied society. Or we will believe we have.

In fact, we shall have a society which is only apparently varied in its cultural life, a society with a range of permitted, safe variations. The old distinctions by class-and-brow may be being weakened, but they are being amply replaced by new status-and-brow distinctions. We may read *The Times* not because we are part of an 'Establishment' but because we like to think we are becoming a 'Top Person'; we may read *The Guardian* not because we belong to a provincial, liberal middle class but because we want to belong to the group with Lively Minds.

But these are at bottom only differences in marketing and brand-image. As the process extends so authentic distinctions become harder to make. The 'highbrow' is as blind here, and as much threatened, as the 'lowbrow'.

So when some of us speak of the need for 'a common culture' we are not seeking a uniform culture. We are opposing that movement towards a uniform culture which is going on all round—towards a culture which looks varied but is the same in spirit throughout. We mean two things by 'a common culture'. We mean a culture not irrelevantly divided by old social distinctions or new status distinctions. We mean also a culture which, though it is varied, and allows a free movement of interacting minorities, has this common ground: that it gives room for individuality, idiosyncrasy, the play of mind true to its own observations and to the substance of the things observed.

1961

MASS COMMUNICATIONS
IN BRITAIN

THE subject of this essay is not 'serious' or 'good' literature; nor is it literature alone. It is that extraordinary range of recreational activities put out by the media of mass communication. Somewhere outside them stands the work of the novelists, poets, and dramatists discussed in the weeklies; so do older forms of popular urban entertainment such as working-men's club concerts, brass bands, chapel choirs, comic postcards, and *Peg's Paper*; so do officially established 'cultural' organizations, such as the Arts Council. But the focus in this instance is on such productions as *Reveille, Sunday Night at the Palladium, The News of the World, Tonight* (the television magazine), *Compact, This Is Your Life,* the *Daily Mirror, Emergency Ward 10, Tempo,* the advertisements on ITV, *Coronation Street, Juke-Box Jury,* the columnist Cassandra and the minor host of 'Paul Slickeys', *Panorama,* television Westerns, *Woman, The Archers, Monitor.* The relation of all these to literature, and to the 'high culture' of which literature is a part, is not immediately clear. But there is a relationship, one which anyone interested in literature and in society should think about.

Many people have been thinking about it; discussion about mass communications has been persistent and heated in this century. But it is not essentially new. It is a development in contemporary terms of a larger debate, with a long history. A recent historian of this larger debate, Raymond Williams, begins his examination with Edmund Burke and moves through, among others, Coleridge, Newman, Lawrence, and Eliot (if we regard Eliot as British). The list runs through more than one hundred and fifty years, and in Britain alone. If we look outside, we can span a roughly similar period by moving, say, from Alexis de Tocqueville to Ortega y Gasset.

The debate is about 'culture' and society; that is, about the quality of the life which democracies encourage. 'Culture' here, then, has to do with the imaginative life these societies express, partly though not only through the place they give to the creative arts and to intellectual inquiry. The debate is also, inevitably, about the relation of culture to 'class', to wealth, to work, and to educational provision. What place, if any, do traditional forms of 'high culture' (those arts and inquiries formerly sustained largely by members of the middle and upper classes) have in a universally literate and fairly prosperous democracy? What future, if any, have the elements of a differently phrased and local 'working-class' culture? Is a good, widely diffused, 'popular' or demotic culture possible in such democracies? What kinds of persuasion, by government or by non-statutory bodies, are legitimate and desirable?

Such a debate is not expressed only in writing. In nineteenth-century Britain the devoted efforts by some members of the 'privileged' classes to disseminate the benefits of education and 'culture' to those less fortunately placed is part of the same movement, an expression of the same concern (as in the development of extra-mural teaching by the universities, which was begun by Cambridge). Similarly, many of those resourceful nineteenth-century reformers who were themselves from the working classes believed they had a 'cultural' as well as a political and economic mission. To take another example from adult education: the universities did not plough a virgin field; many grass-roots organizations for the educational improvement of working-people existed before the universities entered.

So the discussion of mass communications is part of a longer inquiry. But there are sound reasons why the inquiry should be especially active today. The twentieth century is the first century of the truly *mass* media of communication, and this gives a special emphasis to questions of the kind listed above. Is 'high culture' bound to be peripheral to the overriding forces of mass communications? Are all older types of 'culture' likely to be submerged in new substitute forms, in what the Germans call 'kitsch'? What is the relation of the creative arts and of disinterested intellectual activity to these new means of communication?

No definition of the mass media can be precise, but there are workable rules-of-thumb. The chief forms of mass communication, as the phrase is normally used today, are sound and television broadcasting, the press and some periodicals, the cinema, some types of advertising and some kinds of books. In general, all these activities are addressed regularly to audiences absolutely very large and relatively undifferentiated by class, income, background, or locality (so most books are not in this sense mass media). All are products of the last eighty years; before then, broadcasting and the cinema did not exist; the press and advertising existed, but not as mass media.

Several social and technological factors combined to produce these modern forms of communication. Two are usually given overriding importance. In fact, they don't greatly illuminate the more subtle aspects of the problem—those to do with direction and quality. These two factors are technological advance and universal literacy. Obviously the two interact and some mass media (especially popular publications) have particularly developed from the interaction; on the other hand, cinema and broadcasting need hardly attend on literacy. The most striking primary cause for the appearance of contemporary mass communications, then, was the application of new technical knowledge. The last decades of the nineteenth century, in particular, saw an enormously accelerated development in all parts of this field.

In Britain, it is true, these advances roughly coincided with the appearance of a new reading public. Towards the end of the nineteenth century the Registrar-General was able to announce that Britain—no other nation had preceded her— was substantially literate. The population was growing, and has continued to grow. There is plenty of evidence, especially in the biographies of the first press-lords, that some men appreciated the commercial opportunities presented by this large, new audience.

Three further qualifications have to be made, so that universal literacy is not given too much weight in the general development of mass communications. First, it would be wrong to infer that before the late nineteenth century only a tiny minority in Britain could read. Recent research has shown that by the middle of the century a substantial proportion were able to read, even among the working classes. Second, there was a considerable amount of cheap publication for the working class by, say, 1840; these publications divide roughly into two types, the 'improving' and the sensational. Third: if too simple a relationship is assumed between statutory education for the body of the population and the rise of certain types of mass communication, one more easily assumes that these productions are addressed chiefly to working people, that working people, almost alone, are affected by them. This was never substantially true and is becoming less true all the time.

Two other factors lie behind the rise of mass communications and tell more about their nature. The first is the development, in both democracies and totalitarian states, of centralized social planning. In almost all societies, and especially in those which are becoming increasingly industrialized, a kind of national self-consciousness is greater today than ever before. This does not necessarily mean that what is commonly called a 'nationalist spirit' is more powerful, but that these societies need more and more to speak to their citizens as a body, to persuade them in certain directions. This is the public or governmental pressure behind mass communications and can be seen in a great number of forms: in authoritarian countries as a support to state ideologies (Mussolini's Italy, Hitler's Germany, Soviet Russia, Communist China); in democratic countries chiefly in time of war or 'cold war'; but increasingly in the day-to-day peacetime life of any technologically advanced state—to persuade more people to take up a scientific career or wear crash helmets or buy government bonds. A new range of middlemen, professional social lubricators, is emerging: communications experts, public relations advisers, industrial relations consultants, social analysts, all the link-men and anchor-men of the functional society. It would be difficult to decide the relative importance of various factors when comparing the speed with which the means of mass-communication have been adopted in different countries. In democracies we tend to overestimate the effect of commercial forces. We should give more importance to larger social forces, to public and governmental pressures.

Still, there are important commercial pressures in the democracies. In spite of the damage of two major wars and the rise in population, the last half-century has seen a considerable increase in the real wealth of many Western countries. Many more things are being made and have to be sold, competitively. Thus in Britain a lot of people who previously spent almost the whole of their income in providing, and often barely providing, for necessities now have money to spend on goods which are not essential—though they may be pleasant to have. This is generally true, though not evenly spread throughout society. Since the war marginal spending by teenagers, in particular, has encouraged, and been encouraged by, substantial businesses; pensioners and others past working age have not so much benefited from post-war prosperity (compare the attention paid by commercial television to 'youth' with that to the aged). This general improvement may or may not accompany a levelling of incomes within a society. The crucial element is the overall rise in real wealth which has ensured that a large number of people who were previously below the level at which they attracted serious and concerted attention from the makers of non-essential consumer goods are now above that level. These are what market-research specialists call 'new markets', especially for tastes previously enjoyed chiefly by middle- and upper-class groups, or 'potential markets' where a more novel taste or invented 'need' has to be encouraged.

SPEAKING TO EACH OTHER

In Russia and China the mass media are arms of government, with positive and comparatively single-minded functions. In different democracies their use differs, according to the underlying assumptions of each society. In America the main emphasis is on the commercial use of the means of mass communication—they tend to be aids to selling, or profit-making organizations in their own right. In Britain, which is both a stratified society with a still fairly powerful Establishment and yet a commercial 'open' democracy, the use of mass communications reflects this piebald character. The British like to use direct governmental controls as little as possible, but their strong tradition of public service and public responsibility causes them (where it is not possible to support existing voluntary agencies) to establish semi-autonomous chartered bodies under regular, but not day-by-day, government surveillance. The Universities Grants Committee and the Arts Council are typical of such bodies. This tradition helped ensure that, once broadcasting had begun to show its powers, in the middle 1920's, a new chartered body was created—the British Broadcasting Corporation —charged with responsibility for public service broadcasting. After the appearance of television there was considerable pressure for a commercial channel—strengthened by the country's increased prosperity—and so in 1954 the Independent Television Authority was created, to run a second channel from the proceeds of advertisements. Its advocates always point out that programmes on this channel are not 'sponsored' by the advertisers as they are in the United States. This is true, but the similarities between American television and British television on ITA are greater than the differences. And the general tendencies of both are markedly different from those of the BBC. It would be more accurate to call the British second channel 'commercial television' rather than 'independent television'. In media so centralized and which reach instantaneously so large an audience there can be no full independence: one chooses to try to fulfil a definition of public service responsibilities; or one is pulled by the pervasive general requirements of those who pay for the advertisements. At present these two channels,* each competing for the attention of the British people, and each representing one main form of 'dependence', are the most striking evidence for the two themes of this essay: the intrinsic importance of the organs of mass communication; and the curiously piebald relationship of Great Britain to the use of these organs—relationships decided partly by tradition, and partly by new commercial and cultural pressures.

In Great Britain, particularly during the last thirty years, these four factors—technological advances, universal literacy, increased public self-consciousness, and increased consumption of goods—have encouraged two striking changes in almost all forms of public communication. To some extent these changes, towards centralization and concentration, must develop as the means of communication become means of mass communication; in Britain they have developed very quickly.

Centralization denotes the tendency for local or regional sources of communication to give way to one metropolitan source. The metropolitan area itself progressively subdivides into segments, each providing nationally most of the popular material within a given branch (e.g. Fleet Street, Wardour Street, Denmark Street). It is not difficult to see why this process should have moved quickly in Britain. The country is highly industrialized, densely populated, small in area, and has good communications. Practically everyone can be reached instantaneously by sound or television broadcasting, or within a few hours by a national newspaper. The United States has roughly three-and-a-half times the population of Britain but thirty times her land area. Holland and Belgium have most of those characteristics of Britain listed above, but the relative smallness of their populations makes it less likely that massive organizations can be founded in the field of communications. Nor has Britain any strong regional centres of intellectual activity. Edinburgh and Manchester can make some claim,

---

* The situation was made more complex with the appearance of the second BBC channel, of course, but the general line of the argument still stands.

but a comparison with, say, Naples or Milan shows how limited the claim is.

Centralization in communications reflects the centralization in commerce and industry. Similarly, concentration reflects larger economic movements. If centralization makes for the production of almost all material of one kind from one source, concentration makes for a reduction in variety within each kind. In industry, the production of motor-cars is an obvious instance. Several kinds of car are available (family saloon, sports car, limousine, estate car) but the number of different makes and so of models within each kind is small. The large markets thus ensured bring advantages. Occasionally, some of these advantages can be usefully taken in the distribution of intellectual works, as in the issue of good books in paperback. But this is chiefly a matter of 'marketing' an existing product of good quality (and for every publication of this sort the same machines produce several which are worthless). The real problems which concentration in intellectual matters poses lie here: that concentration does not simply distribute existing material but to some extent decides the nature of new material. Motor-cars are not very important; if by centralizing and concentrating production we get workable models cheaply we can be satisfied. But cheapness, speed, smartness are irrelevant to intellectual and imaginative affairs and in these matters are usually bought at the cost of what is relevant to them.

Sound and television broadcasting are products of advanced technology and have been since their birth both centralized and concentrated. The cinema, since it is almost entirely a profit-making industry, has been centralized and concentrated almost since its beginning, and our pleasure when something even mildly exploratory is attempted in a film suggests what a loss this has meant. But changes in the British Press and in periodical publication during the last thirty years show most clearly the trend towards centralization and concentration, since both of these originally had a great variety of outlets and attitudes.

The number of provincial papers still published might suggest that here at least centralization and concentration have not gone far. But a closer look at the provincial papers reveals that centralization and concentration are here too. Ostensibly a paper may belong to a provincial town and the editor live in its suburbs. But in some important respects these papers are no more than provincial outlets, printing offices, for large London combines. Though they include a good deal of local news and views the major comment and editorials, the background articles, the judgments on all topics other than those of purely local interest, are likely to be issued from London each day and syndicated in papers under the same central control all over Britain.

Concentration is even more striking here. Many people still think that Britain has eight or nine national popular daily newspapers, of roughly equal effect. Eight or nine there certainly are, but a glance at the differences in their circulations shows how far concentration has advanced. Among the popular national morning dailies, two alone account for about two-thirds of all sales on any one day. The position is similar in popular Sunday newspapers and in weekly family magazines, and is even more marked in women's magazines.

Some people argue that the mass media are only means of communication, channels for the large-scale distribution of material whose character is not affected by the manner in which it is distributed. I do not agree with this argument, but it does have one use; it points to the more obvious benefits from mass communications. Television, it is true and we are told often, can suggest a range of worthwhile interests and pleasures wider than most of us would otherwise have known. It can give millions of us the chance to see at the same time a really informed discussion on a matter of public interest; it can occasionally give a close sense of the characters of admirably impressive individuals who would otherwise have been no more than names to us; it can present from month to month plays, well acted and produced, which most of us would have passed a lifetime without seeing. In all this television is acting as a transmitter, a multiple transmitter; and it can be extremely valuable.

Some other forms of mass communication appear to have taken over from scattered and varied oral agencies the work of sustaining an elementary folklore. In this shadowy but powerful symbolic world some of the strip-cartoons now work alongside and are probably beginning to replace a network of urban stories and myths. This harsh but pregnant sub-world has not been much examined either by writers on mass communications or by students of literature or—a good thing, since they might make use of it—by the advertising copy-writers.

Most of the work of the mass media is done in a more self-conscious light. The fact that this work is produced for a mass audience radically affects its character. Its situation almost always forces certain qualities upon it; and these are weakenings of the qualities of those established arts on which mass communications must draw.

Mass communications are usually led, first, to avoid clear psychological and social definition. Sharp definition is possible in 'high art', and concrete definition of a certain kind is possible in 'low' art, since each depends on a limiting of the audience. The first audience is nowadays largely self-selected, without overriding reference to social or geographic factors. This is, for want of a better term, the 'highbrow' audience composed of people who, during the times that they are being 'highbrows', are not in a limiting sense also clerks in Sheffield, mechanics in Manchester, or stockbrokers in Croydon—though these may be their occupations and will inform their reading. Yet they are, whilst forming this audience, in a certain sense disinterested. A clerk can read *Anna Karenina* with the same kind of attention as a stockbroker or a mechanic, though the life of upper-class Russian civil servants in the nineteenth century has little social similarity with any of theirs.

The second audience is limited by class or geography or both. It can allow a kind of definition within a specific way of life because this way of life is local or socially accepted. This is the audience of, say, *Peg's Paper* or the *Tatler*.

The mass media can only occasionally accept either of these types of audience. The first is too small to be of much use; the second is a series of audiences, of roughly the same type though divided by habit and custom. The job of the mass media is to weld this second series of audiences into one much larger group. There is an immediate loss. Compare the texture of social life—working class, middle class—in a moderately good novel, or compare even the particularity of social detail in an old-fashioned working-class women's magazine, with the life called up in one of the newer class-less women's magazines, or that in the posters and pamphlets issued by either of the main political parties in Britain.

The overwhelming use of the 'realist' or photographic method in mass art underlines this situation. The mass media, especially in a commercial society, dare not genuinely disturb or call in question the *status quo*. Their function is to re-inforce the given life of the time, to help their new or emerging mass audience accept the 'reality' that is offered them. Everything has to be shown as 'interesting' and yet as equally interesting, since to do otherwise would be to inspire distinctions and so create minorities. By this means most of existence is presented as a succession of entertaining items, each as significant as the next: a television 'magazine' pro-gramme or a weekly illustrated magazine will successively give the same sort of treatment—visual, novel, interest-ing—to a film actress, a nuclear physicist, a teenage singing star, a 'great man of letters'; or similar treatment will be given to close-up photographs of a personal tragedy or a new technique for building roads. Order and significance give way to sheer spectacle, the endlessly fragmented curiousness of raw experience.

So, though they are exceptionally aware of their huge audience as a huge audience, the mass media can only risk a qualified closeness to the individuals who compose that audience. They can rarely be so precise and particular as to inspire members of that audience to say, "There, but for the grace of God . . ." or "This attitude I cannot accept . . ." They are under pressure to retreat from the dramatic immediate presentations of art to the sterilized world of the 'documentary', where the close detail of individual existence is reduced by being generalized to the status of 'problems which concern us all', problems which are examined in a 'neutral' and fair-minded way. This is the foundation of that standardization of character which marks most works produced expressly for the mass media.

We are told the mass media are the greatest organs for enlightenment the world has yet seen, that in Britain several million people see each issue of *Panorama* and several million each issue of *Tonight*. I have already agreed that the claim has some foundation. Yet it is not extensive. It is true that never in human history were so many people so often and so much exposed to so many intimations about societies, forms of life, attitudes other than those which obtain in their own local societies. This kind of exposure may sometimes be a point of departure for acquiring important intellectual and imaginative qualities: width of judgment, a sense of the variety of possible attitudes. Yet in itself such an exposure does not bring those developments. It is no more than the masses of stone which lie around in a quarry and may, conceivably, go to the making of a cathedral. The mass media cannot build the cathedral, and their way of showing the stones does not always prompt others to build. The stones are presented within a self-contained and self-sufficient world in which, it is implied, simply to look at them, to observe— fleetingly—individually interesting points of difference, is sufficient.

Life is indeed full of problems on which we have to make —or feel we should try to make—decisions, as citizens or as private individuals. But the unaccommodating difficulty of these decisions and their severe testing of each individual, are not often communicated through the mass media. The disinclination to suggest complex choices, individual decisions, which is found in the mass media is not simply the product of a commercial desire to keep the customers happy. It is within the grain of mass communications. The Establishments, however well-intentioned they may be and whatever their forms (the State, the Church, voluntary agencies, political parties), have a vested interest in ensuring that the public boat is not violently rocked, and would like so to affect those who work within the mass media that they will be led insensibly towards forms of production which, though they go through the motions of dispute and inquiry, do not break through to the point where such inquiries hurt. They tend to move, when exposing problems, well within the accepted cliché-assumptions of democratic society and neither radically question those clichés nor apply them disturbingly to features of contemporary life; they stress the 'stimulation' the programmes give, but this soon becomes an agitation of problems for the sake of the interestingness of that agitation in itself; they will therefore, again, assist a form of acceptance of the *status quo*. There are exceptions to this tendency, but they are uncharacteristic.

The result can be seen in many radio and television programmes as plainly as in the normal treatment of public issues in the popular Press. Different levels of background in the readers or viewers may be assumed, but what usually takes place is a substitute for the process of arriving at judgment. Mass communications do not ignore intellectual matters; they tend to castrate them, to allow them to sit on one side of the fireplace, sleek, a family plaything.

Similarly, mass communications do not ignore imaginative art. They must feed upon it, since it is the source of much of their material; but they must also seek to exploit it. They tend to cut the nerve which gives it life—that questioning, with all the resources an artist can muster, of the meaning of his experience; but they find the body interesting and useful. Towards art, therefore, the mass media are the purest aesthetes; they want its forms and styles but not its meanings and significance. Since they are mass communications they have a pressing awareness of their audience and a pressing uncertainty about that audience. There is a sense in which a serious artist ignores his audience (assuming that they will share his interest in exploring the subject); or in which a popular artist with a defined audience simply assumes that audience because his work is embedded in, and expresses, attitudes which are never called in question. But the worker in the mass media is not primarily trying to explore anything or express anything: he is trying to capture and hold an audience. Manner is more important than matter. The fact that very often there is not one writer on a specific programme but a 'team', each member contributing his tactical items, underlines how far this process is from a serious artist's single strategy towards his recalcitrant material.

If an artist will co-operate with the mass media on the media's terms (to their credit some artists go on working with the media for the sake of such success as they can gain in their own artistic terms), he may have exceptional rewards. In the age of mass communications art becomes one of the most elusive and therefore most sought-after forms of 'marginal differentiation'. Just as the dilemmas of experience are reduced to a series of equally interesting but equally non-significant snapshots, or to the status of documentary 'problems', so the products of art become an eclectic shiny museum of styles, each divorced from its roots in men suffering and rejoicing in certain times and places. You may buy by subscription and renew, as often as you renew the flowers in your sitting-room, examples of Aztec art or African art or Post-Impressionist painting or Cubist painting or the latest book (probably about the horrors of mass-society) which a panel of well-publicized authorities have selected for you. And all has the same effect as the last instalment of a television magazine. You have sipped and looked and tasted; but nothing has happened. 'Culture' has become a thing for display not exploration; a presentation not a challenge.

The above point needs to be stressed because it is easy to think the mass media affect only 'them'; that the 'masses' are some large body of people in an outer uncultured darkness. But, as Raymond Williams has reminded us, there are probably no masses at all—only operators in the mass media trying to form masses, and all of us from time to time allowing them. And these 'masses' cannot be identified with one social class or with the usual picture of lowbrows and middlebrows (against highbrows). Not everyone who reads the book page of *The Observer* is automatically free from mass persuasions, even in his artistic interests.

We have said more than once that one primary need of mass communications is to reach as wide an audience as possible. Class divides. Where the mass media are commercially influenced this need is all the stronger. To sell their centralized and concentrated goods they must seek a centralized and concentrated audience. So in this the mass media are reflecting and encouraging wider social changes. Centralized production, changes in the nature of work (partly through more effective automatic processes), a higher general level of incomes, greater social mobility, educational changes —all are helping to alter the local and class lines of British life. In part those lines are also related to divisions in types of cultural activity. British society may be forming new stratifications, by brains, education, and occupation rather than by birth and money. But such a society will need, if it is not to be irritated by constant inner dissent, a common meeting ground of acceptable attitudes. In democracies this assent has to be brought about by persuasion. In commercially powerful and densely populated democracies the acceptable attitudes can include a wide range of seemingly varying attitudes. There is room for the *Daily Sketch* as much as for *Vogue*, for the Miss Britain Competition as much as for the Book-of-the-Month Club. But the variety is only apparent; the textures of the experiences they offer do not vary at any point in the spectrum. You have then arrived at a sort of cultural classlessness.

This need to reach a large and (whilst they are listening) classless audience ensures that the mass media can take little for granted. What sort of furniture, of reactions, of assertions may be used here? How far dare one go on this line without running the risk of alienating some group? It follows that mass communications tend to flatter, since they are prone to take a more plainly winning attitude before one which may disconcert. More important, they have little opportunity for taking up a lively relationship towards their material. Some existing attitudes they may use, after a fashion; others they must freshly introduce, with great care. This explains the limited narcissism of the mass media towards attitudes which have been traditionally acceptable to large numbers of people, especially towards attitudes which can be made to assist in creating the atmospheres most congenial to the operation of the mass media themselves. They will accept certain well-established working-class attitudes such as tolerance, lack of meanness, generosity—and import them into a friendly public buyers' and sellers' world in which they look the same but soon wither, for want of the soil in which they had first been nurtured. Programmes such as *This is Your Life* and *Have a Go* are typical instances of this kind of process— so is the whole tone of much popular journalism, especially that in the gossip columns and correspondence columns.

This kind of extension can only go so far and soon risks foundering on the reefs of excessive generality (over-extending the stereotype) or excessive particularity (alienating part of the audience). Therefore, in a society marked with the fine, elaborate lines of class distinction, mass communications have to move towards a world not too specifically recognizable by any one group or class but acceptable by all. They have to invent a world most of us, in the time we are consumers, are happy to inhabit. This is the origin of the advertiser's world, a world with a fixed grin which most of us at times could imagine inhabiting, but which is artificial, 'dreamed-up'. Such is the sophistication of mass communications (they are rarely naïve) that there are also built into this world allowances for idiosyncrasy, for the odd 'highbrow', and even for the 'bloody-minded' individual. But all have in the process been effectively neutered. Mass communications naturally tend towards a nice, harmless but bodiless range of attitudes. For more and more of the time more and more of us become consumers of more and more things—from material goods to human relations.

Here we come to the overriding danger of mass communications, unless they are constantly checked against individual judgment. We are not primarily concerned with whether 'highbrow' books will be read in a society dominated by mass communications; we have to ask what will be the quality of the life expressed through all the arts and at all levels in such a society. It may be that literature will have relatively a much smaller place in the society now emerging than most people who read this essay have assumed and hoped.

The intricate social pattern which produced, among much else, 'high culture' as it is normally recognized is being changed. At the same time great numbers of people are in some respects freer than before. In a changed society the best qualities which inform 'high culture' may have to find other ways of expressing themselves; so will the best qualities in the old local and oral life of people who were not in a position to make much contribution to 'high culture'. At the moment the one seems likely to be bypassed and the other eroded by the impact of massively generalized communications. There is a considerable fund of common imaginative strength in all parts of society. If a thinner consumers' culture is not to spread over all more care will have to be taken in seeking relevant connections, links between things which show this strength (some features of day-to-day life, some work in the arts today, some social organizations, some forms of recreation). It is not possible to define in advance the nature of a good demotic culture. Unless one believes such a culture is not possible, one has to try to keep open all lines which may allow for promising development as well as oppose those likely to lead to a dead smartness. At present most people with literary interests are less effective at keeping lines open than they are at opposition.   1961

THE USES OF TELEVISION

B Y now one feels hesitant about running through the
potential advantages of television, just because they have
been so often and uncritically rehearsed. Yet it does seem to
be true that television can stimulate, does offer 'windows on
the world' and may 'widen our outlook'; and that its intimacy
exposes the usual tricks of crowd-rhetoric. But all this needs
looking at more closely.

It is said that television is an acid-test of sincerity, that it
will increase truth and reasonableness in political discussion,
that the day of the demagogue is over. Certainly it is not
difficult to believe that the McCarthy hearings on television
in the United States helped to accelerate the Senator's down-
fall. But the 'sincerity-test' has become the most common
cliché in writing about television, and we should now make
a self-denying ordinance against using it. I suspect it is true
only at the extremes—with such a man as McCarthy; or with
men of exceptional integrity. Between these extremes, television does not always distinguish between sincerity and
assumed sincerity; it is a blunt and rather bludgeoningly intimate instrument. This stress on not only the importance but
the final value of sincerity (typical of much popular criticism
in all the arts) is not good enough. A man does not need to
be a humbug to be a dangerous fool. Of itself even the 25-
inch screen gives no help in deciding which sincerity is
informed by thought and which is a deluded enthusiasm.

Of its more direct educational possibilities television has
so far hardly scratched the surface. Many people are now
trying to develop these possibilities. Yet I think the gains
they make will be less than most of them assume. I mean
gains from public educational television, not from closed
circuit programmes for precise audiences. In normal circum-

stances there is never going to be enough time on television, and the sense of a huge mixed audience is likely to be too inhibiting to do more than provide a few straight educational programmes and a lot more generally educative programmes. The limits come soon. Television can break down the complicated into a succession of vivid, visual, manageable segments. In presenting the complex it can stimulate by its vividness and immediacy but can rarely go much further. No matter how many people saw a series at any one time, in direct educational terms what was presented was a succession of single half or three-quarter hours to a number of individuals, with no opportunity for discussion, going back on one's tracks, changes of speed, questions or any of the give-and-take of a live seminar. The challenges made to all those individuals were of a limited kind. Group listening with discussion afterwards can sometimes link the two. But the mixture of modes is tricky.

In short, the main advantage of television is that it can, instantaneously and sharply, offer huge numbers of people a sense of the excitement and variety and, possibly, the depths of knowledge. Its limitation, in normal conditions, is that it is a creature of daily or weekly fresh starts. It is like a show which, though it may claim it never closed, yet went on making much the same sort of presentation (in both the usual senses) to new audiences. It can rarely assume continuity; it is almost always making introductions. Television may be —may become—a magnificent gateway. But those who work with it have to spend most of their time oiling the hinges, finding new ways of tempting people to come up to the gate; they are rarely able to plough a pasture within or see a season through on the far side.

Television—and most forms of mass communication—raises old questions in new and difficult forms. There is, for instance, the matter of imaginative commitment. Think of the great number of documentaries on both television channels; on the 'colour problem', nuclear warfare, 'the problem of youth', and so on. They are informed with intelligent good intentions. Yet they are almost always off-key, irrelevant to the lived pressure and depth and grotesqueness of 'problems'. Most of them give as nearly as they can a 'balanced', an 'objective' picture, one which represents a 'fair cross-section' of the 'typical people' involved in the 'problem'. I wonder what effect they have at the level at which we say 'bloody niggers' or 'those damn teenagers ought to be horsewhipped'.

Part of the trouble here is, once again, that the audience is undifferentiated. The truth of the imagination is a committed truth, though not necessarily in a narrowly political sense. If it is broken down into statements those statements look biased because the element has been changed. So, mass communications tend to seek an 'objectivity' which can be pretty well statistically demonstrated, and, if necessary, defended against those literal-minded pressure-groups which haunt all public organs of opinion. It may be, too, that there is a general tendency among individuals—which may well be more widespread today than it used to be—to hold to what is semi-scientifically demonstrable in preference to that which is called 'mere impressionism' or even 'mere interpretation'. Further, writers in Britain are so used to working within known limits, not only of *genre* but of unconsciously-assumed audience, that they feel outfaced by the imponderables within a new medium of communication. What can we assume with an audience that has not selected itself as have those who are regular readers of the weekly journals? What language can we use? How far and in what ways can certain attitudes be explored?

We may get puzzling answers to all these questions, but the point is that they have hardly been asked in Britain. Some people are thinking about the more tractable educational possibilities of television; few have thought much about its imaginative possibilities. So far, we rely mainly on straight translations from other forms of art. I know of no one in Britain (or for that matter in the United States) who has written on the potentialities of a distinctively television drama with the insight and closeness of Mr. Paddy Chayevsky.* He argues that television drama is introspective, Chekhovian; that its strength as a dramatic medium will be in exploring problems of character and personal relationships. He seemed at one time to believe, until the pressure of commerce made him leave television writing, that by this approach he could find a large audience for good drama. It would not be as large as the audiences for the more successful quiz shows. But it would be bigger than any audience that could be contained within the usual highbrow or middlebrow boundaries.

In Britain we are disinclined to spend energy on productions so quickly presented and ended; and we lack the right sort of encouragement from those in charge of the television organizations. The programme companies in ITV spend some money in sponsoring competitions for television playwriting, and argue that this is a considerable fillip to the 'creative cultural life of this dynamic new medium'. But these competitions, as they are at present arranged, are chiefly a means of producing a stock of plays to feed the maws of the drama departments, plays which are usually essays in craft, in working within given and unquestioned concepts; they do not encourage experiments.

Whatever the developments in the imaginative use of television, one of its basic powers is in discursive communication. But it is difficult to develop this power so as to reflect adequately the variety in British life. The fabric of class and culture is so densely interwoven that it is difficult to speak clearly outside one's known groups. By all kinds of characteristics—of which accent is only the first we think of—communication is likely to be blurred: we suggest what we do not mean and create an impression different from that we intend.

Television is often hindered by the association of certain styles in speech with class and status ratings. This is true of many other forms of expression—furnishing, physical movements, emotional reactions; and no doubt there are parallels

* See the foreword to *Television Plays* (1955). Simon & Schuster.

in other societies. But the British situation is peculiarly involved. A few years ago Mr. Joseph Trenaman published some researches into the reception of programmes with an 'educational content' on sound radio. His most striking finding was not that some people are put off because the vocabulary is 'above their heads' or because the background assumed is greater than they possess (both the BBC and ITV have these limitations in mind), but that they resist right from the start the tone and atmosphere of the programmes. It may be too, though I don't think Mr. Trenaman made this speculation, that some people are drawn by this tone, because they identify it with a 'cultured' condition. From BBC programmes in particular, one often feels that too simple an equation is being made: that the tones, styles, attitudes, patterns for emotional expression of 'the cultured middle class' are the norm to which all aspirants for 'culture' should aspire; and that the more these can be transmitted the more will sweetness and light appear in British society.

Of such programmes the outstanding example is *The Brains Trust*. One can enjoy it sometimes, if rather quizzically. But there would not be much gain if most of Britain confronted problems in just this manner; indeed there would be some loss. I don't think I undervalue the qualities which these attitudes can embody: tolerance, reasonableness, disinterestedness. But many of these qualities and others as admirable can be found, unregarded because expressed rather differently, in other social groups. Conversely, we often assume that the display of certain acceptable outward forms is a guarantee of the existence of these inner qualities. It is not surprising that some of Mr. Trenaman's witnesses assumed in advance that such programmes were not for them; they were, rather, for 'Them'. Today 'Them' often means not only the traditional middle and upper classes but the 'grammar school types', those who have been accepted for further education by society.

If we believe 'ability' is more widespread and complex a quality than can be winnowed out by selecting one in five at eleven-plus, if we believe that many more people than the commercial mass-media are driven to assume can think responsibly and feel deeply, then we have to experiment more with the expressive powers of the new media.

I have already suggested that television can be an important primary educator. In a wider sense it will be an important general educator, an educator in manners, a way of transmitting—by implication and suggestion—attitudes different from those many in its audience have previously held. In any society a medium so intimate and pervasive will do this; it is bound constantly to be putting before people other ways of shaking hands, of sitting down, of wearing clothes, of reacting to strangers, of eating, of carrying on conversations; it is bound constantly to be setting in motion numerous slight but widespread reactions.

As British society changes a decline seems likely in the importance of local, face-to-face communities as educators in manners. These communities, whether of a neighbourhood or a work-bench, will obviously remain important: talk at work or round a lamp-post or at the edge of a dance-hall or in a coffee-bar, and the acceptance of the habits of these groups, will all have their primary educative effect. Teenagers in particular pay comparatively little attention to television. But for most of us it will have a relatively more important place as a moderator of manners.

Spend a week regularly watching television on either or both channels and you almost feel the cakes of custom being cracked open. As some of the older ways of transmitting habits, by 'rubbing-off' in comparatively static groups, become less powerful, as more choices become available, so the media of mass communication become more important as guides to choice, that is, as guides to attitudes, since attitudes inform choices.

Dixon of Dock Green is probably a more powerful force in general education than a whole range of evening institute classes in non-vocational subjects. This slightly transmogrified documentary is written by a man with a good ear for the surface of current speech and manners, and an unusual responsiveness to the more evident contemporary tensions. Each instalment is really a dramatized secular parable played by characters who have a kind of life. And all the time, consciously or unconsciously, it is trying to ameliorate manners. I don't mean through the direct injunctions of P.C. Dixon himself (watch your step when you cross the road) but in its whole dramatic presentation of the police. One police force has been recommended to revert to helmets in place of caps, since helmets—it is felt—are now associated with the fine qualities of P.C. Dixon.

Traditional working-class attitudes to the 'cops' were a compound of suspicion, scorn, laughter, and respect. Compare that with the clean, simplified, kindly figure of the 'cop' presented in *Dixon*. Where is the world in which the police beat you up at the station if you've made it difficult for them to get you there? in which you suspect they always stick together and will lie to the magistrates to do so? in which you believe they are lenient with the local nobs? I am not saying these qualities exist all the time and are unrelieved. But one knew and knows that they do exist, within a whole texture of attitudes to the police, a texture that has been formed in the stresses of experience, a texture that is not simply mean and suspicious but is subtle and qualified.

We do not really know how far *Dixon*—and the other programmes for which it stands—affect attitudes over time. Presumably the effect of such half-art is slow, but it may eventually (in combination with the other forces of which it is both part and a reflection) be considerable.

Another part of the process may be seen in the 'commercials' on ITV, which are forms of impure art. It is an irony that the more disinterested workers in television tend to be chary of the murky waters of 'art' and feel safer with a more 'objective' approach; whereas those who are less disinterested forcefully misapply some of the methods of art. If you produced a modern *Merchant of Venice* (Shakespeare's is a 'classic' and so in a special box) you might be accused of anti-

Semitism by several watchful organizations; if you wrote a modern *Othello* you might be accused of exacerbating the colour problem. But you may make an emotional bloodbath so as to sell soap and no one will do more than smile or be mildly irritated.

Admittedly, hardly any of us make most of our choices objectively and dispassionately. Even the professional people who support the Consumers' Association make many of their choices, especially in artistic matters, on prestige grounds. We may tolerate no nonsense about detergents but we'll tolerate a lot in our choice of pictures and books. But for the majority of us the choice of quite ordinary consumer goods has rarely been a matter of weighing up the pros and cons of various products. Small material snobberies apart, we have often sought to buy with these goods gaiety and colour. The success of Lux toilet soap many years ago with working-class women was more sad than comic. It would be inhuman not to appreciate the force of this attitude in a world where material rewards were so limited and the outlook so drab.

The television 'commercials' are the successors to the old coloured mail-order catalogues, but more sophisticated. They do not only exploit old habits; they seek to extend them. In an expanding commercial society they sell people not only the dreams they already seek, but new dreams for new needs or possible needs. In the present situation the single most powerful attempt to alter attitudes—to educate manners—in Britain is made through the imitation art and artificial emotionalism of the advertisements on ITV. It is a pity television isn't allowed to keep its two lines clearer: to find its own forms of free art and to extend rational dialogue. What sort of a world do they portray? It is not a violently crude world; in all sorts of obvious ways it is a very decent world. It is a bright world and a congenitally innocent world, a world prior to the knowledge of good and evil, in which all the young girls have that wonderful Jamesian exclamation-mark between their eyebrows (see the Mirandas of the cocoa-commercials) and even the middle-aged fathers look no more than nicely weathered by sinless winds. But it is a bodiless world.

What goes on in the office where the financial profit-and-loss account is drawn up? It would be interesting to know, but not of crucial importance. It is more important to recognize the childishness and euphoria of this world. There is something remarkably blind in our almost single-minded concern with questions in Parliament, independent committees or dependent committees (willingly set up by ITV) to consider the time allowed to this advertisement or the accuracy of that claim, whilst we almost wholly ignore the harder question— what are the attitudes which are all the time being offered underneath?

These characteristics do not appear simply because some people have commercial reasons for wanting a very large and very quiet audience. As I have said already, one of the strongest pressures on the mass-media—simply because they are mass-media and whether they are public-service or commercial —is their constant awareness of a huge audience of a special kind.

A 'pure artist' may not be unaware of an audience; but there is a sense in which we can say he seems unaware of it. He may write for a tribunal of a few friends or the glorious dead or his own conscience. At his best he respects it and is sensitive to it because its standards are those he respects. Between him and it is the standard itself. He is not aware of a vast, unknown, unassessed, varying audience which has to be *won*. This situation is not wholly limiting, but it can be inhibiting. How will a miner in South Wales or a woman in a North Yorkshire farmhouse or a solicitor in London take this? Will some be dangerously shocked? Dare I assume this? How far will most people go along with me if I risk this? As a result even public-service television tends to take the world much as it finds it, or is very careful in deciding how far it can push out along a path not so far well used.

It can rarely be, in a sustained way, searching. Programmes

such as *Tonight* and *Panorama* show that its procedures can sometimes move a little ahead of conventional expectations; yet if we compare the grip of these programmes with what we know of really rigorous and disciplined enquiry we see how wide the gap is. A programme such as *Monitor* is a 'minority' programme. But it naturally wants to spread further and in any event its 'minority' is immensely larger than the minorities the little magazines talk about. It has to provide a service already acceptable to most of its viewing 'minority', and stimulation or 'stretch' of a kind which doesn't lose as many as it gains. These are among the basic facts of life even for public-service television.

How far television will be able to extend from this base depends on a number of factors. I have already mentioned, in connection with Mr. Chayevsky's work, possible imaginative developments. When it is being discursive, perhaps a disinterested mass-medium will best aim to be a little ahead of the line at which ideas have hardened into clichés or prejudices, and as often as possible will try to speak to groups held together by more than the simple possession of television sets. It is evident that the BBC is better placed to work in this way than ITV. It is in the interests of the advertisers not to break the audience into minority groups; they have to want mass audiences, mass audiences of masses. For American television, Mr. Chayevsky was asked to write no act longer than eight minutes, so that the 'commercials' could be given their place; and there was the pressure to present only themes which reinforced cheerful and undemandingly homely attitudes.

Admittedly, commercial television does not look as nakedly aggressive as this description suggests; and I am sure that many of its staffs are 'sincere' and well-meaning. This is a leathery society, deeply scored with the wrinkles of caution, patience, phlegm and good intentions; and our commercial mass-media reflect some of these qualities and are held in by the structural checks and balances born of them. Yet when we have read the Independent Television Act, and noted the announcements for prestige programmes, and observed the weighty members of their advisory committees, when we have made allowance for all this we have only to watch the programmes in the peak hours on ITV for a few evenings to appreciate which way such a channel inherently wants to push.

If the restraints were slighter the process would be quicker. This has already happened in some Sunday newspapers (who have no similar Act to limit their tendencies). No doubt the press will continue to become smarter, but it has lost most of its contact with significant social debate. It has been caught at a crucial time by a combination of technical advances and financial pressures and so, substantially, defused. Luckily, the best of broadcasting is filling some of its previous functions. For the rest, differentiated publications may have to be born from the grass-roots.

By extrapolation from these tendencies we can easily envision a society rigidly stratified and yet with many common attitudes. I do not mean a society which imposed only a few forms of cultural expression—in which, say, almost everyone watched the same quiz show at the same time. The audiences for such shows would certainly be immense and would cut across class boundaries. But a highly-developed consumers' society can make use of a fairly wide range of status-differentiations within artistic activities. It has room for arts supplements in the posh Sunday papers as well as for chauvinistic tabloids, for the latest experimental writer as well as for teen-age idols. Such a society would not be ostensibly hostile to 'culture'. Nor would it deny the value of radical enquiry; it would be addicted to those discussions or 'panel' programmes which parade a muted radicalism. But the disconcerting force and personal humility of genuine inquiry would surely have been lost.

1960

TELEVISION AS THE ARCHETYPE OF MASS COMMUNICATIONS

Basic Considerations

I T is notoriously difficult to define mass communications precisely, but television, of all the media, has the highest number of those characteristics which feature in any reasonable definition. It has by far the largest audiences of all forms of communication; it sometimes reaches virtually the entire population of a nation—as, in the United Kingdom, during telecasts of great national interest, such as a royal message, a state funeral, or a football final. Radio, too, can have most of a nation for its audience, but cannot cross language barriers. Television, being visual, does just that. Through the use of satellites it is now multiplying its audiences several times over. The same programme that is seen in the United States can also reach huge audiences across the countries of Europe up to the iron curtain or sometimes beyond. Furthermore, television reaches these audiences at virtually the same time; these enormous viewing figures are not made up of successive audiences, as are those of the cinema.

Television's audiences are more amorphous and less self-selected than those of the other media of communication. Most members of the audiences are general consumers of television, people who sit down ready to be entertained for the greater part of an evening, without necessarily having chosen a specific programme at a particular time out of a feeling that it has a special appeal to them as individuals. They do not divide themselves, nor are they often divided by the providers of television, according to sex, class, region or belief. By comparison, the readership of the national press in Great Britain is still roughly assignable to social class, though this is weakening under the impact of the newer 'classless' media.

Television reaches right into the living-rooms of its amorphous audience. It seeks to hold them and retain that hold, rather than being content to be reached for as the mood arises. This becomes less true if there is more than one channel and if the programmes on those channels are arranged so as to contrast with each other and encourage selective viewing. However, when the funds for television come from advertising, the point holds even where there are several channels: they all narrow their programming towards those items which seem likely to keep the average consumer-viewer from switching off or over.

Television is an archetypal form of mass communication also because it is an industry—an industry whose products are recreation, news-reporting and education. Further, the men who produce the programmes—authors, scriptwriters, visual artists, directors, producers, actors, programme controllers—are physically and to some extent culturally separated from their audiences. Mass-communication industries, comprising large bodies of highly endowed professional people with more than average articulateness, inevitably become ingrown towards their own trade. The professionals progressively worship the machine that draws out their talents and are bored at the thought of looking outside their mystery and thinking about its relations to society and individuals. Their link with audiences is indirect; they put their programmes into the camera, and the engineers beam them into millions of separate homes; there is no face-to-face relationship. The programmes themselves may be, for the men in the board rooms, consumer products in time-slots; but the producers have a sort of pure love, professional and aesthetic, for them. Within television there has accrued the folklore and legend common to all highly demanding mysteries.

Like all major mass communications, television has a continuous production belt. It is a recreational, cultural, informational and educational 'sausage machine', which must be fed day after day so as to produce at roughly the same times roughly the same amounts and proportions of material. Inevitably (unless the process is deliberately resisted) it turns out the same kind of material, of the same density and texture although it appears with different packaging—material that is predigested, homogenized, sterilized, artificially coloured and seasoned each and every day. The pressures towards this kind of uniformity arise from the need to deliver immediately-interesting-looking goods day after day, to meet the schedules and keep up the ratings. The servants of the machine may and do change, as the shifts rotate daily and weekly, and as personnel come and go over the years. But the product has a range of established and recurrent characteristics built into it, partly through the organizational structure of the factory, partly through the inherent qualities of the medium itself, partly through an assumed pressure from the audience to provide what has come to be expected. There is, of course, more variation than I have suggested; but there is less than one might have expected in advance.

Questions about television's possibilities for growth as well as its limits are, then, questions about all mass communications. But they are not only questions about the medium in itself. Any discussion about television (about any mass medium) inevitably leads to a discussion of the society television reflects, which uses it in this way rather than that, and so is affected by it in certain ways but not in others.

Although television is important and pervasive in its effects on attitudes and behaviour, it is probably not as important as is commonly thought. There are not at present a great many reliable studies on the effects of television, nor are their results definitive. To sum up briefly what I have said at greater length elsewhere: * television probably cannot change taste radically or upset deep-seated assumptions, but where it follows the grain of personal or social predispositions, it can reinforce them. Recurrent violence on television seems likely to encourage acts of violence only in the psychotic or mentally disturbed. These effects can be increased when a given theme recurs often, is dramatically presented and pro-

* See 'The Argument About Effects', p. 215.

vides the viewer with the opportunity to identify himself with a character on the screen.

Even these limited findings have some implications for programme planning. To what extent can one risk further unbalancing the unbalanced? To what extent should a programme planner settle for meeting the existing expectations of the largest majority? However, these are small questions in comparison with those about which we are still almost wholly in the dark. It may have been proved that television is likely to cause the acting out of violence only in those who are already disturbed: but is it also true that exposure to repeated violence—as a thing simply to be enjoyed—has no effect, at the deepest levels of the psyche, on the millions of us who are classed as 'normal' viewers?

So what should television offer its audiences? There can be no simple answer. In practice, answers differ from country to country according to prevailing ideologies; these ideologies determine the administrative and financial structures of the various television systems and so determine their patterns of programming.

What functions in relation to their audiences might be said to be more or less fundamental to any television system in a democracy? First, it should provide substantial services for the known needs of the majority of the population. The broadcasters have to amuse most of us in the periods when we most seek amusement, and have to keep us (though it can only be sketchily) abreast of what has been happening in the world. Thus they have to provide entertainment ranging from the equivalent of a variety show to that of a concert hall, as well as a range of informational services varying from the equivalent of a morning newspaper to that of a weekly journal of opinion. All this must be done in the light of the fact that television is very expensive and that the number of channels available (so far as we can see at present) is not likely to be sufficient to allow fine breakdowns by audience taste.

These considerations might seem to justify the pattern of programming dominant in those countries where the audience sought virtually all the time is the largest possible majority of the total population. It is not sensible to oppose this view with the notion of television as the servant of small minorities; but even with only one channel a television system can serve a range of overlapping sizeable minorities much of the time. The word 'overlapping' is important. Large minorities are not discrete sections of the total population. The same people can belong to different large minorities at different times, depending on how they are feeling. Of course, programming can be so arranged as to hit the centre of average taste most of the time and so discourage any form of selectivity in viewing. If the broadcasters are successful in obtaining this kind of consistent attention, then they are tempted to decide that their audiences are as uniform in tastes as their own programmes. The history of some unexpectedly successful programmes, which were not designed for a 'mass audience' but nevertheless got surprisingly large minority audiences, challenges that thinking.

The taste of today's audiences is potentially more varied than programme planners are led to think or often lead themselves to think. The existing tastes of most of us are a product not simply of irremovable hereditary factors; they are to a large extent a product of our opportunities, education, social class, available money, and where we happen to be born. It seems reasonable to ask whether broadcasters should simply reflect those average ranges of interests which a great number of other environmental forces have together produced at any particular time. If they decide to do this, they should realize that their role only appears to be passive. They will, in fact, be harnessed to the service of, and made to pull in the same direction as, many other forces whose natural aim—in commercial democracies—is to exploit the existing range of tastes and interests. In that apparently passive role, television will therefore not be passive at all; it will reinforce the existing limits in range of taste. Should the broadcasters not be free to cater to the potential as well as the actual tastes of their audiences? Thus they might decide to offer programmes which some people, though not as yet a large majority or even a sizeable minority, already find imaginatively exciting, in the hope that others, who might not have had a chance to know of such possible interests, may become interested too.

This part of the argument is confused by the clash of slogans. Shall broadcasters 'give the people what the people want', or shall they 'give the people what they ought to have'? The Pilkington Committee on Broadcasting, in its Report published in 1962, pointed to an area of possibility between the two: "The broadcasting authorities certainly have a duty to keep sensitively aware of the public's tastes and attitudes as they now are and in all their variety and a duty to care about them. If they do more than that, this is not to give the public 'what someone thinks is good for it', but it is rather to respect the public's right to choose from the widest possible range of subject matter and so to enlarge worthwhile experience."*

Any decision to put on programmes other than those apparently justified by simple 'feedback' from the market or by obvious consonance with existing taste can be called paternal, patronizing, or propagandist. Indeed, all such decisions are risky. Programme planners are mortal men with circumscribed views and assumptions that are not always examined. Their interpretation of the need to offer their audiences the chance to widen their tastes may, for example, amount to no more than the desire to make as many people as possible into 'middle-brows'; planners may have simple views of the relations between social class and cultivation.

So it is difficult to define a 'good' programme. 'Counting heads' is not a sufficient test of a programme's success, but is not altogether irrelevant. When a programme attracts an unexpectedly small audience, this may indicate that, though the producer did all he could to make it interesting without compromising the integrity of his subject, only a tiny minority of people are at present willing to be interested; on the other

* Report of the Committee on Broadcasting 1960 (London: H.M.S.O., 1962), para. 49.

hand, it may indicate that not enough thought—not enough of the right kind of thought—went into the effort to communicate widely. Again, technical competence is important and technical brilliance admirable. But, in the face of the difficulty of defining 'good television' without seeming either patronizing or a victim of the market, many television producers hold on to technical virtuosity or 'professionalism' as an end in itself. There are certain programmes where the possibilities of the medium are being extended through an exploration of its inherent characteristics. But it is a good working rule that, in general, technical skill should be the servant of the subject or theme which is being presented.

In presenting that material, the broadcasters are required to aim at 'objectivity' and 'balance'. This is often said, sounds fairly straightforward but is very difficult. The two words are not synonymous. 'Objectivity' means the decision not to push a particular editorial line, but rather to present the odd contours of truth as accurately as possible. 'Balance' means ensuring that all sides have a fair and reasonable chance to be heard. Both 'objectivity' and 'balance' have to be positively interpreted, or they become polite synonyms for sitting on the fence and balancing each side against the others so nervously that all sides lose their force. The problem is to avoid propaganda or partiality, to suggest the complexity of truth, and to retain a sense of the importance of making choices.

'Objectivity' and 'balance' are useful. 'Catholicity'—remembering that tastes do differ—is a good check to narrowmindedness. But still all the difficult questions about standards remain virtually unanswered.

Television is not a home industry or a folk industry. Even its conventional art has to be carefully planned; it doesn't just happen because someone just happens to feel that way. Television is a many-layered industry with stage after stage interposed between an original idea and what eventually appears on the screen. Production is a several-stage process, and thus is even more complicated than producing a finished performance of a dramatist's script in the live theatre. Moreover, this medium often uses several writers at the same time on the same script or teams of writers working concurrently on a number of scripts or a series; in other instances a story line and thematic pattern is established and different men take over the work of script-writing at different times; and the relationship between a writer and his producer is all the time dialectical. All these differences between television and live theatre need not restrict a dramatist used to the ways of the theatre; he may gain from them so long as he recognizes their possibilities as well as their rules.

The medium has qualities which restrict those who use it, or at least closely define their areas of movement; but so do all art forms and channels for artistic expression. As in other fields, the tension between the given limitations of the medium and its peculiar possibilities challenges the imagination and suggests different ways of exploring experience. The restrictions of budget for particular programmes, as well as problems of available space and personnel, are similar in kind to those technical and commercial pressures which were felt, say, in the development of the novel during the nineteenth century. The relevant considerations here can range from the simple and obvious to the most psychologically obscure: from merely circumventing a shortage of cameras to discovering new possibilities within the medium through a creative response to the challenge of that shortage. The parallels with, for example, the writings of sonnets are obvious.

About the qualities of the medium itself not a great deal that is authoritative has been written, but there are some useful hints and guesses. Television has a peculiar 'immediacy' and 'fluidity'; it strongly suggests that 'it's all happening', gives a sense of 'thereness', 'thisness', and 'nowness', and it tends to break down existing categories. It resists stage acting and even cinema acting, breaks through the picture frame or mental proscenium arch, and merges the spectator with the picture, on its sidelines if not at the centre. On television everything tends to become an instant report from the front-line. Television tends to seek 'personalities' of its own. Of course, television personalities help to build up 'channel loyalty' and link disparate items, and so programme planners like them. But the power of personalities is more than this: they are part of the engrossing, internalizing nature of television.

Television has an exceptional sense of immediate history. When a great public occasion or terrible event—a state funeral such as Sir Winston Churchill's or the murder of Oswald—is seen on television, the sense of immediate historical presence is overwhelming. Or television can make a funeral in a back garden seem heavy with the meaning of life. It heightens even the most 'ordinary' ordinariness of life and seems to give it dramatic significance. Because of its sense of actuality, of its Brechtian breaking of distance, we are all sidewalk spectators of the drama of life when we watch television. Sometimes one really believes in the reality of an event only because it has been validated through being seen on television. It is too early to determine how far television may be encouraging a more fluid psychic responsiveness, or how far it may be the agent of a disconnected, discontinuous flow of value-free sensations. About both the medium itself and its deepest relationships with its audiences we still know too little to be dogmatic.

There are three main kinds of formal structure for television, as for all broadcasting: the state-controlled, the commercially impelled, and the in-between, or—as I would prefer to call it—the potentially democratic.

In the first, the communications system is an arm of government and so, at bottom, propagandist, no matter what its apparent face. It can be found in one form or another in communist, fascist and other types of authoritarian countries, especially those in which the Roman Catholic church is strong. It stresses the party line and the national philosophy and keeps a tight hold on the channels for debate. Under this system the greatest sufferers are information and education, since both are consistently distorted. Television is regarded chiefly as a channel through which things are done to people rather than as a medium with its own characteristics and possibilities. State-controlled television tends not to be experimental either about what the medium can best do or about what audiences might enjoy if they had the chance.

In the second system—the commercially impelled—television is tied to commerce, usually because it makes its money by selling advertising time. Such systems can vary from those in which advertising is regarded (or said to be regarded) chiefly as a convenient means for financing the programmes to systems in which (public professions notwithstanding) the main feature is advertising. In the former type of system, the programmes are still professedly the most important thing, whereas in the latter type they are regarded as carriers or bait for the commercials; but in the end the pressures on all such systems are much the same. The pull of commercial values will tell on any system which allows advertisements but obviously is likely to be more extreme under direct sponsorship.

The drive is to maximize profit by increasing the number of impacts delivered or persons reached; the audience is seen as a vast number of possible consumers whom it would be advantageous to hold as one group. The basic urge of this kind of television is, therefore, to hold the largest possible number of people for the largest possible amount of time. Its natural drive is the reverse of that of state-controlled systems; it stresses entertainment rather than information and education. It tends to narrow the range of programmes offered, so as to concentrate on types of programmes considered likely to attract a mass audience. Thus it tends to ignore minorities, because minorities are subdivisions of the potential single mass audience. The commercially-impelled system also reduces the urge to experiment, whether in regard to the potential tastes of audiences or to the more freely imaginative possibilities of the medium itself; it inherently seems to exploit existing tastes.

I called the third system the 'potentially democratic' because I doubt that a fully-fledged democratic broadcasting system exists anywhere in the world. At its best, the BBC gets near to it. In such a system the state does not have day-to-day supervision or any executive control (though in the public interest there must be some overriding guardianship); nor is the advertiser able to distort the uses of the medium, since there is no advertising.

The two chief difficulties in such a system are paying for it and providing the necessary minimum of supervision without inhibiting the broadcasters. Advertising—with the advertisement-revenue-receiving body formally and genuinely separated from the programme-providing body—might just be possible at one end of the financial spectrum; the danger here is the steady spread of the pressures of advertising into the planning of programmes. Mass-media advertising is like a seamless garment, and to think you can seal off a part of it is to daydream. At the other end of the financial spectrum is a system of direct payment from public funds to the broadcasting authority, who would be entrusted to use it in the public interest, with 'public interest' not too restrictively defined. This has various possible forms, too, and some are less tricky than others. The danger here is that the state will exercise an increasing, creeping pressure, since it is the direct provider of funds.

In between these two ends of the financial spectrum there are, again, several different ways of paying for broadcasting. On the whole, the most successful is the licence fee, because it gives most scope for the broadcasters to serve the public interest in the wide and responsive sense described earlier. Although there are arguments against this approach—for example, that it is a form of 'poll tax', or that it is too expensive because the money has to be collected in millions of small packets—the arguments in its favour seem overwhelming. The licence fee falls on all, and almost all use broadcasting; furthermore, it multiplies and subdivides the sources of money so that no one large agency is tempted, because it is footing the bill, to try to exercise consistent strong pressure, or feels cheated if things do not go in just the way it wants. However, once practically every family has a television set, the ceiling on new licences has been reached, and from that time on, the amount of the licence, if it is to serve its purpose, may have to be tied to increases in wages and incomes.

The supervision of a 'democratic' (non-state and non-commercial) broadcasting system is even trickier than the problem of paying for it. There must be a buffer between the broadcasting professionals and whatever party happens to be in power at any time—a buffer which allows the broadcasters to exercise proper editorial independence but which also stops them from too narrowly, too remotely, or less than responsibly defining the public interest. Countries trying to operate this system vary in the buffer they use, but the BBC's Board of Governors, for both its strengths and weaknesses, is one instance worth more study than it has received.

Below the government level, it is important that broadcasters are kept responsive to public need. But 'public need' is not easy to define and some quite large bodies which claim to speak for 'ordinary opinion' are philistine and restrictive. There seems to be a need for a range of responsive and well-informed bodies which would form links between the producers and their audiences; not pressure groups in a political or economic sense, but interest groups, specialist groups, professional groups—all helping to form a web of relevant understanding, of challenge and response between the two sides of the operation.

In all this, the overriding need is to find a structure that will let professionalism in broadcasting (in the sense defined earlier) grow and be, as far as ever possible, responsible for itself. The fully democratic broadcasting system which might emerge if the twin pressures of the State and the advertisers were thus avoided is difficult to define precisely (and even more difficult to put into practice). But a rough workable definition is certainly possible. Such a system would not make an automatic correlation between 'cultivation' and social class;

it would not think of itself as offering some fixed socio-cultural images downwards to the masses. Nor would it reject the standards of civilization in its pursuit of popular support. Nor would it peddle 'culture' as a form of marginal differentiation in the 'affluent society'. It would be a varied and pluralist organization with a strong but dispersed life. It would be highly professional in that it would be technically efficient and would have devoted a great deal of thought to the possibilities of the medium and to its own varied and changing relationships with its audiences; and it would regard its audiences, too, as varied and changing. It would be editorially objective but not given to fence sitting. It would combine a high degree of freedom with a clear sense of responsibility.

1966

THE BBC AND SOCIETY

OF the three main kinds of broadcasting system*—state-controlled, commercially impelled and democratic—the first two are easy to set up and the world is full of them. The last is less often achieved.

Each system has a distinctive relationship with its society. The first is a branch of government and 'gives the public what the public ought to have': that is, what the state thinks is good for it. In the distribution of bread and circuses, it lays special stress on handing out bread: state bread—the party line, selective news, direct exhortation.

The second kind makes broadcasting into an extension of advertising. It claims to 'give the public what the public wants'. In the distribution of bread and circuses it is inherently disposed to reduce the ration of bread but increase the circuses: large-audience circuses are good for sales. It tends to narrow range, ignore minorities, and reduce experiment, since all these divide the mass audience.

The third kind of broadcasting is by its nature harder to operate and is not really loved by the establishments and big battalions, political or commercial, since it can be awkwardly independent of them. The essence of democratic broadcasting is the effort objectively to serve as wide a range as possible of diverse interests. I do not know of one wholly successful example of democratic broadcasting in this sense; but I would argue that the BBC has a reasonable chance of growing into such a system if it is given the right opportunities and has the wisdom to take them.

Democratic systems have trouble, to begin with, in finding their money. A state will pay readily for a system which is wholly obedient, being an extension of itself into the field of public persuasion. The advertisers will pay handsomely for

---

* For a fuller description of these three systems, see 'Television as the Archetype of Mass Communications: basic considerations', p. 163.

a very large number of exposed viewers. The third system has to fight for its cash, and often fight against distortion and misrepresentation. From the noise made in some quarters about the 1965 increase in licence fees you would never guess that the BBC provides three sound and two television channels* continuously for the larger part of every day, for half the annual cost to a family of its daily morning and evening newspaper, or for less than the cost of a single weekly packet of ten cheap filter cigarettes shared between the whole family.

More difficult: democratic broadcasting has no plain and built-in impetus. It cannot ask simply 'what best serves the state?' or 'what delivers the largest numbers to the TAM meters?' It has to ask 'how can broadcasting best serve the community in all its variety and capability?' The answers are complex and riddled with difficult evaluations.

At their most schematic, these are the three main direction-givers in broadcasting. In practice, naturally, things are not so clear-cut. No sizeable group of well-endowed individuals will let the logic of an administrative machine be a remorseless logic. Men break out, experiments *are* made under systems one and two; broadcasters in the third system often settle for something easier. In other words: ITV does have some good programmes, Granada does experiment and the BBC does sometimes go after big audiences for the wrong reasons, or becomes portentously official. But any discussion of broadcasting, if it is to break out of short-sighted anecdotage, must start by recognizing that these are the main structural types, these the dominant tendencies and these the fundamental relationships to society.

In fact, discussion about broadcasting in Britain today starts in confusion. In the national folklore, the BBC is a scapegoat, a celibate priest (nowadays often attacked as a fallen priest), a father-figure, and everybody's Aunt Sally. We fight out over the body of the BBC many current confusions about class, authority, the place of the arts, and the rights of free expression.

* Now four sound and two television channels. The comparisons still stand.

Almost every Hansard debate on broadcasting, in Lords or Commons, is dispiriting. A sizeable number of members would like the BBC to be, if not a disguised arm of government, at least a respectful channel for received opinions. They resent the decline in the power of the traditional Public Voices and would like the BBC to get it back for them. In one mid-sixties Parliamentary debate on broadcasting a speaker suggested that broadcasters be forbidden to interview Ministers at airports.

The popular press (most of it with heavy stakes in commercial television) still plays up the old 'Auntie BBC' image, regardless of the fact that the label would stick on ITV more easily today. The *Daily Mirror* now and again tries to prove that the BBC grossly wastes money. The evidence of at least three independent inquiries runs against them. The 'quality' press is sometimes more helpful, especially if it doesn't have commercial television interests. But some writers on broadcasting in the 'quality' press are still too much wedded to the old divisions by brows, or the new smart trend-hunting game. Yet some also think the commercial channel must be doing the better job, since it gets 55-60 per cent of the available audience. Whereas if the BBC sets out to provide democratic programming—wide-ranging, aware of different sizeable minorities as well as majorities—it will automatically, in competition with a commercial channel, have an overall lower audience figure. Equality would be failure.

Meanwhile a new force has come up recently, in the shape of movement for censorship.* These people don't attack the commercial channel as much as the BBC. After all, they say, we expect more of the BBC; it's paid from public funds, not advertising. This does at least pay the BBC, backhandedly, the compliment of giving it a special role, as the only system free to try to put mass communication at the service of the community without ulterior motive. It's a sort of tribute.

These people have a crude view of broadcasting and its effects; they assume a direct relationship between what is on

* See the essay 'The Guardians and the New Populism', p. 205.

the screen and what people then do. A reading of the relevant research would tell them that we still know little about how effects are made, but what we do know suggests that the relationship is rarely a one-step affair. When they call on the BBC deliberately to put on programmes that will 'build character' they are showing ignorance as well as incipient authoritarianism.

With little help from the old Authorities or the new Popular Spokesmen, the broadcasters have to work out largely for themselves the relations between freedom and responsibility in their work. Some exhaust themselves trying to do so. Some act as though nothing has changed since the Golden Age of the thirties. But most—predictably, since they are particularly responsive to the prevailing climate—are in retreat from the idea of 'public service broadcasting'. They suspect its paternalistic overtones and adopt 'professionalism' as their motto. The poor overworked word has to serve a multitude of uses. If it means a good sense of one's subject, and of one's audience, plus thought about the right relationships between the two, then three cheers for professionalism. But it is used to mean anything from that interpretation to a totally uncommitted technical virtuosity. I don't underestimate the difficulties in working for the BBC, especially since it is so much under criticism. Still, there are compensations, particularly today. Before the war it performed, all in all, a very responsible job; but its style smacked too much of offering something to 'the people' down there, of well-meaning paternalism. The social changes of the last two decades (and the shock of competition) have given it the opportunity to reinterpret its role in a more fully democratic sense. No other broadcasting system is poised before such a prospect.

Experiments, especially if they are controversial, get most public attention. But more than 90 per cent of BBC broadcasting time goes, must go, on straightforward servicing—providing a service for known and existing needs (news, music, sport, background information). People usually talk about the BBC as though it were a monolith, and often its own public utterances reinforce that impression. But it would be just as true to think of it as a lot of different institutions under one name, a cross between a zoo and a Tower of Babel, an almost unbelievably polymathic, culturally polyglot organization, an Ark of journalists, poets, variety artists, teachers, straight actors, musicians, 'presenters', anchor men, comedians, natural historians, astronomers—all pouring out material almost round the clock every day.

Ninety per cent of broadcasting time on straight servicing to existing tastes sounds easy. But whose taste is to be mirrored? The 'average man's'? And shall the 'unaverage man' have a turn now and again? How often is 'now and again'? How do you decide proportions? Or choose between an enormous number of not-quite-average tastes? You must choose as a broadcaster, must make judgments of value, since the channels are few and time limited. Then the trouble begins. The world is wider than most of us know or want to admit. When we agree that the BBC should most of the time reflect existing tastes we usually mean that it should reflect our tastes, the dead-centre taste of our particular social group. We correlate good taste with what we happen to know and already approve. So some people think that all broadcasting should aspire to the condition of a permanent Palm Court Orchestra or White Heather Club.

A great many people assume that if, whenever they happen to turn on the radio or television, they don't find something that chimes in with the way they are feeling at that moment, then the BBC has somehow failed and is drawing part of its licence money on false pretences. This is one instance where the 'freedom of the switch' argument—often employed speciously—has real point. Otherwise we will not encourage good broadcasting but will push broadcasters towards providing unexceptionable middle-range material all the time. The BBC is not a continuous cornucopia built just for us: it is more like several different kinds of cinema, several different kinds of newspaper and magazine, several music halls and concert halls, a school, a university, a club—sometimes running concurrently but more often successively.

Some people also assume that any programme which is not to their taste is not only a boring misuse of their licence money but immoral. I do not think discussion about the 'moral quality' of broadcasting programmes is irrelevant. It is essential—but very difficult to do properly. I am myself less disturbed by, say, satire programmes than by some of the pallier audience-participation shows. I say this not to seem paradoxical or suggest that one man's meat is another man's immorality, but to stress two provisos: any discussion about the 'moral quality' of a programme will be useless if it is crudely moralistic and external: and most attacks on the BBC's 'immorality' prove not that the Corporation is actively seeking to pander to a depraved section of the public but that it is accurately mirroring prevailing differences and contradictions in taste. I do not assume that the producers of *This Is Your Life* (any more than those of *TW3*) said to themselves: 'This is a load of rubbish, but the dopes seem to like it.' I think they probably 'believed in' the programme. That's what makes the debate more difficult, and more important, since it goes wider than any issue the BBC can in itself resolve.

Of course, there are deeper waters. Some of the sharp anger directed at satire programmes or those portraying violence is inspired by a freshly disturbed fear that the world is more difficult to understand, come to terms with, or control than we have wished to think. 'Leave thou thy sister when she prays': disturbance for kicks would be hard to justify. But there is as deep a ditch on the other side of the road, one in which the rugged contours of reality are submerged.

A democratic broadcasting system cannot rest with mirroring its society, even if mirroring is defined as widely as I have proposed. It has a more positive element, one very difficult to define today because so many people react against the notion of 'doing good'. This is understandable: the phrase suggests patronage; and the man who seeks self-consciously to 'do good' takes his eye off the object to look at his audience, and before long is manipulating both. But if 'doing good' means believing that your subject—current affairs, the arts, astronomy—is interesting and worthwhile and wanting others to be interested too, then that is one basic element in successful broadcasting. The range of interests enjoyed by most of us is largely a product of historical and social chance; even I.Q. is more fluid than we used to think. There are many more possible activities—interesting, useful, imaginative—than most of us have had the opportunity to realize. Has a public-service broadcasting system to ignore this fact for fear of being accused of 'going back to Reith' or 'bringing back Haley's pyramid'? Has it to settle for mirroring the average level and range of taste which happen to pertain at this time, even though it is so well placed to call in question what class and cash and geography have decided shall be each individual's limits of response?

The BBC has made and is still making many mistakes, some of them grievous; there is no need to stop criticizing the Corporation. But we hear an inordinate amount these days (often on stupidly inaccurate grounds or for self-interestedly irrelevant purposes) about the BBC's failings. It is time to count its gains and estimate its promise. More consistently than any other broadcasting system, the BBC has tried to take a fresh look, not settled for known recipes for success, banked on latent tastes, believed that what its diverse producers find interesting and valuable can be found interesting and valuable by sizeable audiences too.

Compare the BBC's coverage of news and current affairs with that of much of the press. Recall the class-bound and chauvinistic tone of the middlebrow press, and the elementary assumptions about taste and capacities in the popular press. When the ritualistic jokes about news-announcers in evening dress or Richard Dimbleby's style are over, remember the BBC's tradition of objectivity in reporting, which was built up through the thirties, often against government opposition, reached a high plateau during the last war, and a peak over Suez. Add the developments in television news and current affairs during the last few years, the range of programmes which run from *Tonight* through *Panorama* to *Gallery* and *Twenty-Four Hours* (and *This Week* on the other channel). What seems important about these programmes at their best is their common central objective—to find a direct, accurate, unstuffy way of treating matters of public interest, one which assumes common sense, patience, and judgment in viewers. Granada's *World in Action* is sometimes telling. But those people, and they include a number of television critics, who rate its febrile life above the less dramatic achievement of the BBC in this field are confused about values in communication. To use the 'hard sell' manner of soap commercials for programmes on current affairs neither assumes good sense nor assists judgment.

Similarly, the initiatives of BBC television comedy over the last few years—Tony Hancock, Harry Worth, Eric Sykes, Benny Hill, *Steptoe and Son*, *Meet the Wife*—are important because they have broken out of the dreary old 'pro' routines, and have made more difficult the patronage of *Workers' Playtime*. Or compare the assumptions and expectations behind a typical B-feature gangster-film with those of *Z Cars*, or *Softly, Softly*.

The audience for *TW3* cut across social and brow divisions, chiefly because satiric (nonconforming, mickey-taking) jokes have been a staple of English urban working-class life for generations, part of a tradition of dissent. Above all, this tradition deflated humbug, especially the humbug of public pretensions. *TW3* was often silly and sometimes cruel; given the newness of the enterprise on television this was likely. But to talk only of 'destructive cynicism' and fail to see the sceptical intelligence which was also at work, and meeting a response throughout society, is to confuse axe-grinding with social observation. *TW3*'s natural successor was the more consistently intelligent *Not Only . . . But Also*, and a comparison of that with *Sunday Night at the Palladium* or *The Eamonn Andrews Show*, a comparison of different levels of imagination and intelligence assumed, is to wonder whether we are in the same country. We are, and roughly with the same audience; and this underlines the case for going out on limbs against routine show-business and social-class expectations.

There is much more evidence—*The Newcomers, Diary of a Young Man*, some of *Monitor*, sport, some documentaries. Initiatives like these are good because they do not accept a preconceived idea of what audiences can take and trim to that; they respect their material, won't compromise it but want to communicate their interest. This is the right creative tension in broadcasting. No feedback from past successes or audience research can take its place.

All this is only a beginning. But it is something. The BBC is still feeling its way, more often unfairly harassed than usefully criticized from outside (you wouldn't have guessed from press comment that BBC-2 is so different and so interesting), still struggling for a range of voices between those of the Headmasters and the Fast Sellers. Sometimes the BBC's mistakes are so bad you wonder how they could ever have come about, what possible view of broadcasting or of audiences could have generated them, why they were not laughed out of consideration at the start. One cause is the freedom rightly given to producers; another is the inherent in-grownness of broadcasting. In television especially there is a strong temptation to mistake self-absorption for a critical professional dialogue. The noises from outside, seeking to censure or censor, are usually so irrelevant that the broadcaster's self-defining tendency is increased: he is tempted to reject all outside comment as the stuffiness of Establishments or the vulgarity of the market-place or the bleatings of old puritans.

'Professionalism' has to be better defined by the broadcasters themselves so that internal criticism improves; and criticism from outside needs to be more informed, responsive, and varied. With these, we might get quite near to having a democratic broadcasting system.

1965

DIFFICULTIES
OF DEMOCRATIC DEBATE

The Reception of the Pilkington Report on Broadcasting

G OVERNMENTS in Britain seem to be getting into the habit of setting up departmental committees to review the record of broadcasting and advise for its future roughly every decade—that is, well before the BBC's licence and charter fall due for renewal. The last renewal was timed for 1964, and the Act which had created the BBC's competitor, the Independent Television Authority, fell due for renewal in that year also. The Pilkington Committee was thus given, in 1960, the following terms of reference:

> To consider the future of the broadcasting services in the United Kingdom, the dissemination by wire of broadcasting and other programmes, and the possibility of television for public showing; to advise on the services which should in future be provided in the United Kingdom by the BBC and the ITA; to recommend whether additional services should be provided by any other organization; and to propose what financial and other conditions should apply to the conduct of all these services.

The language is necessarily formal and its implications somewhat opaque. But they were powerful implications. A number of new elements made the work of this Committee, on which I served, more challenging than that of its predecessors. This was the first committee to review British broadcasting since the establishment of television. It was the first such committee since the arrival of competition (with the creation of the second system in 1954), so it had to assess the performance of the new Authority and the effect of competition on the BBC. At least two new television channels were likely to be available within the next few years, and recommendations about their uses and about the desirability of moving into

UHF had to be made. The 405-line standard for television was in dispute, and colour television was being powerfully urged. Systems of pay-TV were proving workable, and there was strong pressure to license them. Finally, there was a demand for the authorization of local sound broadcasting from about one hundred hopefully-formed commercial companies and from the BBC itself.

So the Committee had a lot to do. It sat for about 22 months, tried to digest several million words of written and oral evidence, had 78 whole-day meetings of the full committee and 43 sub-committee meetings, took evidence in all parts of Britain and some foreign countries, visited all kinds of broadcasting installations, and finally produced in June 1962 a report of 150,000 words, followed by two large volumes which contained a representative fraction of the written evidence.

The Report produced at the end was, when we looked back to our own attitudes at the start, as surprising to the Committee members as it was to many other people. Set off by the wide-ranging evidence of public dissatisfaction (which was reinforced by our own inquiries), we had gradually but firmly and unanimously come to believe that something was badly wrong in British broadcasting.

The Committee's most striking conclusion was that the commercial television 'experiment' (the word is the Government's) had proved substantially a failure. On the whole it had resulted in competition for large audiences; and this kind of competition, the Report argued, was different from competition in good broadcasting. The Report recommended a radical reorganization of independent television, the award of the third television channel to the BBC, and of the fourth to the ITA only after it had been reorganized and settled down again. Finally, it was argued, there should be no pay-TV and no commercial sound radio.

At first hearing, these recommendations sound restrictive. In fact, they all follow from the aim of encouraging greater freedom and flexibility in broadcasting, and the arguments on which they were based were given in the Report. It became plain early in the inquiry that, before it made any specific recommendations, the Committee would have to try to establish criteria for democratic broadcasting in the public service.

The Report suggested that such broadcasting requires the broadcasters to put on in peak time a fair range or variety of programmes, varied in both subjects and moods (rather than to think of viewers as one large relaxed mass). It suggested that the minorities broadcasters should think of are not only minorities in the usual intellectual and 'cultivated' senses, but minorities actual or potential in the great body of people; a great many people are specialists or enthusiasts in something, whether in carpentry or music or gardening. Most of us, it was argued, do some things more intensely than others; but if broadcasters do not plan their programmes so as to cater for these different intensities of concern, they will only hold people in a lukewarm bath of low-level interest— though their audiences will be larger than if they do cater for different tastes. The Report suggested that broadcasters should from time to time gamble on our willingness to try something different—or they will come to assume that today's average levels of taste are immutable, facts of nature. By assuming this, they will tend to reinforce those levels, to make them 'set' rather than support growth and difference. Dissent, the freedom to differ, had to be built into broadcasting systems because, left alone, they tend to accept the status quo, to overlook small growing points in favour of established or popular big battalions. Finally, the Committee argued that greater power in the control of broadcasting should go to the professionals, power to aim solely at good broadcasting in all fields, from current affairs to comedy.

All the Committee's recommendations were designed to give a greater range of better choices to the viewer and greater professional freedom to the broadcaster. Pay-TV was opposed because such a network, which would be established only in urban or well-populated areas, could be profitable to its owners only if it took some of the best existing programmes from the present networks by out-bidding them. Pay-TV would thus ensure that many people in country districts would no longer have the chance to see these programmes at all, and that others who now see them as part of what are called the 'free' services would have to pay heavily for them, item by item. The Committee rejected the proposals for local sound broadcasting under commercial auspices because the desire to make maximum advertising revenue would cause such stations to concentrate on packaged and uniform programmes of the disc-jockey type, at the expense of a balanced service which, throughout the day, sought opportunities to cater for a variety of local interests. Last, the Committee asked for the reorganization of Independent Television because there is, under the present system, a conflict between the demands of varied broadcasting and the drive for maximum advertising revenue. In all these recommendations the Committee aimed to increase the right kinds of freedom in broadcasting.

Opposition to a report of this kind was to be expected. Some people would lose the opportunity to make a lot of money, even more than they had already made, if its recommendations were accepted. Still, the Committee did not (or, at least, I did not) expect so sharp a reaction. Many articles in the Press had urged the Committee to be fundamental in its thinking. The *Daily Telegraph*, four months before the Report appeared, urged its authors to inquire into why the commercial channel lacked initiative in comparison with the BBC, said in the next paragraph that the commercial companies were primarily in the business for money and proceeded to be acutely critical of them. Mr. Altman, a journalist who subsequently brought up to date a pamphlet on broadcasting in which he supported the commercial channel, said in the *Contemporary Review* for March 1962 that Independent Television was perfidiously greedy and terrifyingly smug, that television provided a basic diet of trivia and was ruled by ratings. He added to the broadcasters:

Subject all you have created to an agonizing reappraisal. Because unless you remedy some of the more glaring faults, do not be surprised if the recommendations of the Pilkington Committee deal a crushing blow to your pride and in your case, gentlemen of the programme companies, to your pockets too.

When the Report was published in June the response was immediate and very violent. The members of the Committee were described as authoritarians, socialistic, round-heads, do-gooders, highbrows, puritans, and paternalists; they were, it was said, polemical, smug and naïve.

No doubt there were some faults of presentation, of phrasing and of organization in the Report. But I do not think they significantly account for its hostile reception. Many a report is not as well organized or expressed but does not attract a hundredth part of the criticism the Pilkington Report attracted. The reasons for the opposition range from the most obvious—cash—to some very much less obvious. The argument was at bottom about freedom and responsibility within commercialized democracies. It touched on the interrelations between cash, power and the organs for intellectual debate; it had to do with a society which is changing rapidly and doesn't understand its own changes; it had to do with the adequacy of our assumptions and vocabulary to many current social issues.

The Report's reception by the Government is not particularly illuminating. Probably the Postmaster General (to whom the Report was presented) was shocked, and no doubt he was not alone. It has been said that the Government had expected the Report on the whole to confirm the rightness of prevailing arrangements, that no government expects a committee it has itself set up to be really radical, that no government will officially promote dissent. So, this interpretation runs, when setting up a committee any government ensures that there are no members, or only a manageable few, who are likely to take a strong dissident line. But this sounds too simple. Departmental committees are not intellectually fiery organisms; but they have disinterested collective minds and make them up for themselves.

Rumour said that several members of the Government, when the Report reached them, were in favour of accepting it either as a whole or substantially. Some others were as strongly against the Report; others, no doubt, didn't much care. There was plenty of pressure against it from outside, so that in the end the Government took only a few of the recommendations and ignored or watered down the others. In this, its reaction seems to have been not sinister but predictable, and not of great cultural significance.

The popular Press was almost uniformly violent. "Pilkington tells the public to go to hell", screamed one paper in enormous headlines. "Given a chance, Pilkington would recommend the suppression of your favourite newspaper", yelled another. Mr. Woodrow Wyatt, a wealthy socialist MP who was interested in the possibilities of commercial radio, told the readers of the *Sunday Pictorial*, "You trivial people will have to brush up your culture." Another paper shouted that 'Big Brother TV' was round the corner; "If you think you're enjoying yourself too much, they'll soon put a stop to that", they added. Others spoke of "arrogance . . . this amazing document . . . a haughty conviction that whatever is popular must be bad", and claimed that the Committee wanted compulsory ballet and chamber music for all and would like to close football clubs. Hardly one bothered to give even a minimally comprehensive or balanced account of the Report's findings.

The provincial Press was more in favour of the Report and, whether in favour or not, these papers dealt more responsibly with it than the nationals. This was agreeably surprising because it suggested that provincial papers had more editorial freedom than one had begun to believe (since most of them are owned by the national Press or by financial groups which own national papers, provincial papers and—sometimes—shares in commercial television).

But why was the national Press so angry and one-sided?

Partly, it is obvious, because the Report ran against most newspapers' financial interests, since most of them, at one remove or another, have stakes in commercial television. In both the popular and the quality Press there was a fair degree of correlation between the reception of the Report and the existence or not of financial interest. The *Mirror* had large stakes and was strongly opposed; the Beaverbrook Press had at that time no stakes and welcomed the Report. There were one or two exceptions, such as *The Guardian*, which has shares in a regional television company but dealt fairly (and favourably) with the Report.

Yet I do not believe that the popular journalists who reacted so sharply to the Pilkington Report did so just because they were employed by organizations financially opposed to the Report's finding. They were being true to their trade in a deeper sense. Some of them attacked with what seemed genuine feeling; they were not putting on an act of the sort they employ when they pillory some politician or local councillor or attack immorality in Piccadilly. The Committee members did not expect the Report to be handled with kid gloves and had all seen unfairness in the Press before. But this was an exceptional demonstration of distortion, tendentiousness, personal abuse, half-truth, straight misrepresentation, disingenuousness, pseudo-honesty and irresponsibility. It all added up to an indictment of the claims of much of the British Press—not only of the popular Press—to be a Fourth Estate, except when this role suits its own book. The Press will play with top-surface dissent but will not tolerate substantial criticism of those social assumptions which allow it to have its cake and eat it, to pose as a public benefactor while exploiting the accidents of social and educational history. When the interests of the Press are criticized—as they often are, though it is hard to find evidence that most papers have seriously considered these criticisms—it reacts with vehemence and refuses to reconsider its prosperous apologetics.

With few exceptions popular journalists accept the social system or are not given to serious questioning of it. It treats them well, or they are built that way, or they think they can 'play' it and retain an out-of-office-hours inviolability. So they fight back very hard if the system is challenged at the roots. I think they were deeply disturbed by the Pilkington Report because they felt themselves indicted by it. If Pilkington's analysis of the tension between freedom and responsibility demanded by good broadcasting in a democracy was sound, then it had some relevance to the Press also; and the Press would not come out of such an examination lightly.* The late Arthur Christiansen, an ex-editor of the *Daily Express* and the man to whom is usually given the credit for raising that newspaper to the height of its glossy efficiency, asked, "Is the free Press in danger?" He went on, "After the Pilkington Report, anything can happen." He at least saw the relevance.

The attitude of some social scientists was more difficult to explain. A few reacted sharply because the Committee had not itself commissioned 'any solid original research'. I wish this had been possible, but there were overwhelming reasons why it was not. Still, here is a field which was, in its more objective aspects, intensively worked over all the time by TAM and Nielson and BBC audience research; the Committee did take account of this and other available evidence, British and American; it consulted specialists and made its own analyses of viewing as it went along. But the more difficult and relevant kinds of research—into subjective areas— could not have been done in the time the parliamentary timetable allowed. The Report had to be ready in 22 months.

One or two of the social scientists who objected sounded personally affronted. I wondered whether they were angry because they felt their discipline had once again not been sufficiently called in on issues where it was clearly relevant. Sometimes they seemed to suspect that evidence is offered to such committees only by professional do-gooders who do not speak for most people; and they seemed convinced that social

---

* The Press is not as limited in its number of possible outlets as broadcasting is, so has some grounds to claim more freedom to do as it likes—since, in theory, all sides can have a chance to be heard.

scientific studies can in all things provide a better guide than the *ex cathedra* opinions of laymen witnesses. But the witnesses the Committee saw did not seem particularly stuffy; and no committee worth its place simply takes over opinions given in evidence. And though social science can be invaluable and *ex cathedra* opinions often misleading, yet social science, while it may give a great many useful 'is's', cannot give a single 'ought'.

Some social scientists talked as though, if you scientifically studied the evidence—of audiences, responses, and so on—then value-judgments would emerge from it. This view is less tenable than the narrower one which was also put forward—that a government committee ought to restrict itself to collecting and ordering objective evidence, to making recommendations on objective matters (e.g., use this line system or that colour system), and to laying out the social alternatives neutrally. Some of the commercial companies joyfully took up this criticism of the Report's approach. They knew that if you studied the data till the end of the century, no judgments of value would emerge. You would be left with inert masses and would probably, in the end, accept the built-in assumptions of your particular society as a means of ordering them.

That is why the Committee had realized quite soon in the inquiry that, whatever else it did, it had to write a kind of essay in social philosophy—on the place of mass communications in a democracy—before it could begin to make sense of the conflicting evidence. People could disagree, but at least they would know the assumptions behind the recommendations.

Most interesting of all was the reaction to the report among recognized 'intellectual' voices. They included some who would call themselves 'progressives' and some of the more intellectual Members of Parliament, whether of the Right or Left.*

* Christopher Mayhew, the Opposition spokesman on broadcasting, gave up that position because of his Party's treatment of the Report. He strongly favoured Pilkington.

Among the journals which spoke perceptively of the Report's aims were the *Birmingham Post, The Guardian,* the *New Left Review, Peace News* (whose three successive articles made up, in my view, the best of all the immediate assessments of the Report), and *Contrast.* (The last, a quarterly which used to be published by the British Film Institute, was almost wholly concerned with television criticism. It was good to see people with professional knowledge saying that the Report made sense for those who work in the field.) There were also impressive individual tributes—impressive for their particularity; they were not just messages of generalized goodwill and approval. But all this is incidental. I am concerned with what the attacks on the Report indicated about the general condition of 'the cultural debate' in Britain.

A great many people seemed unwilling to rethink in the way Pilkington had tried. There is a favourite intellectual cliché which allows people to feel progressive, and runs: the BBC is a stodgy old Auntie and, in spite of its obvious faults, ITV is 'the people's channel'. At the beginning of the Committee's work some of the members felt like that; they were anxious not to seem 'highbrows' (not that all of them were, but they knew many people had assumed the Committee would start with a bias in favour of the BBC, and wanted to avoid any such bias). But by the time they drafted the Report they had come to the conclusion as a body that, all in all, the BBC is a highly professional organization with a comprehensive sense of its job, and that the commercial channel could not in any authentic sense be said to 'speak for the people'. This opinion startled many reviewers, caught with their clichés unready, and they reacted by standing even more stiffly in their habitual postures.

There was further confusion over that hoary *pons asinorum,* the apparent conflict between 'giving the people what the people want' and 'giving the people what they ought to have'.* Most critics bypassed the early section of the Report, in which

* See 'Television as the Archetype of Mass Communications', p. 163 of this volume.

the two statements are examined, as though a look at it would have taken a 'good root-confusion' away from them.

Similarly, some people became stuck in the proof-of-the-pudding dilemma: "After all, people watch the commercial channel more than they watch BBC, and therefore it must be for them the better channel. The proof of the pudding . . . You and I may think that some things are better than others, but wouldn't it be undemocratic to try to force these things down people's throats, etc., etc." Not that the Report had suggested any forcing. Still, most people do not seem to find a dilemma here. Four or five public opinion polls, taken just before or just after Pilkington, showed that a majority of people make the distinction Pilkington made between the channel you watch rather more often, because it is more frequently relaxing, and the channel which you think is doing the better job over-all and which you watch with more interest.

Again, in the chapter about advertising on television, the Report distinguished between two kinds of criticism in the evidence submitted to the Committee. First, were 'objective' criticisms—that some advertisements were untruthful or misleading. Second, were less tangible criticisms about the effects of advertising on individuals and on society—about the instincts it plays upon, the images it suggests as desirable, and so on. This second kind of criticism is part of a general critique of advertising which has been deployed for several decades, and one would have expected it to be known to anyone interested in social questions.

Many of the Report's critics seemed never to have heard of this analysis or, if they had heard, to have dismissed it immediately. I do not mean only men in the advertising industry; they tended to look at the criticism as though it had been written in Sanskrit—and then quickly walked around it. Others balked for a moment, as embarrassed as though the Committee had been discovered in some extraordinary ingenuousness. Then they said, "Really! What sort of a world do these people think this is? Let's at least be realistic." In the House of Lords debate on the Report a Bishop remarked that one could hardly expect advertisers not to use whatever devices were available. One couldn't ask too much of people. After all, one had to be . . . realistic.

When the Report discussed the actual quality of programmes it got away, as I have already suggested, from the old distinction which puts serious = highbrow = good in one box, and light = lowbrow = bad in another. It said, of course, that light and serious programmes each had their place, that goodness or badness was not a matter of height of brow but had to do with the quality of the imagination and the response to life in any work, whatever its mood. It attacked a particular fault which seemed to run through some programmes of all kinds and was probably due to excessive fear of the audience. This the Report called 'triviality', meaning to indicate by the word the way in which technique, gimmicks, can become dominant, the packaging more important than the product. "A trivial approach," the Report said, "can consist in a failure to respect the potentialities of the subject matter, no matter what it be, or in a too ready reliance on well-tried themes, or in a habit of conformity to established patterns, or in a reluctance to be imaginatively adventurous. . . ."*

This is only a summary statement of what good television critics have long recognized. But most critics of the Report shied nervously away from analysis like this, as though they were afraid of its implications. They tended to define the Committee's position as an attack on 'the ordinary man's' freedom to relax, a puritanical mistrust of lightheartedness.

The response was much the same to the Report's discussion of violence on television. The Committee had received a great many statements about what witnesses regarded as excessive violence. Some of the statements were crude, assumed that there was a close correlation between every act of violence on television and every act of juvenile delinquency, and hammered at this 'social evil' in a way which made it

* *Report of the Committee on Broadcasting 1960, op. cit.,* para. 98.

certain that, if Shakespeare had been writing today, hardly one of his plays would have had a showing. So the Committee tried to define the tension between imaginative freedom and social responsibility—a difficult job and one they could hardly do adequately. But because the Report did not simply say "Freedom is all, and any qualification is a surrender to the Mothers' Union", many commentators called the Committee fuddy-duddy. Here more even than elsewhere these commentators seemed just not to have read the relevant chapter, but to have attributed to it what they assumed would be there. Much the most interesting of all aspects of the response was the 'moral condition muddle'. The Report argued more than once that broadcasters have to recognize that, whether they like it or not, they are in "a constant and sensitive relation to the moral condition of society", and that this gives them responsibilities difficult to define but not easy to shrug off. Not felicitous phrasing, perhaps, but the quoted passage—in particular, by the meaning it assumes for the word 'moral'—belongs to a fairly common kind of discussion, is an instance of what Lionel Trilling has called 'the cultural mode of thought'. It means that the quality of the life of a society as expressed in its texture—its assumptions and values as bodied out in its habits and ways of life—that these will be reflected and to some extent affected by broadcasting as by other forms of mass communication.

The Committee knew that a few people would think they were defining a crudely moralistic relationship, were saying that broadcasters had a responsibility for the direct propagation of the Ten Commandments. But the members thought the sentence quoted above would be clear to informed people, whichever side of the argument they were on. The Committee was mistaken. *The Times*'s leader writer was among the first to assume that the Committee meant that broadcasting has a duty to promote ethical precepts; in this error he led a fairly large chorus of respected organs of opinion, including some of the educational Press.

That word 'moral' affronted them like a Gideon Bible

found at his hotel bedside by a roving atheist. It became a term of irony, scorn and contempt. In all the debate, I only once saw it used seriously by any of the Report's critics, and this was in the *Investor's Guardian*. The writer noted that most investors assumed the Pilkington proposals for re-organizing Independent Television would seriously damage profits, but said his calculations suggested that profit levels under the new system (if it were accepted) would be adequate. "But even if the commercial viability of the proposed scheme is accepted," the article went on, "it does not necessarily follow that the system is desirable from the political and moral point of view." But that use of the word 'moral' is hardly an instance of the 'cultural mode of thought'.

The heat engendered by the use of 'moral' was reflected also in the reaction to almost any phrase which suggested responsibility or commitment. Here the criticisms tended to focus on style. You felt these critics were determined to 'mistrust the big words'; and, remembering Joyce and Hemingway on the need to do just that today, you might at first have supposed their attitude was fed by an admirable ironic refusal to strike large postures. On a closer look you noticed that these people mistrusted only certain big words, such as 'moral' and 'responsible'; but they loved others, such as 'anti-humbug', 'forward-looking' and 'realistic'.

Equally, they mistrusted certain manners. This was a soberly written Report. A few people remarked that it was unusual to see a case firmly argued, without a gimmick in three hundred pages. But most of the critics I am discussing could only respond with the old, expected, big words of dis-like: 'censorious', 'pompous', 'priggish', 'prim', 'governessy', 'ponderous'.

Just as these people seemed habitually to mistrust certain manners, so they habitually approved of others. They liked, for instance, what they would call irony; but in fact they did not distinguish between an ironic style and that of the smart alec. Perhaps a knowing manner was felt to indicate that they were free of 'Establishment' stuffiness, or perhaps it helped them feel at one with their audience, whom they assumed were congenitally anti-Them. Whatever the reasons, most of the critics would not have been seen in print before they had put on a peculiar kind of sophisticated tone.

The Pilkington Committee walked a rough road in trying to find a plain voice; it ran right between professional narks and trigger-happy shooters at clay feet, on the one side; and, on the other, the organ-voiced and archaic chauvinists—one or two of whom, as though to redress the balance, favoured the Report by misreading it in their own way. In the weeks after the Report came out, I often remembered Auden's line about the lack today of any 'sane affirmative speech'. There is not even a moderately precise vocabulary for discussing the cultural questions raised by the study of broadcasting. There is no adequate terminology, no adequate sense of the history and process of this kind of cultural change, and no adequate language for discussing the popular arts.

The Pilkington Committee made mistakes; and it was severely criticized for them. But my argument has been that the reception of the Pilkington Report illustrates more than the errors of a committee. It was attacked so sharply because most of its critics were not ready to admit 'the height of that great argument', to admit that this was an argument about freedom and responsibility in a democracy. The Report did not match the demands of the times, but it did recognize something of its scope, and tried to conduct a social, cultural, personal, and moral as well as economic, political and technical argument.

The Report tried to define a democratic position. It tried to challenge, in its discussion of actual programmes and of broadcasting structures, that socio-cultural stratifying of British society which thinks all demands are satisfied if there are symphony concerts for the highbrows and quiz-shows for the masses—and never the twain shall meet (except in a few muzzy areas of togetherness, such as when we all hear the Queen's speech on the afternoon of Christmas Day).

In all its recommendations the Report sought to extend

intellectual and imaginative freedom, to give more room for variety and dissent. Its view of society was based on the idea of change and possibility, on the view that there are within the huge majorities lots of overlapping minorities, on thinking not only about what we are but of what we might become if we were given more varied chances. By contrast, many of the Report's critics—for all their claims to be smarter and more progressive—had, below the obvious debating levels, deeply static and conservative attitudes.

The greatest disappointment in the reception of the Pilkington Report was not that so many publicists disagreed with it, but that they approached its themes so shoddily prepared. Here was a confrontation of an unusually searching kind, and few were ready for it. This has depressing implications, and they go far wider than broadcasting matters alone.

1963

THE *DAILY MIRROR* AND
ITS READERS

THE trouble with the *Mirror* is its smugness. It is forever telling us how 'irreverent—forward-looking—cheeky—earthy—brash—in tune with the people' it is and in the end sounds like an overgrown, undeveloped lad playing to the gallery. This is a pity, because it can put you off from recognizing in what ways the *Mirror* is in fact preferable to most of its rivals. The 1945 election was a good instance. The *Express* campaign then was distorted and virulent. But more decisive than its tricks, such as the Laski scare and the use of Churchill's wartime reputation, was the *Express*'s inability to sense the changed mood of the country. Its view of English society was chauvinistic, ridden with privilege, patronizing and mean-spirited. Churchill himself was, of course, better than this; but he, too, had hardly any sense of the need for change in domestic affairs.

By contrast, the *Mirror* was much more in touch with the prevailing mood, and in particular had recognized that the servicemen abroad wanted things to be different when they came home. The *Mirror* had a kind of generosity in its view of what 'ordinary people' might reasonably expect. It did not defer to the totems of a paternalistic society. It was ready to stand up to government and bureaucracy and kick hard at instances of caste-thinking. Its reception of the Beveridge Report (Churchill's reaction to the Report was, again, remarkably unperceptive) shows the *Mirror* at its best.

It is important to get this part of the record straight if we are to understand the *Mirror*'s relation to its readers, and its sense of the society which it reflects or helps to change. Research suggests that the media of mass communication reflect prevailing attitudes more than they change them. This apart, they apparently tend either to reinforce existing attitudes by going with the grain of them or, where opinion

is just on the point of change, can—if they catch that wave—
help to tip it over. This is probably what happened between
the *Mirror* and its readers in 1945.

The point is worth making since most writers on the
popular press tend to look two ways. When the paper they
are writing about takes up a position with which they themselves feel uneasy, they remind us that a popular paper predominantly reflects its readers' attitudes, cannot go too far
ahead of them, and so on. When the paper advocates a
position which seems intellectually respectable and worthy,
they talk about the way it leads opinion. The question in the
background is: how long and how firmly will a mass circulation newspaper stand out against what it takes to be majority
opinion after that opinion has begun to reflect itself in sales?

We need a dispassionate analysis of these relations. Such
an analysis might start with the *Mirror*'s treatment of major
issues and the shifts in its attitudes to them. I am not thinking
of individual authors on the *Mirror*, of whom Cassandra is
the most notable. He seems clearly to be his own man, and
the *Mirror* has been sensible enough to let him say what he
will, even when he is opposed to the general line of the
paper. I am thinking of larger movements in the positions
taken up by the paper as a whole, and of the forces which
cause those movements.

Trickier and more important would be an analysis of the
Mirror's attitudes to its readers. We can agree that the *Mirror*,
more often than the *Express* or the *Sketch*, has been on the
side of the angels, in that it has attacked humbug and pre-
tension, and has shown a generous indignation about in-
justice and want. Hence some writers about the Press almost
exempt the *Mirror* from criticism or even hold it up as a fine
example.

But this is not good enough. This is to reject one kind
of belittling only to fall victim to another. The crucial point
is that the *Mirror* does not—one or two instances apart—
allow its readers to think for themselves, or help them to do
so. It blusters at them, hammers them with slogans, treats

them like kids. Its rhetoric can be brilliant—brilliantly effective in its own terms, that is, in its ability to produce the kind of emotional shock it seeks. Its cartoons can be brilliant, again within its own terms—they hit you over the head so as to shock you.

It has recognized certain attitudes which do exist in working-class life, has inflated them, and ignored others just as important but not so melodramatically usable. The tradition of dissent and non-conformity becomes—as, admittedly, it sometimes does in real life—big-mouthed bluster; warmth and charity become—as they sometimes do in life—loose-mouthed sentimentality; the friendship of workmates becomes—as it sometimes does in life—an over-easy heartiness. Edith Sitwell once rebuked someone who wrote an article about 'working chaps' and talked about 'Bob, Jim and Ted'. She had more respect for these gentlemen, she said, than to arrogate to herself the right to refer to them so intimately without knowing them. When its friends say of the *Mirror*: "It was vulgar: it spoke for the crowd," we have a right to ask: "What crowd?" Whom do they think they are talking about? Truer to say the *Mirror* often fathered its own vulgarity and silly little tricks on its readers. In its own way all this is as belittling as the approach of the press of the Right, which patronizes its readers as though they were lower orders or other ranks.

The combination of an inflated-caricature view of your reader, and of inflated rhetoric to carry that view, means that the *Mirror* hardly less than the *Express* tries to decide for its readers, rather than to help them decide for themselves. One can't help remembering Cecil King's fantastically superior—and wrong—pronouncement: "The popular press taught ordinary people to question and make up their own minds. They are still not very good at it. They still come to decisions emotionaly rather than by reason, but they are immeasurably better informed." Thus the voice of Winchester still breathed o'er Britain.

The logic of the commercial newspaper world ensures that

there is no effective counterpart from within that world to these two opposed and unsatisfactory positions. For that we have to go outside, to the much-derided BBC. To the BBC which the *Mirror* has long enjoyed attacking, but which will always give fairer treatment to news unpalatable to itself than the *Mirror* does.

It does not treat its audiences as children to be hectored and jollied, even for good causes. It tries to respect them; it assumes that they can be more widely and more objectively interested in affairs than the popular papers have assumed. Hence its news treatment has set a new standard of breadth and fairness.

When it sets out to explore issues in depth and without deference to established authorities (as in programmes such as *Panorama, Tonight* and *24 Hours*) the BBC does so with an informed sharpness that the *Mirror* hardly ever reaches. The real 'news revolution' (though I think the phrase is extreme) of the first half of the twentieth century, lies just here; and today more than ever the BBC is close to this change and one of its agents. Opinion surveys on mass communications reveal that most people make distinctions between things they enjoy—and go on reading and seeing—and those they respect, as fair-minded and straight. In such surveys the BBC comes out very well indeed. The *Mirror* might reflect, in the light of this distinction, on its own relation to its readers.

1966

THE GUARDIANS
AND THE NEW POPULISM

OVER the last few decades there has been a slow but steady movement in Britain towards rather more openness in public debate, rather more freedom in themes and language for the arts, rather less recourse to euphemism. The causes are complex, but probably include increased higher education and, perhaps most notably, broadcasting. Broadcast debate and broadcast drama may not often impress intellectuals, but they are reaching millions of homes in which the notion of open discussion and of exploratory art have not been known before.

By all this the Guardians, as is usual at such moments of change, have been taken by surprise. I say Guardians so as to distinguish this body of people—senior clergy, leader-writers, presidents of national voluntary bodies, headmasters —from what Coleridge called 'the clerisy'. The clerisy maintain the cultural standards of a society by virtue of their disciplined intellectual and imaginative energy. The Guardians may think of themselves as the upholders of cultural standards but usually lack the qualities of mind necessary to fulfil that role. They are, rather, public expounders of public assumptions, of what has officially been felt to be 'in the country's best spirit and interests'; they tend to be paternal and act *de haut en bas*.

They have hardly realized that people are listening less, are often listening out of politeness or phlegm, or listening quizzically. This, as some critics said at the time, was the significance of the *Lady Chatterley's Lover* trial, its culturally-representative significance, not the debate about the quality of the book as literature. The twelve jurors were required to read the book immediately before the trial began. Nine of them were willing to acquit it on that reading. This figure would presumably have seemed unbelievable to the Senior

Treasury Counsel. In his conduct of the prosecution he showed no sense of changes in the climate of the country since he first took silk.

Such a man does not work alone; to some extent he represents the assumptions of his group. The direction of the *Lady Chatterley* case (and more recently of that against *Fanny Hill*) suggests a persistent failure on the part of the Guardians to understand the changes in English opinion. This view is reinforced by the evidence of almost any Lords debate on a matter of intellectual, artistic or moral concern, and by the pronouncements of most major advisory bodies.

The irony is that, at this moment in which the Guardians are losing effectiveness, a counter-movement has started which is probably more unpleasant (because the Guardians at least respected the idea of 'culture' and knew something of its need for freedom). It looks superficially like a grass-roots movement, but isn't; it can best be called Populism. So we look like going in one move from Vestigial Guardian-ship to the New Populism, bypassing the alternatives a literate democracy is supposed to offer. Increasingly the practice of the arts and of free debate are coming under violent attack from groups which do not claim to be Guardians but do claim to 'speak for the body of ordinary decent people'. Even though it may have no formal existence this can obviously be a dangerous form of censorship—censorship which works through causing risks not to be taken, by artists and by entrepreneurs.

As usual these people claim to be broadminded and tolerant but find themselves 'forced to take a stand against' *unnecessary* dirt, *gratuitous* sex, *excessive* violence, *destructive* irony. But look at the specific instances they cite and you see they will attack whatever does not underwrite a set of prior assumptions, assumptions which are anti-intellectual and unimaginative.

Presumably they would, like Pip's sister, really go on the rampage if they were to look at much good modern fiction (apart from the books the Director of Public Prosecutions brings to their attention); and recent English poetry would have them calling for tar-and-feathers again. So far only a television executive has been threatened with that.

Their happy hunting ground is among the more public forms of art—the theatre and, best of all, broadcasting. It is not difficult to see why. Its potential audience undifferentiated by location or class or taste or age, broadcasting—and especially television—is the most diffused of all mass-entertainments. It is a 'family' entertainment. It operates under public-service regulations. The Populist can attack the broadcasters energetically because—as he says—since they are 'our servants' broadcasting to 'our families', they have no right to present anything other than what we already recognize as healthy and irreproachable. So far the BBC has come under fire much more than ITA. Though ITA also operates under public service regulations (in fact, under slightly more stringent regulations than the BBC), it is explicitly recognized by the Populists as responsive to the market and isn't expected to toe the line quite so properly. This easy accommodation to the profit morality is the nastiest item in the record so far. No wonder the shadow of Moral Rearmament is not far off.

There is a more interesting reason why public service broadcasting—and subsidized theatre—are bound to aggravate the Populists more than commercial organizations are. It is a matter of their different natures. Organizations not tied to the balance sheet are more likely to experiment, to make genuine rather than pseudo experiments.

The Populist movement started a couple of years ago, with the attacks on *That Was The Week That Was*. It has gained force in the last year, notably in the nation-wide campaign to clean up television launched by two housewives in the Midlands, and in several other organizations. To some extent their behaviour is comical; but it would be foolish to underestimate their determination and nuisance value. Whom do they speak for? So far as they speak for anyone I should think it is for people much like themselves—middle-aged and middle class and genuinely worried about 'the way the world is going'—but probably not even for a majority of such people. Their movement finds no serious echo in the body of other social groups. But they may be unrepresentative and still, because broadcasters are occupationally vulnerable and Parliament thin-skinned in these matters, do damage to the free expression of opinion.

The biggest irony of all so far lies in the emotional link between these people and the commercial wing led by Mr. Peter Cadbury and Mr. Emile Littler, who have recently attacked dirt and violence in the theatre in the name of the ordinary man's right to entertainment which doesn't upset him. That link accurately illustrates the world without art that could emerge under Populism . . . with a neutered art keeping cosy the big audiences commercial entertainment needs. It is going to be harder after this for us to laugh at the cruder forms of Populism in the USA. Now that Vestigial Guardianship has weakened we are showing, not the lineaments of civilized democracy but the false democracy of aggressive philistinism.

Of course the recent increased freedom has gone to the heads of some writers, so the New Populists have a grain of truth. This indicates the most important reason why it would be good to think we could find an alternative to both Guardianship and emergent Populism—because this kind of pervasive control is so bad for British artistic and intellectual life. It makes all art 'social', even the apocalyptic. A British writer, when he is writing about something 'shocking', usually has the air of being shocked by his own cheek, of being 'in company', of not facing experience on his own. This is another dissociation of sensibility. It is difficult to write about the extremes of, say, sexual life without feeling a close relationship—cagey or defiant, or coy—to a certain kind of audience outside. Prufrock could assume a self-deprecating irony, in a similar position; for an artist such all-embracing social awareness can be disabling. It makes even his most fundamental experiences seem slightly suburban.

1964

THE CASE AGAINST ADVERTISING

B Y turns hurt, defiant, apologetic and self-justifying, advertising men seem particularly sensitive to criticism just now. Criticism has certainly been heavy in the last few years, perhaps because the number of reasonably well-informed people is somewhat greater than it used to be. You need a fairly widespread critical public opinion to get the Consumers' Association, the Advertising Inquiry Council and similar organizations started. Yet few people in advertising have taken the measure of this development. Some have seen its superficial aspects and made their advertising more self-conscious and sophisticated; but the moderate widening of critical opinion has so far escaped almost all of them.

I will try to sum up as directly as I can the case against advertising. Even so, I do not expect to have much, if any, effect. None of us likes our profession to be attacked, and we fight back when it is. But usually someone somewhere in a profession steps out of line and says that he does see some justice in the criticisms, that some things in his particular house do need to be put in order. This can be seen in the quite fierce arguments about the function and financing of universities today. But I have not heard any spokesman of the advertising (or public relations) industry admit to other than minor faults (that claims are sometimes a bit exaggerated, say, or not strictly truthful); I have not heard any spokesman of the industry take the full measure of the case against advertising, let alone answer it.

Why is this? Is it because a profession which lives by manipulating reality, by weaving attractive but deceptive verbal links between products and potential consumers, gets taken in by its own sleight-of-hand? And that, by-and-large, such a trade gets the servants it needs, who fit its demands and are suited by them? For such men, when they find themselves criticized, the temptation to sell themselves a rationalization, like an outfitter clothing himself from stock, must be strong. Still, if the case against advertising is going to be seen (not necessarily accepted, but at least seen), then people in advertising have to make a harder effort than they have made so far. The time for easy rides, especially for the big public spokesman of advertising, is past.

To get a few red herrings out of the way first. There can be some unexceptionable advertising (and it need not be dull). It has not been proved that advertising in its present form (the kind of advertising that is being criticized) is essential to the economy, or reduces costs. It is true that the industry has done some self-policing; but only at an innocuous, true-or-false level. Last, no one in his senses is proposing censorship; anyway, the important problems could not be touched by censorship.

The really serious questions raised by advertising are much wider than advertising itself. If critics spend a lot of time attacking advertising this is not because advertising is a peculiar kind of vice, but because it is a symptom, because it exhibits more plainly and persistently than anything else the issues raised by mass persuasion. At bottom the case against advertising is the same as that against political propaganda, much religious proselytizing and any other form of emotional blackmail.

The case is this: that advertising tries to achieve its ends by emotionally abusing its audiences. Recognizing that we all have fears, hopes, anxieties, aspirations, insecurities, advertisers seek not to increase our understanding of these feelings and so perhaps our command of them, but to use their existence to increase the sales of whatever product they happen to have been paid to sell at any particular time. They exploit human inadequacy, and we have the right to say to them what Hamlet said to Guildenstern: "Why look you now, how unworthy a thing you make of me; you would play upon me; you would seem to know my stops; you would pluck out the heart of my mystery; you would sound me from my lowest note, to the top of my compass . . . Why do you think that I am easier to be played on, than a pipe?"

There is no point in illustrating, since illustrations are all around, nor in elaborating on the occasional exceptions. The basic charge is indisputable, unless you adopt a purely predatory—every man for himself—attitude; in which case there is no basis for argument. But if you accept some responsibility in your conduct towards others then you have problems, in advertising, which verbal manoeuvres can only evade, not solve.

Some apologists seek to rebut all this by taking up the Stance of the Licensed Pantaloon. You are too solemn, they argue. No one really believes what we say. The ordinary chap is much more subtle than you give him credit for. He recognizes that we add to the amusement and colour of his life—and that's all there is to it.

Coming from anyone who has read the research literature this is disingenuous. The evidence shows, and a reasonably close acquaintance with 'ordinary people' will tell you anyway, that a lot of people do literally believe what they read in the ads. A surprising number, when you think of the effort which goes into training in literacy. Still, that effort has been long delayed and is still small in proportion to the need. Most men in advertising are, of course, more effectively trained, more articulate and mentally quicker than their audiences—which doesn't make the business any pleasanter. What usually passes for sophisticated advertising (e.g. in the Sunday glossies) is at bottom as simple in its appeals as the stuff in the mass circulation papers; its stage-properties and snobberies are different, that's all. Outside that range there is, I suppose, a small core of self-aware intellectuals who do enjoy, or claim to enjoy, advertisements as aesthetic objects, as sources of verbal, sociological or psychological fun. Most talk of this kind strikes me as disingenuous; but men in advertising are grateful for it. It confirms their status as harmless amusers and pays tribute to their verbal inventiveness. Since there is a poet or novelist manqué inside many a copywriter, this is a benison. And an outsider may feel that, though it is a sad little claim they are making, at least it isn't portentous.

It is easy to appreciate the excitement, even the glamour, which advertising can have. Playing with words, making them do tricks for you within narrowly prescribed rules (this product, this target audience, this number of words), is obviously fascinating and in some ways similar to working within the rules of a simple literary form. I once passed hours, on a sticky hot journey by troop-train from Italy, inventing copy (with a man who is now a very popular columnist) for 'Critch', a mythical powder which would eliminate the awful persistent itch in our crutches. Still, how long can that sort of fun satisfy a man? A long time, I suppose, if the rewards are good, and if you find something cathartic for your spare time. But it's a shabby business.

Which is why the least attractive people in the whole advertising business are the front men with the public relations voices—the men who cheer up conferences with fighting keynote speeches about the public-service element in advertising and make prepared palliative statements on all other suitable occasions. Their routine is usually predictable. They assert that advertising is the linch-pin or lubricant of a modern progressive economy. They use words like 'creative', 'dedicated' and 'sincere', so much that you remember Hemingway's *A Farewell to Arms*; "I was always embarrassed by the words. There were many words that you could not stand to hear and finally only the names of places had dignity. Abstract words were obscene . . ." They take a few cheering-up-the-troops swipes at critics (this is a fairly recent development), and offer the services of advertising to promote any good cause the community can name—citizenship, education, religion.

With people like that you are really up against it. They seem to have no sense of the difficulty of truth and of the need to respect other people's effort after it: "There's no limit to the wonderful things advertising can be made to sell . . . religion, social conscience, racial tolerance, education. . . ." How do you explain that if religion is to mean anything it must be founded on personal commitment, arrived at with any help others can disinterestedly give, but in the end arrived at personally and in the fullest possible emotional clarity? Or how do you explain that illicit manoeuvres (associating religion with togetherness or smartness) cannot really convert anyone and only prepare the ground for equally illicit manoeuvres with more questionable ends. As 'professionals', Goebbels' ad men were very efficient indeed.

There is, of course, good persuasion as well as bad persuasion; and advertisers keep the debate murkier than it should be by sliding between the two types. In one sense, any good book is an act of persuasion. But the gap between that and the persuasion of advertisers is so large as to make virtually a difference of kind. Good persuasion, whether in dispassionate argument or in a powerfully moving novel, has two root qualities: respect for the reality of the subject, and respect for the listener's right to judge for himself his attitude to the subject. This definition does not rule out emotional engagement; any important commitment is a mixture of emotion and intellect. But it insists on emotional relevance—that the emotion, in both its nature and its intensity, fit the theme.

Naturally, the line between this and illicit emotional persuasion is a continuous one, and it is difficult to decide just where the watershed comes. But look at each end of the line and you see the distinction at once, and see its importance; and this makes it all the more important not to blur distinctions in the large middle area (which is where most of the battles about persuasion are fought), but to try to make them clearer.

It is important for outside critics not to use advertisers as scapegoats for bigger social problems; they reflect more than they affect in society. There are a lot of reasons why a society such as this throws up so much persuasion, and so to many people in advertising theirs seems as respectable a trade as many others.

That much can be granted. But it is just as important not to make easy accommodations. The overriding fact is that much of the work of this profession, as it is at present practised, consists of exploiting weakness, through language. Anyone who thinks it is better to try to understand one's weaknesses than to indulge them, anyone who thinks that language (the articulation of our thoughts and feelings in communicable form) can help in that better grasp, anyone with these two premises must regard most modern advertising as, at the best, a waste of good human resources and, at the worst, a misuse of other people.

1965

THE ARGUMENT ABOUT EFFECTS

SOME people think mass communications can have, over time, profound effects on individuals and on society; and that on the whole (perhaps chiefly because of the way they are organized) these effects are likely to be harmful. Incidentally, such people should remind themselves more often that the mass media can have some good effects. Professor Hilde Himmelweit's study of a few years ago suggested, for example, that television can make children more objective, less prejudiced, about other nations. And it would be interesting to know whether, as some people claim, film and television have generally sharpened our visual responsiveness.

There are, of course, much more favourable attitudes to the mass media, and they provide a useful way in to the discussion of effects. Here, it is argued that the media have little or no effect; or, if they do, that the effects are quite likely to be for good. Predictably, this line is often taken by those who are operating mass communications, or are financially involved in them. But that, and the fact that a fashionable anti-puritanism puts some intellectuals in the same camp, shouldn't make anyone dismiss their arguments out of hand.

Their case rests on five main statements. First, that mass communications are in themselves neither good nor bad, but simply vehicles we use for our purposes. It is therefore up to us to use them properly. Second, we must trust people more and not, under the guise of appearing to care for them, patronize them by assuming they are silly enough to be taken in by the sillier excesses of mass communications. Third, it is said that, even though many regrettable things appear within mass communications, they are only reflections of society; and you can't blame the mirror for reflecting the warts on your face. At a famous NUT conference in London some years ago Cecil King and Norman Collins used this type of argument, and one of them turned it back on the teachers themselves. If taste seems terrible as it is mirrored on your screens, he asked, surely the people who should be blamed are the teachers, those who train the young people who eventually become our audiences? The fourth defence claims that the media of mass communication have virtually no effect. They roll off people's backs. They are entertainment, relaxation, time out. More important, they are only a minute part of the whole fabric of any individual's personal or social experience. Finally, it is argued that though the mass media may have some effect—especially when they portray violence —this kind of thing is cathartic. Perhaps 'emetic' would be a more apt word for what they mean—which is that if the consumers were not able to discharge their aggression through these harmless channels they would do so in real life.

It is a defence of varying strength. But one's first reaction is simply to wish that the problems were as simple as the defence makes them. It is true that some critics of mass communications over-simplify the case. Defenders simplify it at least as much. If we say, for example, that the media are in themselves neither good nor bad but merely what men use them for, channels down which they pass this or that kind of information according to choice, we are dismissing one of the most interesting and difficult areas for analysis. Among the things for which we have cause to be grateful to Professor Marshall McLuhan one of the most important is this; that he has tried to make us see that the media of mass communication have qualities of their own which affect the messages we transmit through them. Actually, he says more than that. He says that "the medium is the message". The media have themselves inherent characteristics, and though you may think you are sending the same message down several different media the fact that they are going down different media affects or—he would say—decides what is being communicated. The news on radio is different from the news on television, even though the words may be the same (though they are not likely to be, since visual possibilities will make the pattern of television news items different from that of radio news). The 'same' play seen on television or in the theatre, or read, is three different plays. I do not go the whole way with McLuhan on this. But the drift of what he is saying is important. It turns our attention to the specific qualities of television—its peculiar immediacy, its overwhelming 'this-ness', the extraordinary sense of involvement it gives, though involvement of a certain kind. McLuhan helps make better sense of the narcissism of television. Since each medium has its own characteristics and since human imagination can flow in many directions, television naturally attracts to its service people whose imaginations are moved by its particular possibilities. The peculiar qualities of each form of mass communication are only brought out by men with relevant imaginations. This is a sort of aesthetic play, and begins long before one talks about the relations of the mass media to society.

This is a long way from simple assertions that the mass media are neither good nor bad but only vehicles. When we go further, the discussion becomes similar to the old argu-ment about the relative influences of heredity and environ-ment on human beings. In this instance the heredity side is made up of the inherent qualities of the media themselves; the environment side is represented by the way the media are organized within each society. Depending on the ways they are established, their characters differ. If you set up ideologi-cal, state-controlled television you have television of a certain texture (though the aesthetic pressure of the producers them-selves will produce ambiguities—as you may see in France). If you set up a competitive commercial network you will have yet another kind of television. Or, to move to another medium, one won't understand much about the Sunday colour supplements without relating them to consumer adver-tising in Great Britain; one won't understand, that is, not simply their economics but the texture of their prose and the inner nature of their illustrations, even the illustrations to their most 'serious' articles.

Or, take a relatively small issue in broadcasting but one that has been current throughout the sixties, in Britain: local radio. What should be its structure? My argument is that the structure you choose partly decides the medium you create. There is strong pressure to license local radio and finance it by advertising. Most of those who seek franchises do not convince one that they are particularly interested in either the possibilities of local radio in itself, or in the communities they claim to be going to serve. One has to start with the most simple and direct questions—What can local radio do best? What structure will give it the greatest freedom to do it? What structure allows it to express the variety of a community's life and to encourage energies still only potential? What best allows it to be independent and responsible, neither timid nor callow? Clearly, too close a structural link with the local powers-that-be would be dangerous. Just as clearly, tying it to advertising would be dangerous. The dream of combining public-service radio with advertising is the dream of the young lady of Riga.

Or look at the way mass communications are staffed. Some of us tend to slide easily into a form of conspiracy-theory. We imagine hard-faced financiers at the top controlling these things for their own ends. We think of journalists out to make money or reputation by cynically playing upon their publics. This is too crude and misses an important functional element. As I argued in discussing the reception of the Pilkington Report on Broadcasting* most popular journalists are not, with cynical and detached intent, peddling a certain view of the world; this is their world.

Every activity within a society gets the recruits it needs; and the nature of that activity is to some extent decided by the structure it is given. Some doors open, others close. It is therefore always tricky to argue from journalistic practice or opinion back to general statements about 'the nature of journalism'.

* In 'Difficulties of Democratic Debate', p. 185.

Herbert Gans, in a paper analysing the image of man in American television news, concludes that the great freedom allowed to broadcasters can be largely explained on these grounds: "Broadcasters are familiar with the major taboos, and unless the issue is very important, will observe them rather than antagonize powerful figures or large audience sectors. . . . The kind of people who choose to become journalists and broadcasters in America today are enough like the audience they serve so that they can be left free to work as they see fit." All systems tend to be self-perpetuating; they produce justifications for their own continued, unchanged existence.

So the first defence—that the media are merely vehicles—is untenable in the face of what I have called the facts of both heredity and environment. The mass media have characters of their own which affect the 'what' we communicate through them; this character is further affected by the structures within which we set them to work.

The second line of argument was that, though mass communications sometimes seem to promote regrettable attitudes, it is not necessary to worry. People know better; they are not taken in; they know a joke when they see one. Only humourless, academic moralists would so underestimate the people they are supposed to respect.

One feels guilty of presumption and arrogance. But then one begins to look around. At, say, the level of sophistication assumed in most television advertisements. It is hardly high and doesn't support the argument that most people know the advertisements are hoaxes, a huge joke they share with the advertisers and which has no relation to persuasion and sales. A few years ago, programmes called Advertising Magazines were a feature of commercial television. Some were a kind of serial, each with its own locale and sometimes a slight story-line, and the advertisements were injected into these situations in as natural a way as possible. The Pilkington Committee suggested they should be prohibited on the ground, among others, that they blurred the distinction between programmes

and advertisements which the Television Act requires. Naturally, the advertisers and programme companies objected. One
of their defences was a form of the one I am discussing now:
that few people would be taken in by the Magazines and
fail to recognize them for what they were—advertisements.
One programme-company commissioned a survey of the response to four such programmes in the London area. It
showed that, of those who had ever seen these programmes,
two out of three thought the performers were giving the
advertisers' selling points. Of the rest, the majority thought
the products were actually used by the performers, and the
remainder had no opinion.

A further version of this defence—that in the end people
always know better, and that in any case it is sound democratic
practice to let us make our own mistakes rather than to try
to coerce us into good sense—centres on 'the freedom of the
switch' argument in television. If we don't like a programme
we can always switch off, it says, and most people have the
sense to do that. In some ways this is a valuable argument,
especially against those who are both morally censorious and
imaginatively narrow. It is on the side of 'fair shares' and 'live
and let live'. Yet we know by now that certain kinds of programme can dangerously disturb certain types of people. And
we know that these are just the people who, once they have
been emotionally engaged by a programme, find it difficult
or impossible to switch off. At this point the 'freedom of the
switch' argument doesn't seem wholly adequate. So that, all
in all, the second defence, that hardly anyone is ever taken
in, doesn't stand up well.

The third, fourth and fifth defences have much in common
and can be taken together. They were: that mass communications only mirror the society they exist within; that they
have no serious effects on their audiences; or, that if—for
example—scenes of violence do have an effect it is likely to
be cathartic and therefore socially helpful, since it pipes
off violent actions. We might set these against social scientific

findings to date, all of them necessarily tentative.* They are compressed here, but not seriously misleading:

(a) Mass communication ordinarily is not a sufficient cause of effects on its audiences but functions within a range of other influences. That is to say, it is part of one's whole environment and its effect is influenced by that environment.

(b) Where it does have effects it tends rather to reinforce than to change. It is most successful in affecting people when it goes with the grain of existing assumptions.

(c) Where mass communication does resist change it does so either because the environment is not providing its penumbra, so that the impact of the mass communication is direct; or because the environment is itself, abnormally, favouring change rather than reinforcement.

(d) Therefore, in certain situations, the mass-media can directly and of themselves serve certain psycho-physical functions. They can provide directly for the needs of certain kinds of people and can do so the more readily if the environment of those people does not provide a sufficient bulwark or network of supporting values. Thus they can affect directly, and more powerfully than they affect other people, the very young, the very old and the mentally ill, people for whom the sustaining network of social values is either not yet fully woven, or has fallen away, or has not been formed.

(e) The efficacy of the media as affecting agents is influenced by various characteristics of the media themselves and of the communication situation. This supports what I said at the beginning about the inherent qualities of the media and about the effects of the structures we give them. Certain kinds of mass communication can affect

* The best brief guide to this work is, so far as I know, J. D. Halloran's *The Effects of Mass Communication* (Leicester University Press, 1964). See also the same author's and publisher's *Problems of Television Research* (1966), and *Attitude Formation and Change* (1967). New York: Humanities Press.

people more than others. Stylized violence is less likely to affect even the mentally disturbed than 'real' violence. Violence in a recognizably domestic situation is more likely to disturb children than that carried out with full conventions in a Western. A dramatically powerful scene is more likely to affect people than one with the spirit of reasoned documentary.

How do the three final defences look now—that communications only mirror, that they do not affect, or that, where they do affect, they are cathartic? They get some support. Research underlines that mass communications do not write on the blank sheets of our minds. This is not a simple, one-to-one, process. Except for the marginal cases I have mentioned, mass media are not likely to bring about marked changes, but they work within and along the grain of an elaborate pattern of attitudes, assumptions and habits. Here, research does tend to support the argument that mass communications mirror rather than initiate and that their effect is less, and more indirect, than many people assume.

This part of the findings also points, by implication, to a wider question about mass communications, one which isn't enough looked at. The question is not: "What do the media do to us?" but: "What do we do to the media?" To what extent can audiences affect the media? There is not only a two-step but also a two-way process in this matter of effects, and what social scientists call uses-and-gratifications studies have done something to plot it. Several other dimensions need to be brought in though. Can you adequately explain—say—the emergence of the Beatles by a one-step or one-way Denmark Street conspiracy theory or by a two-step uses-and-gratifications study?

Yet research supports the 'mirror' argument only so far. Mass communications are likely to mirror rather than positively to change. But, after all, they don't simply mirror; by repeating, by going with the grain of existing presumptions, they tend to reinforce. Suppose you are living in an area where colour-prejudice is strong. If you mirror that prejudice day after day you will not only mirror it; you will increase it. An already narrow population will have the tight boundary of its prejudices made stronger and higher.

Though the argument that the media have little or no effect stands up reasonably well for most people who are in touch with their environment and so are sustained by it, on quite a number of people who are not so supported—the very young (especially if they are left on their own or have a disturbed home), the very old (especially those who live alone), the mentally ill—on people like these the media may have a direct and positive effect. The possibility that some person who is already mentally disturbed will be even more disturbed by any particular programme can hardly define the bounds of programming for everyone else. Such a person might be disturbed by something which for hundreds of thousands of others would be a worthwhile widening of the bounds of experience. But where to draw the line? What is the maximum number of traceable suicides due to shock one can tolerate before deciding that the invigorating effect of a 'shocking' drama for hundreds of thousands of others has ceased to be, on balance, worthwhile?

Take the question of whether the BBC did right in its handling of *The War Game*. Most people who criticized the Corporation seemed to do so not because they thought it had made the wrong choice, but because they did not accept the BBC's right to make a choice, because they thought it had no right to feel responsible about whether or not the film should be shown. Suppose you were Director-General and had to think about the film. You knew research suggested that there might well be some people—though only a small handful of children, old people, nervous people—who could be pushed into depression or even suicide by seeing *The War Game*. You knew that 'the freedom of the switch' argument didn't apply to them. But you thought the film important, challenging, probably valuable for a great many people. What would you do? Which side of the line the decision falls on matters a lot. It is just as important to recognize that an editorial decision has to be made, and is not easy.

In the light of all this, the 'catharsis' argument begins to look dubious. Apparently, acts of violence experienced in the mass-media may in some marginal cases act as triggers, increase the predisposition towards violence. The most recent research I have heard of suggests much the same: that from such scenes, especially if they are realistic, we can learn how to act out violence rather than experience catharsis. But we can't be sure; research of this kind has tremendous difficulties and, so far, tremendous limitations. What we can say is that current results leave us a long way from the extravagant assumptions about direct imitation made by some people: "After seeing that programme she got so worked up that she went out and gave herself to the first man she met." It may be that for some people violence experienced vicariously can be a release; perhaps the same programme can work in opposite ways for different people. What we know is not sufficient to justify wholesale alterations in programming; it does begin to help define outer boundaries.

There is a further turn of the screw. The last two in the list of tentative research conclusions were: that situations which seem 'real' are more emotionally effective than stylized or conventionalized situations; and that dramatically successful situations also are more emotionally effective than stereotyped situations. Yet these are among the qualities for which we value works of literature: their fidelity to experience, their power to recreate the pressure of experience, and so on. It seems to follow from the evidence, however, that Shakespeare, Dickens, Ibsen on television may be as disturbing emotionally, to some people who come upon them by chance, as any other works.

Faced with having to justify the appearance of violence in works of literature we value, we normally use arguments like these: that a good work of art implies a world in which, though violence exists, there are also other dimensions; that the violence is not introduced for its own sake; that we experience pity as well as terror; that this is not simply a two-dimensional world of predatory assaults one upon the other but a world in which charity and love can also appear. This argument makes one crucial assumption: that works of art are seen, read, heard 'whole', in the way a serious critic himself thinks he experiences them or constantly tries to experience them. Or in the way an ideal common reader might be assumed to respond to them. But here again the social sciences are troublesome. They point out—and perhaps we always knew somewhere, but it is easy to forget—that we all exercise 'selective perception', that we tend to take from a work what we need emotionally at any particular time. Learning to become 'a good reader' means above all learning to control our bias towards selective perception, towards raiding a work for our own ends; means learning to listen to it disinterestedly and fully. This is very difficult and I do not expect any serious reader would claim more than partial success. Yet think of television: great dramas can be seen by millions who are certainly not 'ideal common readers', yet who can and do exercise selective perception. It follows that, though you may put *Macbeth* or *Troilus and Cressida* or *Oliver Twist* on television with the best intentions and with as much fidelity to the work as possible, those works may be used, unconsciously, by someone disturbed and out of touch with his environment, to strengthen a predisposition to violence. I do not think this is a reason for wholesale retreat. But again it provides essential background for understanding the context of programming.

The fact that so many research findings are tentative and small-scale underlines how little we can so far actually verify about the effects of mass communications at deeper levels. What we know is useful. But it does not yet go far into the value-laden, emotional complexity of the matter; nor has it measured changes over time. I have recalled elsewhere that one of the difficulties here, apart from the evident ones, may be that really slow psychic changes are matched by changes in linguistic use, so that we never quite see ourselves as others see us; we alter the language to match.* Yet it is at this point that the subject becomes most interesting and important. It is here that one tries to get as close as possible to the inwardness of day-to-day life, to its 'feel'; and then moves outwards from it, from the intuitions it offers, to hypotheses about change. It is here that one begins to speculate on the psychic effect of, for instance, the style and content of the endless flow of news and current-affairs coverage on television. Is it gradually making us accept even human beings, other people, as parts of sensuous experience, as parts of aesthetic patterns? Do we gradually become spiritual voyeurs, present at tragedy at the moment it happens yet incapable of being committed to it? Do we begin to see men as objects —for our use? Some recent Australian work—obviously its span has had to be relatively short—suggests that children, to defend themselves against shock from mass-media, may give themselves a sort of patina, acquire a kind of insensitivity.

And though, as I said earlier, stylized violence seems to affect people less than 'real' violence, one is then measuring more or less immediate responses. But what does the exposure to stylized violence on the screen do over a long period? Does it articulate and order inner conflicts? If so, is this valuable? Does it, seen so often and with such style, progressively seem to sanction violence, make it seem socially accepted and even useful, lessen its horror? Or does the first experience of horror and violence in real life dispel at once the world of stylized screen violence? We can't answer any of these questions, but we ought to look at them more. Too many of 'the intelligentsia' hate serious analysis of the mass media. They prefer them to be kept in a compartment labelled 'For Fun Only'; and they dismiss attempts to discuss them as 'puritan', 'over-earnest', 'old-fashioned moralizing'. A few months ago an article about broadcasting in a Sunday supplement began one of its sentences: "Radio, which is the most dated medium in the country, inclined to take an unfashion-

* See 'The Literary Imagination and the Sociological Imagination', in Vol. II of this collection.

ably puritanical view of events . . .". The most advanced
exponent of this position today is Marshall McLuhan. No one
wishes to seem Methodistical; but this kind of free-wheeling
is no more attractive, and is inconsistent with such evidence
as we have.

To talk like this is not to ask for censorship. If we had to
choose between some form of official censorship, by no matter
what body, and the freedom of action—and freedom to criticize—we now have, I hope we would stay as we are. But we
need better criticism. If we do not think about these questions more, we shan't be giving freedom to the mass media.
We will be handing them over to uses which conflict with
their fullest possibilities. We will tell ourselves we are playing it cool and being broad-minded; we will really be rein-
forcing, by default, some major tendencies in society. On the
whole those tendencies narrow the media's possibilities; they
therefore work against us all. We can't have it both ways.

1966

THE ARTS AND STATE SUPPORT

THE British have been habitually chary about providing public money for the arts. But in the last few years the climate has begun to change. The Labour Governments of 1964 and 1966 gave greatly increased grants to the Arts Council and appointed a Joint Parliamentary Under-Secretary of State with special responsibility for the arts.* The politicians were recognizing a process which had been under way for some time. Several Local Authorities were already very active: for example, in the North-East; there was some increased public pressure: for instance, for better local theatres in the Midlands.

So the arts are in the air, more and more regarded as matters of public concern and subvention. Lectures, conferences, day-schools, pamphlets, feature articles, symposia from all parties and all kinds of organization take up the theme. With the exception of a few out-and-outers at each end of the scale (local councillors who don't want a penny of the rates spent on the arts at one end, artists who insist that all public money for the arts is tainted money at the other end)—with these exceptions, the tide is flowing strongly in one direction and taking all sorts and conditions of people, apparently happily, along with it. They all think that we— our corporate public 'we'—have spent too little on the arts and must spend more, probably a lot more.

In its spirit this general good will is extremely practical. We all agree on aims, it tends to say, so let's get on with the job; don't let's get bogged down in theoretic arguments. Still, assumptions decide the way money is spent. When conflicting assumptions are embodied in brick, stone and organizational structures they become obvious and troublesome. Below to-day's unanimity are major differences of view about the

* Who has, predictably and confusingly, come to be called a 'Minister for Culture'. Throughout this essay the word 'culture' will be used in its anthropological rather than aesthetic sense.

nature of the arts and their place in society.

Two main kinds of attitude, one static and the other expansionist, often share a platform and for much of the time appear to be talking the same language. Both say that no 'civilized society' should be as mean as Great Britain in its public provision; both add that, with increasing prosperity, the arts should have a much higher priority. The 'statics' go on to say that this will encourage the really intelligent members of society—for example, the executive class—and is important if these top men are to consolidate our competitive position internationally. There the split begins. The static attitude assumes that only a small minority in any society can ever appreciate the arts, that appreciation is the product of a certain level of intelligence and sophistication, a level virtually pre-ordained. True, it is allowed that this proportion can be slightly increased, chiefly by recruitment through improved higher education and hence some social mobility. But for 'statics' this is, by and large, where we start: with a small proportion, but one regarded as so important to a society that public funds should be made available to provide for it those arts which are too expensive to be wholly paid for privately. Here the argument looks like a small mirror-image of the case for reducing high rates of income-tax, on the ground that they discourage initiative in just those people on whose initiative society most depends.

Conversely, the expansionist attitude assumes that the appreciation and indeed the practice of the arts is potentially within the power of all men. "The artist is not a special kind of man; every man is a special kind of artist," expansionists are likely to quote. That only a small minority have so far appreciated the arts is, on this view, almost wholly to be explained by limited opportunity. So for them it is good practical sense to talk as though everyone could potentially appreciate the arts.

Since in most discussions even this level in examining assumptions is rarely reached, both types can appear to agree. But in practice their differences are crucial. They affect the size, the direction, the stress and the shape with which public support is actually planned for the arts. In one form or another contrasts of this kind run right through the British debate. It is a long and complicated debate.

Perhaps there was a time when all classes appreciated the same arts together, groundlings with aristocrats. But fully to sustain this case would require more knowledge of the inner nature of 'response' at different periods and in different kinds of people than most literary critics who have accepted the argument possess. And even they tend to use, in conjunction, the onion-skin argument: that people of different levels of intelligence and sophistication have at some periods been able to appreciate different layers of the same great works of art, the number of layers increasing with increasing sophistication. Again, the argument is more often asserted than explored. It would not carry far with the 'statics' who would reply that to appreciate some forms of 'high art'—chamber music, say—requires considerable musical sophistication and intelligence; and that only a minority have ever been able to bring these qualities to bear.

Some forms of 'high art' are expensive to nurture and have always needed patronage, patronage hitherto provided mainly by the aristocracy and high bourgeoisie. The vast majority of people had no opportunity of learning to appreciate these arts or money to pay for them. But this kind of patronage was not strong in Britain. Compare, say, the German principalities in their heyday. There, for whatever mixture of reasons and motives, there were some courts which felt themselves committed to the furtherance of high art, to having their own composers and orchestras, to commissioning the best living painters. I am not being normative, but giving a thumb-nail sketch of an elaborate process. As the mercantile upper middle class assumed power in Britain it did not take over a strong sense of the peculiar claims of high art to its patronage. Its urbanity, though impressive, was of a different, a more puritan, kind. The German high bourgeoisie turned its energies to governing the growing cities within a context

which assumed that a distinguished city should have a symphony orchestra, an opera house, an art gallery; that, though
all these cost a lot of money, they had claims as great as more
obvious socially-beneficial initiatives. There were all sorts
of hidden assumptions here, assumptions which to some extent seem still to exist within German society, Germany having rebuilt her theatres at great expense since the war, often
before her dwelling-houses. I mean assumptions about the
existence of firm links between middle-class status, authority,
and the patronage of the 'high arts'. These assumptions make
me at least, whatever the splendour of the new German
theatres, prefer the more confused British situation.

I live in Edgbaston, the nineteenth-century prosperous-
bourgeois district of Birmingham. Walking through these
tree-lined roads only two or three miles from the centre of a
large city one is constantly reminded of its post-Industrial
Revolution civic tradition. Here the Chamberlains and their
kind lived, and from here took carriages into the town they
ran, in which they created a highly efficient municipal government. That tradition has had its day. It was in some ways a
dull tradition, imaginatively; but it had compensating
strengths. The fine Art Gallery apart, those strengths were
not notably in the public promotion of the arts. This tradition
had a strong interest in the natural and mechanical sciences
and a well-developed domestic sense: Edgbaston's private
gardens and voluntarily-supported Botanical Gardens are
beautiful. But the Birmingham middle class paid comparatively little attention to the practice of the high arts. In
Manchester the Hallé Orchestra was the creation chiefly of
European refugees, many of them Jewish, who settled in that
city in the nineteenth century. At least since industrialization,
the British themselves have not had an adequate framework
of assumptions within which to give public support of the
arts a higher place.

Oddly, the United States, for long regarded as artistically
barren by the British, in some respects surpassed us, not only
absolutely but proportionately, in the provision of large

capital sums for the arts. But their route was different. Funds were rarely provided by public subvention. They are still fighting in that particular sector of the battle and, now that the impetus of President Kennedy has gone, are inclined to use our own new impetus as a stick with which to belabour later cabinets—which, in search of the Great Society, are paying some attention. But money in large sums did appear for some of the arts. It appeared because America was so wealthy, so wealthy in individual entrepreneurs; many of them, in the late nineteenth century, of European stock. Typically, the great German-Jewish self-made millionaires gave the art galleries and financed the symphony orchestras. Thus they killed two birds with one stone: they created a monument to the gods of the old country and at the same time asserted the power of the new over the old, since they could buy bigger buildings and better pictures than the old could now afford. It was the best act of distinction they could make, a free gesture. That race of men is not so evident now, and here is another reason for the increasing pressure on recent governments to spend more on the arts, a pressure supported by both good and bad justifications.

Hence, the debate has some common qualities on both sides of the Atlantic. On balance we in Britain seem to be making the running on this side. France and Germany are objectively ahead of us, Germany in the way I have indicated, France with her Minister for Culture and other powerful initiatives. But French governmental provision for the arts sometimes becomes entangled with a revived political nationalism, and that of a restrictively bourgeois kind.

The British unwillingness to vote public money for the arts has been strengthened by a suspicion that the arts are soft if not sinful, and probably both. This attitude, too, has a long history and dies hard. The present century opened with the trial of Oscar Wilde fresh in people's minds, and more recently saw the symptomatic case of *Lady Chatterley's Lover*; and, now, the 'Clean-up TV' movement, whose members are particularly shocked by what they think is outrageous drama on television.* Behind attitudes like these is the belief that any deviation from their own highly-conditioned and rigid norms is immorality. A Franklinesque ethic of industry and sobriety also lies in the background. The mention of art prompts a series of stock responses about drink and sex and wastefulness, about getting up late, staying up late, and not paying your dues. Objectors tend to insist, sincerely, that they do appreciate the arts. But they also insist that life is 'not like that', not as shocking as that; that though they know that dirt exists it doesn't have to be dwelt upon ("surely, that's morbid"). It is here that some local councillors, of all political parties, are likely to dig their heels in hard and declare they will stand no more nonsense.

A section of the press plays up to this outlook; indeed, shares it and displays a cock-sure philistinism. They can call in aid a large range of British clichés, items of cultural folk-lore: about bohemian artists, cissy poets, sexual deviations and actresses who are no better than they should be; or about putting first things first and getting the house built before thinking about frills.

The situation is further complicated by the way in which some artists play up to their opponents, enjoy the histrionic image which this attitude fathers on them and make it a substitute for the more difficult search for artistic identity. They enjoy too much shocking the bourgeoisie, and so spend more time responding to social incidentals than to the demands of their art. It is quite difficult for most artists not to be at least slightly disabled by accepting one of these melo-dramatically-attractive social stances.

To return for a moment to the Press. Range upon range of reach-me-down responses are available to them: that all that highbrow stuff is a load of rubbish thrown in the public's face, that though we know nothing about art we know what we like, that one man's meat . . . , that there's no arguing about taste, that you can't force things down people's throats,

* See 'The Guardians and the New Populism', p. 205.

that you can't eat art, that you've got to give the people what
the people want.

Still further behind is a body of casual intellectual 'demo-
crats'. Since they are knowing, they could if required write an
essay on British philistinism, lightly and ironically as well as
allusively. Deeper down they are still part of the British
condition. They have replaced the common clichés of attitude with others which, though more sophisticated, do not
challenge basic assumptions. They have learned to live within
the situation, not stood outside it. They have convinced
themselves that they are being intellectual, democratic and
realistic. A recent P.E.P. pamphlet* shows this attitude clearly.
Fundamentally, it draws on what I called earlier the static
attitude:

> A large selection of the population is completely indifferent
> to anything that comes under the general heading of 'culture'
> and they have every right to stay in that state of non-grace. . . .
> The appetite for culture in this country is less voracious than
> many of us pretend.

That passage unites the 'static' outlook with that of the
casual but knowing democrat: the flip, 'realistic' tone, the
assumptions taken over without examination of their origins
or limits, the contemptuous irony by deflation ('less vora-
cious . . .'), the awful patronage which allows the allusive
inversion 'a state of non-grace'.

At the very end of this line is a cluster of intellectuals who
are likely to call themselves 'objective' and 'value-free'. Claiming that all artistic judgments are reflections of different social
conditions, they conclude there can be no objective standards
or valid judgments between levels in works of art. Best, therefore, to leave people alone. All attempts to encourage the
appreciation of the arts by a wider circle will be misconceived,
because trammelled in their own socially-determined assumptions.

* *Public Patronage and the Arts*, P.E.P. *Planning*, Vol. XXXI (1965), 492.

Yet the climate is changing. Why? There are several inter-locking causes. A more widely diffused prosperity encourages the sense that the arts should be promoted lest we become 'crudely materialistic'. There is a feeling that a prosperous society 'owes it to itself' to be cultivated as well as comfort-able; that for a society in the condition of 'the man who has everything' this is the right next stage, a qualitative change in the style of life. And this in itself contains a range of atti-tudes, from reasonable civil aspirations to crude new forms of acquisitiveness. A hundred years on, the cruder forms are linear descendants of the attitudes of those Bradford business-men Ruskin rebuked for calling in an 'architectural man-milliner' when they decided to have an Exchange consonant with their newly-acquired sense of prosperous dignity.

There is also a feeling that the working classes in particular need to be brushed over or more than brushed over by the arts. Again, this unexamined assumption covers a range of attitudes. Some draw on a tradition of love and respect for the arts and a desire to make them more widely available; some are more than usually puritan, see bingo as the great enemy today and the arts as a counterweight; some are new forms of the view that 'we must educate our masters'. Today this last takes the shape of saying that though working-class people are now literate they remain socially crude; let us therefore 'embourgeoisify' them. And far back in that particular atti-tude is sometimes the unconscious feeling that an embour-geoisified working class is less likely to become difficult.

This leads naturally to what is coming to be called 'the problem of leisure', inspired by the progressive shortening of the working week and the working life. In fact, for most people the shorter statutory working week is not shortening the actual length of time worked but increasing the hours worked at overtime rates, or the number of people who have two jobs, one full-time and one part-time. Advocates of the need for 'education for leisure' argue that this reinforces their point, that because people fear vacancy and don't know how to amuse themselves creatively they seek further work which fills time and provides money for more possessions.

All the above approaches assume the importance of the arts as socially civilizing, as helping to make society more humane. In one way or another they all arise from an extraneous interest in the arts, as something a society needs or other people need. But behind the demand for increased public support there seems also to be a more direct interest, from people who themselves enjoy the arts and find local provision inadequate. A new audience seems to be emerging all over the country. Slowly, better education, the increased availability of many kinds of material (long-playing records, good books in paperback), and some types of broadcasting are all helping to create an audience more informed and aware than we have so far realized, an audience whose members give the arts an important place in their lives, and who are now steadily insisting that better provision be made for their tastes. In this respect, one of the most interesting sights in Britain today is the audience at the theatre in one of those provincial towns which, though it has some fierce opponents of the 'waste of public money', has finally paid for better quality. The audience is likely to be mixed, of course, but a high proportion will usually be young people, clearly interested and well-informed. A sizeable audience of this kind did not exist in the thirties; it has emerged in the last decade. It presumably overlaps to a large extent with the audience for the more imaginative and ironic programmes on television. This audience largely looks to the BBC although in some respects commercial television, had it been willing to take the risk, might have gained it. In gaining it, the BBC forfeited some of the confidence and good will of its traditional audiences. In this respect, the BBC now finds itself out on a limb. It has lost some of its reputation with the older establishments; its new supporters are appreciative, but scattered and without immediate public influence.

What I have been calling the static attitude is, in its view of the nature of the arts and their dissemination in society, a somewhat debased form of élitism. But at its best it is rooted in the view that to practise or appreciate the arts is a discipline, requires attention and intelligence. The expansionist attitude is, by contrast, democratic. It rests in the assumption that everyone needs the arts, deserves the arts and to some extent can practise or appreciate the arts. At its best today this is the mid-twentieth century version of that spirit which founded the Mechanics Institutes, the public libraries, the adult education movement and was fed by Morris and Ruskin. At less than their best both attitudes, as they are usually expressed today, are confused. They exhibit what an American observer, speaking about his own country, has called 'social good will and cultural myopia'. The good will will be useless if the cultural myopia is not corrected.

What are the relations between social class and the appreciation of the arts? Is some sort of mediating group—an élite, a clerisy—always necessary? If so, how is it to be defined today? What effects does the operation of the market in centralized open societies have on the practice and appreciation of the arts? What alternative structures are possible and desirable? These are vast questions, and there are others. But we hardly ever look at them, and so the tones of voice in which we declare our support for the arts betray us.

One tone is still too much conditioned by the historical correlations between height of social class and appreciation of the 'high arts'. It is difficult enough to trace and assess these links even in earlier periods. In today's more fluid situation the difficulty is compounded. Hence, it is particularly depressing to hear people talking about the arts in so unthinkingly class-bound a way. This kind of talk neglects art that cannot be associated with acceptable social signs; it accepts even dead conventional art which has the right cachet; worst, even when it praises good art it mixes relevant and irrelevant reasons. The reaction to that writing in the fifties and sixties which was about, and often by, working-class people is a typical case. The inability to deal in other than 'carriage-trade' or 'smart metropolitan' terms, to conceive other audiences or criteria, meant that this writing had to be reduced to a manageable curiosity. It was consistently simplified, seen as excitingly melodramatic or unacceptably crude. Whatever the angle, it had to be made odd, marginal to 'real' literature and to art's engagement with life.

We are, it is true, somewhat more aware of these risks than we used to be. Even the Arts Council seems less often to be staffed by, speak to, and provide for a certain middle level in social class. But there is still a long way to go. At its most banal this attitude boils down to a form of salesmanship or public relations, to selling not so much the artistic appreciation of a certain class as the mores of that class itself. The hidden and often unconscious assumption is still that the respectable working class or lower middle class wish to become like the middle class, and that one route is by learning the 'cultured' language of this class (in this sense, to be 'cultured' means to appreciate the arts).

Attitudes within this group are not necessarily sinister; sometimes their disposition is positively amiable. But they are rigid and unfruitful because their mental picture is pyramidal; they are monolithic and hierarchic. They think of the diffusion of the arts in a paternal and presentational way ('bringing art to the people'). They are made uneasy by the thought of plurality, of a diverse range of tastes and voices not easily related to known social norms.

All this has a practical point, since it affects the administrative and physical structures we devise for supporting the arts. Take a new provincial theatre, one which is attracting larger audiences than anyone could safely have predicted. No point in naming it, since the issue is typical. In some respects (not in all) this particular theatre has had incorporated into its layout assumptions about the role of the theatre in provincial life which its actual audiences refute. Of course, one might argue that it nevertheless works, since audiences are large. But it might have worked even better—in important new ways—if the design of the theatre had been more relevant.

You go there, let us say, with little money but reasonably civil requirements; you are a young man with his girl friend, or a family man with his wife and children; and you want some food. Apart from the bar, you have two choices. You can have a full dinner, served by men in tail-coats for a basic charge of about £1 a head. This rules out all but a minute proportion of families. So you look around. You find that the only other provision is in the Snack Bar. So you go in one step from tail-coats to tea-ringed plastic tables, to the hamburgers, hot dogs, eggs and chips, to the glass counter inside which sausage rolls are warmed and, inevitably, to the pervading smell of hot groundnut oil. You know at once where you've been assigned. If you can't afford the full leisurely treatment with damask tablecloths and tail-coats then you must get on with it as quickly as possible in what is no doubt thought of as a garish but bright-and-serviceable décor for the masses. In this instance the separation is even more marked, since the posh restaurant is inside the theatre itself and so part of the whole theatrical occasion. The Snack Bar is at the end of a terrace jutting from the theatre towards a public road. As you sit there you feel like a pensioner waiting to be allowed in when the doors open.

This kind of thing is not ill-meant; it's just thoughtless and blind. We find it difficult to imagine a decent middle-ground for people to stand on, or a range of styles not ranked in caste-order. But the new audiences do seem to some extent less bound than their elders by assumptions about links between social class and the arts. Perhaps only to some extent, perhaps only on occasions, perhaps only during their twenties. But it could be a start. One of the opportunities of a time such as this is to let the planning of theatres and other such places express and encourage these new possibilities. Too often we plan according to models which are out of date, socially and artistically.

The fortunes of some of the civic Arts Festivals which now dot the country are a rich source of even odder evidence. Or consider Cannon Hill Park. There, in the mixed suburbs of Birmingham, Mr. John English is building the Midlands Arts Centre for Young People. This is an ambitious and imaginative scheme to provide a variety of buildings in which young people can practise and appreciate the arts. But all voluntary organizations begin to take on a definite character from the moment they open their doors, a character decided by those who form the first managing group. That character attracts some and keeps out others and so tends to be self-perpetuating, unless there is a revolt. Mr. English is anxious that perceptive young people from all parts of society shall look to the Midlands Arts Centre as a natural home. He also knows that because the practice and appreciation of the arts is largely a middle-class preserve, because middle-class teen-agers are socially more at ease in these situations than working class, it is unlikely that he will, without considerable efforts, attract more than the rarest of working-class children, no matter how talented they may be. Even then, they may look like the odd trade unionist in the central councils of the Conservative Party. Mr. English is certainly trying very hard, particularly to reach children, children too young to have had their appreciation spoiled or over-socialized. Whether the effort will be disproportionate to the result remains to be seen.

A not unsympathetic article about Cannon Hill, in a Birmingham University students' magazine, ended: "So, go to the Centre, certainly go to see *Thunderball*, but above all Keep on Running." It was an intelligent conclusion: it acknowledged the potential value of Cannon Hill; it refused to get caught up in habitual but peripheral assumptions; it insisted on its right to find its own position before the attractions—many spurious, some genuine—of that mass art and pop art which traditional rankings ignore or despise. Whatever its phoniness or manufactured quality mass art does sometimes blow the gaff on the old correlations, and part of its attraction lies in just that.

It is against this background that one can understand better some of the impulses behind various attempts to link the arts with working-class life and with earlier oral traditions. I am thinking of Arnold Wesker's Centre 42, Charles

Parker's radio-ballads and the contemporary folksong movement. Their historical perspectives and emphases are different, but they all try to bypass the conventional links.

As we have seen, to some extent this correlation between
the appreciation of the arts and the level of social class
continues. Coming up strongly and to some extent interlocking with it is a newer type of association. This sees the appreciation and sometimes the practice (even the amateur practice)
of the arts as a form of consumption, of status consumption.
In a prosperous society one of the last differentiating things
you can buy—apart from a public school education for your
child—is artistic kudos. Inevitably, such an attitude attracts
the world of commercial persuasion and learns its language.
It insists that to enjoy the arts is fun; it has a whiz-kid air,
rather like an advertiser writing free copy for his local church,
telling you that religion doesn't hurt a bit; it argues (borrow-
ing its phraseology from parts of the debate where it is more
carefully used) that you should not decide the value of imaginative expression by the height of brow assumed or by social
class but rather by 'the quality of life within it'; it asserts that
it not only enjoys Beat as well as Beethoven, strip-cartoons as
well as Turner, but will make no distinctions between them.
This is a foolish muddle: one enjoys brass bands and should
not feel snobbish towards them; but they clearly have a
different imaginative intensity from Bach. This smart style
can sound even less attractive than the conventional mandarin
manner. It is a pity, though, that we have to choose so often
between the stiff guardians of the traditional gate and the
all too fluid cheer-leaders for the new era.

The Labour Government's White Paper *A Policy for the
Arts, The First Steps*, published in February 1965, has many
good passages and, taken by and large, is a remarkable step
forward for a British Government. But some passages show
uneasiness before the dilemma I have described. The writer
wishes not to sound patronizing, creeps near to the new ad-
man's tone and so begs the difficult questions:

There is no reason why attractive presentation should be left to those whose primary concern is quantity and profitability. They ['the younger generation'] will want gaiety and colour, informality and experimentation.

All that is needed is to find models that can be given the gay 'Come to the Fair' atmosphere essential for recreational purposes.

One paragraph manages to use both styles, the gentility of the old and the smartness of the new: it talks of "Making Britain a gayer and more cultivated country".

The intentions are good but the muddle is great. We could easily jump out of the frying pan into the fire. If we reject the long-standing correlations between social class and the appreciation of the arts without sufficiently considering what appreciation of the arts really involves, we shall swop the first set of assumptions for others which regard the arts as guides to glossy consumption. Appreciation of the arts will become a status mark, and new status mark is only old class writ large, old class distinctions under a new name. The kind of energy which had been employed in retaining class-distinctions can then be used to maintain the idea of an artistic pecking-order. If we learn to look afresh, new forms of art might emerge: they certainly need to.

These misunderstandings apart, why should the arts be valued by a society? What distinctive qualities, if any, give them claims on corporate spending? The answer has to begin in a few fundamental statements about the nature of the arts.

The first is that the arts celebrate 'life', that they play around with it or recreate it, in awe or curiosity or pleasure. 'Life' in this context can mean all forms and aspects of experience, and can inspire all forms of art, from the most abstract and non-representational to a portrait of Rembrandt's mother. At this level the arts are without functional purpose. They are about love and are themselves acts of love. They transcend the limits of our creatureliness by creating something new. They start in the will to make something good in itself, and for its own sake; and those phrases cover all their aspects, from the concern for good craftsmanship to the highest imaginative disinterestedness.

But to be disinterested, to stand back that far from day-to-day life, may be the beginning of wisdom, of a greater sense of perspective and depth. Which is why it is said that the arts can never be finally tamed, that they must sometimes be disturbing as well as rewarding to us. No other experiences outside our own personalities offer this kind of exploration into what it means to be 'human', what it can mean in sadness and in joy. These are large phrases but none smaller meet the case.

We can then go on to say that the arts are nevertheless about truth:

> It is the glory and the good of Art,
> That Art remains the one way possible
> Of speaking truth . . .

They are immersed in the sense of relative values, in the ordering of experience, in rejecting this and asserting the worth of that; in celebrating, they inevitably criticize. This criticism may well be by implication; the artist himself may not be conscious of it; his work may contain no direct moral judgments, let alone simple ethical precepts. Yet his art will be engaged, on some points and at some levels, with assessing the quality of different kinds of human experience. It explores and sees as if afresh, and its usually unspoken question is: "Is such a life after all worth living?"

It is in this sense that the arts can be liberating. One has to say 'can be' because we do not have to go to the arts, we do not have to allow them to affect us in this way. We can even 'appreciate' them without, so far as we know, any effect at all on our 'moral being'. Yet in so far as we allow them, working in their own way, to affect us they may, it seems, help us to see better. But, to repeat (since it is so important), not necessarily by making statements. They will often work obliquely, by myth or symbol. And, again to repeat, everything starts with them as they are, with celebration, play and awe. They may make their best 'criticism of life' simply by being; they may best state by not stating. Of all the possible meanings of that unforgettable but almost impenetrable phrase of Keats 'Beauty is truth, truth beauty', this is one clear candidate.

It follows, if even only part of all this is true, that the arts do have an important social function. Yet to put it in that way sounds unbearably crude and likely to lead to shallow optimism. Thus, some supporters of the arts claim that a wider appreciation could blow away that damp, illiberal quality which so often seems characteristic of this island. One has some initial sympathy. Yet the exploration of British society today, in art of any depth, would make that kind of formulation impossible; it would see not only the dampness and illiberality but complimentary strengths—tolerance, non-conformity, irony—strengths almost entirely neglected or misunderstood by even the most well-intentioned publicists for the arts. This is worth stressing since it illustrates how art can give greater depth to a society's sense of itself. The arts therefore—and perhaps we can properly use these phrases now—are fundamental to civilized life in a civilized society: a country without great art might be a powerful collection of thriving earthworms but would be a sorry society.

Next, we need to look closer at a paradox which has been glanced at before. The practice and appreciation of the arts demand effort; they are not a veneer one applies effortlessly. In spite of the way some people talk today, they are not something simply given to us but a process in which we take part. Suspicion about, for instance, the current stress on enthusiastic amateurism in the arts is not necessarily intellectual snobbery; it may just as well be a recognition that worthwhile engagement begins at the point where self-indulgence ends.

But how does this recognition, that the arts make considerable demands, square with the belief that they should be more widely spread? On the view* that a great many more

* This is a hypothesis, but there is some evidence to support it.

could enjoy or practise the arts than we have been used to assuming, and that they are spread throughout society. This hypothesis therefore assumes that there is no necessary link between the appreciation of the arts by some and the existence of a fixed mass who are, by definition, incapable of appreciation. It also assumes that there is no inherent connection between the maintenance of the arts at a high level and the maintenance also of a particular kind of social élite, that Mannheim was wrong in saying "The social value of intellectual culture is a function of the social status of those who practise it". We are left, of course, with difficult questions about transmission, about who—if mediators are essential— are the mediators in the new situation. To answer these properly we will have to learn to read the evidence afresh. Last, the key hypothesis assumes that the imaginative and intellectual life of a society can be more diverse and open than we have habitually thought. For some people, including me, this hypothesis forms the basis of the case for spending more public money on the arts. Those who do not accept it will have to decide that public money should not be spent or find other grounds for doing so.

But how does one convince enough people that more money for the arts is an essential form of public provision? There is little, if any, objective proof. Bridges don't fall down or roofs leak because a society fails to support its dramatists. To try to convince the really hostile is like talking from behind to a totally blind man. Still, to say it once again, the climate is visibly changing; new audiences are emerging; cracks are appearing in some of even the least promising city councils; and the Treasury has been persuaded to give far more than one might have imagined a few years ago. Still less than is needed, so the momentum must be kept up, very hard. No new principle is involved, since the provision of public baths, public libraries, public parks and much else all rest on similar assumptions about legitimate extensions of public spending. They had to be fought for in their time; much better provision for the arts is the inevitable next step. But it must be argued on the right grounds. A case argued for quick returns on the wrong reasons will rebound and we shall have the wrong kind of provision.

It is only then that we can begin to be precise about the nature and scope of public provision. First, physical factors. The practice of certain forms of art requires very large capital and recurrent sums: for example, opera, symphonic music and ballet. We recalled earlier that arts of this kind have never paid for themselves but developed under patronage. Nor are they likely ever to pay for themselves at the box office; the cost of seats would be beyond all but a tiny minority, and quite hopelessly beyond many who badly want to attend them or the new young audiences who are just learning to appreciate them. One has simply to recognize that such enterprises must have a solid foundation of assured public money; after that, there is room for manoeuvre and for accountability as close as that used in commerce. Even if only half-a-dozen major centres in Britain were regularly to house productions of this kind, the capital outlay would not be small.

The smaller-scale matters for which more public provision, priming of the pump, or financial readjustments, are necessary vary from art to art. Here our backwardness has produced all sorts of hindrances and hardships, small in terms of the total sums involved but large to the people directly affected by them. An obvious example is the treatment of authors as to income tax, copyright and public lending; and each of the arts has its list. To amend any of them would involve, at any rate in the short term, some loss of revenue and the Treasury would presumably feel bound to object. It is wrong to ask a Chancellor for intermittent acts of what seems like charity. We have to decide as a society to move provision for the arts higher up the scale of priorities.

Or one can, even more precisely, define public intervention according to the types of work which it should support. There are two aims: to preserve and to extend. A society must sustain its own artistic heritage; and it must encourage

246

the new, since to do so is to understand better its own present and future. The classical repertoire of great art, of all kinds, has to be kept up for each generation and this too is expensive and never likely to pay for itself. It should be unthinkable that at any time in Britain there was not, say, a body of actors capable of interpreting—and reinterpreting—at the highest level the whole of the Shakespearean canon. To do less is to let part of the national heritage fall into disuse. This is one of the artistic achievements of the Soviet regime. It has financed the Bolshoi Ballet and the Arts Theatre in a way which ensures that they maintain their standards at the best pre-Revolutionary level.

Mention of the Soviet regime points to the second and more difficult job of the State. Though the Soviet leaders have kept the classical repertoire at its peak, they find it more difficult, because of the nature of their society, to allow the contemporary arts freedom to explore. To ideologically-centralized societies, exploratory art is always a nuisance if not dangerous. This is true even though an art may appear to explore only in technical matters; technical invention moves out to affect the style of life itself. We can believe that the Soviet regime under Stalin did wrong to inhibit the arts. But since it had decided to restrict them the regime showed great subtlety (or out of stupidity stumbled upon subtlety) by including in those restrictions musical experimentation as well as the verbal arts; to let jazz into Russia is to alter more than the style of dancing. The explorations of art are indivisible.

It does not follow that in a mass, commercial democracy such as Britain the scope for exploration is assured. No Establishment likes to be criticized and no society likes its citizens to be too disturbed. To some extent every culture provides its own opiates, its own explanation of life, and dislikes having its accommodations challenged. Commercial providers cannot underwrite long-term experimentation for which an audience is not already available and able to pay; nor are commercial providers much attracted to those kinds of experimental art which make people unhappy or puzzled.

247

Of course, some kinds of experimental art are silly, but there are risks of this kind in any important area of experience. A society which is trying to be democratic, which does not wish its tones to be set by either the ideology of an Establishment or the pressures of the market, must provide room for the arts to experiment and explore, not simply encourage them to mirror existing or earlier tastes—even taste at its traditionally 'highest'.

The condition of Britain two-thirds of the way through the twentieth century has made this difficult prescription even harder because there has emerged a pressure which is restrictively petit-bourgeois, sure that the particular level of intellectual and imaginative awareness it possesses is an ideal standard and that the job of art is to reflect that. This is something of a nuisance, since it may inhibit public support for experimental art.

A greater problem is to give room for experiment and revolt without institutionalizing and so neutralizing even them, without allowing them to become accepted minor variations or marginal oddities, in which artists themselves co-operate by striking public postures. One cannot blame a politician for not loving the arts; if they are alive he should often find them subversive. One can more easily blame an artist for selling them short.

Given the relations between art and society during the last 150 years, the danger for a serious artist is less that he will settle for such a bogus bohemianism within society than that he will feel driven to take up a self-destroying defensive stance right outside it, one not nourished by a considered criticism of the society. In such a situation a sense of fellow-feeling with other individuals has little chance to develop. For the arts, we like to say (and it is probably the most important thing we do say about their social relevance), are a way of speaking to each other. There are many substitutes for a sense of community, and they are more easily acquired than the real thing—patronage in many disguises, and false palliness of several kinds.

All these imitate but do not replace or deny the sense of common humanity. We have to try to learn, partly through the arts, what that phrase can mean. We can only discover slowly. Before making larger gestures or assertions, we have to learn to talk to each other, and that includes listening to each other, more simply and directly.

1967

INDEX

INDEX

INDEX